CW00765499

SONS OF WAR

First published by Affirm Press in 2022
This edition published in 2023
Boon Wurrung Country
28 Thistlethwaite Street
South Melbourne VIC 3205
affirmpress.com.au

10 9 8 7 6 5 4 3 2 1

Text copyright © Paul Byrnes, 2022

All rights reserved. No part of this publication may be reproduced without prior written permission from the publisher.

A catalogue record for this book is available from the National Library of Australia

ISBN: 9781922992000 (paperback)

Cover and internal design by Karen Wallis, Taloula Press © Affirm Press
Typeset in Sabon 10/17
Printed and bound in China by C&C Offset Printing Co. Ltd.

SONS OF WAR

Astonishing stories of under-age Australian
soldiers who fought in the Second World War

PAUL BYRNES

For my father, NX103384

CONTENTS

FOREWORD 6

INTRODUCTION 14

CHAPTER ONE
THE LOTTERY 24

CHAPTER TWO
THE BOXER 40

CHAPTER THREE
THE BABIES OF TOBRUK 56

CHAPTER FOUR
THE BULLDOG AND THE BARRISTER 90

CHAPTER FIVE
BOYS OF THE GOLDEN WEST 102

CHAPTER SIX
THE GREAT ESCAPER 130

CHAPTER SEVEN
MISSING PERSONS 144

CHAPTER EIGHT
THE BEST OF FRIENDS 162

CHAPTER NINE
NO PRISONERS, NO WOUNDED 184

CHAPTER TEN
FORTUNATE SON 204

CHAPTER ELEVEN

A NICE OLD BLOODY MESS. 216

CHAPTER TWELVE

PARADISE LOST. 234

CHAPTER THIRTEEN

HAWKS AND SPARROWS 256

CHAPTER FOURTEEN

HEART OF DARKNESS 276

CHAPTER FIFTEEN

SHAPING THE TRUTH 296

CHAPTER SIXTEEN

PARADISE FOUND. 314

CHAPTER SEVENTEEN

BREAD AND BUTTER AND JAM 332

CHAPTER EIGHTEEN

THE MURDER OF INNOCENCE. 352

CODA. 372

ACKNOWLEDGEMENTS AND THANKS 374

PHOTO CREDITS. 376

INDEX 378

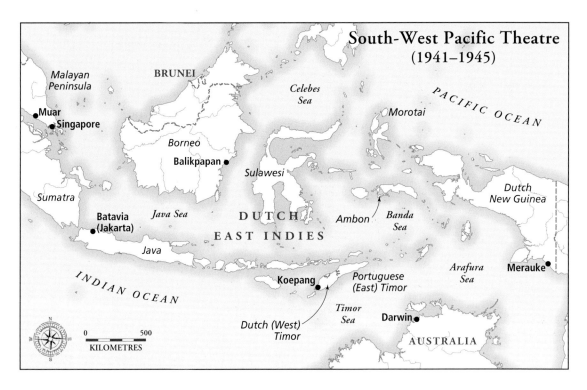

South-West Pacific Theatre
(1941–1945)

Malayan Peninsula

BRUNEI

Celebes Sea

PACIFIC OCEAN

Muar

Singapore

Morotai

Borneo

Dutch New Guinea

Balikpapan

Sulawesi

Sumatra

Batavia (Jakarta)

Java Sea

D U T C H

Ambon

Banda Sea

E A S T   I N D I E S

Java

Arafura Sea

Merauke

INDIAN OCEAN

Koepang

Portuguese (East) Timor

Timor Sea

Darwin

Dutch (West) Timor

AUSTRALIA

N

0   500
KILOMETRES

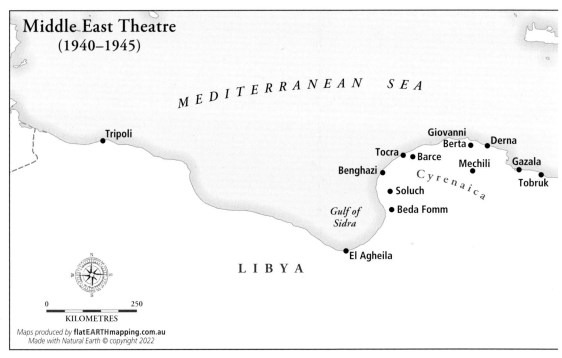

Middle East Theatre
(1940–1945)

M E D I T E R R A N E A N   S E A

Tripoli

Giovanni Berta

Derna

Tocra

Barce

Mechili

Gazala

Benghazi

Cyrenaica

Tobruk

Soluch

Beda Fomm

Gulf of Sidra

El Agheila

L I B Y A

N

0   250
KILOMETRES

Maps produced by **flatEARTH**mapping.com.au
Made with Natural Earth © copyright 2022

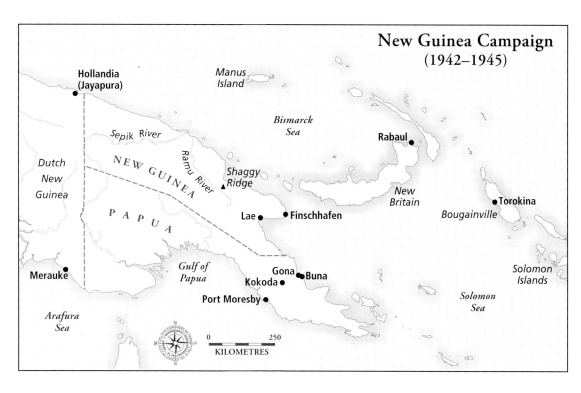

New Guinea Campaign
(1942–1945)

Hollandia (Jayapura)

Manus Island

Sepik River

Bismarck Sea

Rabaul

NEW GUINEA

Ramu River

Shaggy Ridge

New Britain

Dutch New Guinea

PAPUA

Lae ● ● Finschhafen

Torokina

Bougainville

Merauke

Gulf of Papua

Gona ● Buna

Kokoda ●

Port Moresby ●

Solomon Islands

Solomon Sea

Arafura Sea

N
W   E
S

0   250

KILOMETRES

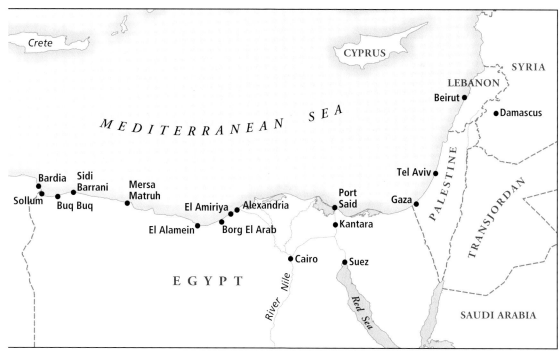

Crete

CYPRUS

SYRIA

LEBANON

Beirut ●

● Damascus

MEDITERRANEAN   SEA

PALESTINE

Tel Aviv ●

Bardia   Sidi Barrani

Mersa Matruh

Port Said ●

Gaza ●

Sollum ●
Buq Buq

El Amiriya ● ● Alexandria

Kantara ●

TRANSJORDAN

El Alamein ●   Borg El Arab

EGYPT

River Nile

Cairo ●

Suez ●

Red Sea

SAUDI ARABIA

FOREWORD

ELSON EVERED BELL was known as 'Ding Dong' in the 2/17th Battalion. His father George had been twice wounded in France, in 1916 and 1918. Elson enlisted at Randwick on 23 May 1940. He claimed to be almost twenty-one, but he was seventeen. He arrived in the Middle East in November 1940 and was hit in the left leg by shrapnel during the Siege of Tobruk, in June 1941. He was 'mentioned in despatches' in December 1941 for his bravery, during an operation in which three men went out to try to find a sniper. The officer was killed by a mine; Bell and the other man were wounded. Bell lifted his wounded comrade onto his back and carried him back to the post. Bell also served in Syria, where this picture was taken in May 1942. He was wounded again at El Alamein in October 1942. He returned to Australia and was wounded for the third time, in late 1943, in New Guinea. Bell was shipped back to Australia from Borneo in 1945 with dengue fever and malaria. He was discharged in late 1945 – one of the few to have seen action in most of the major Australian theatres of war in the Second World War. He returned to Sydney and became a carpenter. Elson Bell died in 1995.

In early 2020, when Martin Hughes at Affirm Press suggested that I look at under-age boys of the Second World War, I resisted. I was tired after two years working on my first book, *The Lost Boys*, about under-age Anzac soldiers in the First World War. I didn't believe the problem could have persisted, unchecked and unfixed, into a new conflict. Surely not.

I assumed there would be a few cases, but not the thousands who went overseas in 1914–18. Australia had changed by 1939: patriotism and ideas of 'King and Country' were not so prevalent, nor our leaders so wedded to Britain's cause. Rules and regulations for the new army would certainly be stronger

and more difficult to flout. Recruiters who turned a blind eye to fourteen-year-olds would be found out and disciplined. More people had birth certificates. Surely the government would have required some proof of age for new recruits?

Almost none of that turned out to be a hindrance. Thousands of young men – and some women – lied about their age, forged a parent's signature, or simply found a back door into the armed services, just as their fathers had done twenty-five years earlier. In fact, many did it because their fathers had done it. These youngsters had grown up on tales of the First World War. There is a strong correlation between

> Thousands of young men – and some women – lied about their age, forged a parent's signature, or simply found a back door into the armed services, just as their fathers had done twenty-five years earlier.

Ready to serve ... New recruits leave Melbourne Showgrounds in November 1939 for Puckapunyal camp.

generations: 'I wanted to go because my dad went'. If war is hell, it's clear that old men's stories were not always perceived that way by the coming generation. The more I looked, the more I found.

It was harder for the under-aged to get into the services in the Second World War, but these boys still found a way. They had to be more cunning and resourceful than their fathers. They stole papers from their older brothers or from strangers; they moved from town to town to find the lax recruiters; they figured out ways to game the system, often entering via the militia and then transferring to the Australian Imperial Force (AIF). Astonishingly, in some places and at some times, the system was as porous as it had ever been. Once in, boys as young as fourteen were protected by a culture of silence. The young did not want to be found out and the old did not want to know.

For a long while I assumed that the numbers could not have been as great as in the earlier war. I still don't know how many under-age soldiers there were, nor does anyone else. No-one has figured out a way to count them. They lied about their ages to get in, so the records are a jumble of half-truths and misdirection. It would be hard to find every lie. It's possible that more under-age boys went in the Second World War, simply because there were more than twice as many Australians across all the services. I found under-aged boys in every battalion I looked at. Some of the unit histories proudly point them out as a defining feature, even claiming distinctions that can never be tested: 'surely this was the youngest platoon in the army'. Nor do we know how many died. I hope the Australian War Memorial will eventually compile a list, as they have done for the First World War.

There were significant differences in the research and writing of this book. The service records of 550,000 men and women who served overseas are still being digitised by the National Archives of Australia, so it took longer to access the records. The more significant difference is that some of the under-aged soldiers are still alive. If I could find them, I could talk to them about what they did and why. Much of the second half of the book consists of interviews with these old men, most of them aged north of ninety-five.

School boys at Abbotsford in Victoria display their fathers' medals on Anzac Day 1943.

For the first time, AIF recruits were photographed at enlistment for official records. **STAFF SERGEANT ALAN WHITING** captures **NOEL ERNEST COLLINS** at Royal Park in Melbourne.

They were a revelation and a joy to meet. Some were in dire health and some were as fit as mallee bulls, to use their own words. Some have died since we spoke. For some, the memories had faded; others could recall details and dates as if the events happened yesterday.

I was humbled by the generosity and honesty with which they answered my questions. Some of the memories were painful and private, yet most were willing to share them. They made this book harder to write, because I didn't want to disappoint them. For all of them, the past was not the past. They did not 'get over it', as promised. For some, the emotional wounds were as strong as the day they were inflicted, even seventy-five years later.

I was struck by the fact that none blamed the authorities for letting them go as boy soldiers. They wanted to go and were proud to have done so. Almost none of them cited patriotism as their motivation. Several admitted they needed the money. They were the sons of the Depression, in that sense. Most felt they were lucky to make it through the war. Their stories make this book more directly personal than the earlier one. Their voices come through more clearly, opening a door that was closed in my previous research. For that, I thank them. I could not have been more wrong about the potential for a second book.

I am indebted first to Martin Hughes and the most excellent staff at Affirm Press. They are an exceptional outfit – dedicated, creative, patient. I thank them for believing in me and the project. My agent Jeanne Ryckmans paved the way as ever with grace and good advice; Deonie Fiford was the most sympathetic editor, once again. Michael Grealy's help with research was invaluable. John Rogers gave me a title.

Covid-19 made this book harder, in terms of logistics. I was less able to travel within Australia, which meant that I could not interview everyone I wanted to. Through it all, family and friends have been supportive and encouraging in so many ways. I thank you all at the back of the book. To my partner, Mary Dickie, who has endured me being in another century – at least in my head – for almost four years on these two books, there are no words.

INTRODUCTION

A MELANCHOLY DUTY

Australia in 1939 was not the same country that had rushed gleefully into war in 1914. Hard lessons and disillusionment had furrowed Australian brows after twenty years of economic downturn and polarising politics. The once unbreakable bond with Britain had been weakened by a series of shaky imperial promises about defence. If Australia had once been more innocently patriotic, it had also been more gullible. Attitudes were changing, alliances were shifting.

Recruitment in 1914 had been chaotic and enthusiastic, full of the sense that adventure awaited those of stout heart. The first batch of 20,000 men had taken a few days to recruit. In 1939, for several weeks, there was nowhere to join up. Thousands fronted at Victoria Barracks in Melbourne and Sydney, only to be sent home. The Royal Australian Air Force (RAAF) was flooded with men, most of whom were disappointed.

> If Australia had once been more innocently patriotic, it had also been more gullible. Attitudes were changing, alliances were shifting.

The Prime Minister, Robert Gordon Menzies, blueblood lawyer and diehard royalist, declared in a national broadcast on 3 September that Australia was at war – his melancholy duty, he said. For some weeks, he could not decide what to do next. While other parts of the British Empire announced expeditionary forces of arms and men to Europe, Menzies said there was no indication from London that such a force would be required. Australians should adopt a 'business-as-usual' approach. The Country Party members, who kept Menzies in power, were concerned that war would obstruct the export of a bumper wheat crop. In *Australia in the War of 1939–1945*, the 22-volume official history, Paul Hasluck writes that the government in late 1939 worried more about exports than self-sufficiency in arms: 'Marketing came before munitions'.

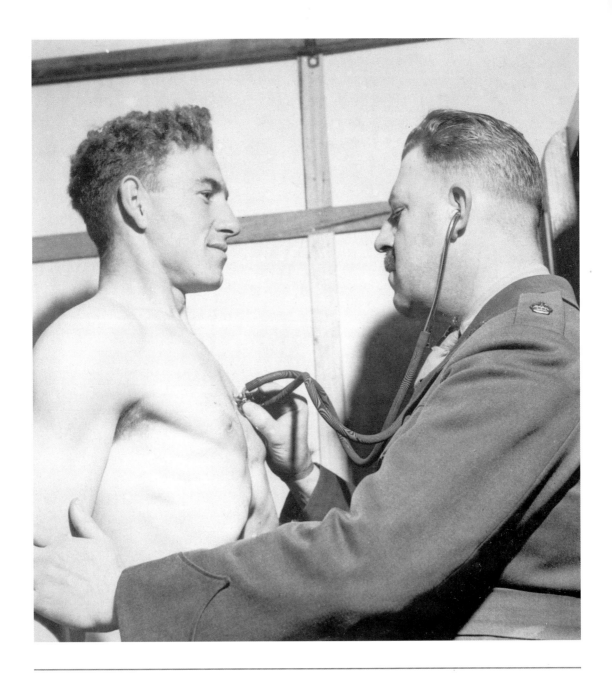

In August 1941, new recruit **BILL DAVIS** has his chest checked by an army doctor.

To some extent, this was because of lessons learned in the First World War, where Britain redirected its peacetime orders for food and materials away from Australia once war was declared. Those who now governed Australia knew that the new war would come at a high price in prosperity, as well as humanity.

For the seven million Australians who did not run the government, the lessons had been just as painful, but different in focus. It was only twenty years since a war that was supposed to end all wars. The wreckage was everywhere to be seen – repatriation hospitals full of frail, coughing veterans; limbless men working as lift-drivers; men in wheelchairs begging on street corners or lying drunk in alleys behind pubs. More than 60,000 Australian soldiers died in the First World War. Nobody knew how many had died since, their wounded bodies giving up the ghost, unseen by the statistics. Every family in Australia had been touched. Now it was happening again. Mothers, fathers and grandparents wept at the thought.

Others saw an opportunity, especially if they were poor and young. The Depression had scalded a generation. At its worst, more than a third of eligible men were unemployed. For some, the worst was over by 1939, but not for all. The National Register of July 1939 reported that 264,000 men aged between eighteen and sixty-four were out of work – approximately 12.5 per cent of all wage-earners. The real figure was much higher. Children could leave school at fourteen and work if they found a job, but they weren't even counted. For some, the army was a more attractive proposition than a badly paid job herding cattle or sweeping floors in a factory.

It is not true that the under-aged had no knowledge of the effects of the earlier war. Many went because of that war, not despite it. They had fathers who went and uncles who did not come back. They grew up listening under the table as the old comrades talked of Passchendaele and Palestine. Some wanted to measure up to their fathers' standards. Others just wanted to get away from sometimes dangerous homes. The war had damaged these older men in so many ways. Such was the misery of their sons that

This happy breed ... Some of the first men to enlist, at Melbourne Showgrounds in November 1939.

enlistment, for some, seemed a better option. They really were the sons of war.

In 1914, many men had no idea of why they were fighting, beyond vague sentiments about German aggression. In 1939, the motivation was clearer: Hitler had to be stopped. But as yet, there was no guarantee you'd get a crack at Hitler if you joined the new army. The Labor Party was opposed to sending any force overseas, as were many powerful unions. If Labor won the coming election, a man could end up guarding an oil refinery in Darwin rather than potting Germans in Europe.

By law, the militia – the part-time Citizen Military Force (CMF) – could not be sent overseas, except to Australian territories like Papua and New Guinea. To fight anywhere else, a second AIF would have to be enlisted, trained and equipped. When Menzies did finally succumb to pressure for an expeditionary force, he capped it at a mere 20,000 men – the same as in 1914.

There had been five Australian divisions in the earlier war, so this new outfit would be called the 6th Division. When they finally set sail, they were diverted to the Middle East, just as their fathers had been. They occupied some of the same ground in Egypt and Palestine, with the same misgivings – many thought they were short of the real war. Just as in 1915, they were ill-used by Winston Churchill, thrown into fights they could never win, with inadequate resources, planning and leadership. Many of them lie there now, in graves in Libya, Greece and Crete.

Distinctions between the militia and the second AIF became blurred as war went on, but there was one important

> Just as in 1915, they were ill-used by Winston Churchill, thrown in to fights they could never win, with inadequate resources, planning and leadership. Many of them lie there now, in graves in Libya, Greece and Crete.

difference. Menzies announced compulsory conscription late in 1939 for the militia. It only applied to unmarried men who would turn twenty-one before 30 June 1940, and initially only for three months' training, but it provided a back door for the under-aged. They could register a form, with a fake age, at the post office, as all eighteen-year-olds were required to do. Proof of age was not necessary. All they had to do then was wait for a letter from the government, telling them to report at an appointed date for militia training. In effect, they tricked the government into demanding their enlistment. From the militia, it was fairly easy to transfer to the AIF.

Once in, the under-aged boys dared not tell anyone their real age, but they didn't need to. The older men, including the officers, usually guessed and said nothing unless circumstances provoked some action. Nicknames like 'Junior' and 'Baby' were often applied to the very young. There is some evidence that they were protected by the older men, sometimes covertly, against the boy's own wishes, but that could only go so far: when a platoon charged into battle at El Alamein or Shaggy Ridge, every soldier had to pull his weight. Inevitably, they died in the same ways as their older compatriots. Although the reverse is also true. Some survived because they were younger and stronger than the older men, especially when it came to disease or being a prisoner of war.

The army's age policies in the Second World War were just as confused as in the First World War. Many under-age soldiers were sent back to Australia from the Middle East and New Guinea, but the process was often flouted. One boy who should have been sent home was asked instead if he would like to join his brother's unit. That cost him his life. Another boy lies in Bomana War Cemetery in Papua under his brother's name.

The persistence of some of these boys was remarkable. Weeded out once or even twice, they would go to a different location to try to fool the recruiters, or try another service. Some didn't bother enlisting: they just showed up at an army camp and joined a line, without papers or numbers, blending in. A few

They grew up listening under the table as the old comrades talked of Passchendaele and Palestine. Some wanted to measure up to their fathers' standards. Others just wanted to get away from sometimes dangerous homes.

pretenders ended up in courts in Australia at different times during the war, charged with impersonating a soldier. Two young soldiers were so bored with their duties at Aitape, on the north coast of New Guinea, that they took up with American soldiers who were flying to the Philippines. Aided and abetted by friendly GIs and officers, these two fought in American uniforms for some months, before being sent back to Australia to be tried as deserters.

Many of the stories in the book have come straight from families, handed down from one generation to the next. Others turned up in printed records, battalion histories and accounts written after the war by under-aged soldiers.

As always, the staff in the research library at the Australian War Memorial and at the Australian National Archives in Canberra gave great assistance with records. Friends and family passed on names gleaned from their friends and family, although some of these illustrated the idea that truth is the first casualty of war. A number of old soldiers who claimed to be under-age turned out not to be. It was clear from talking to descendants that many of them felt pride, rather than regret, that their father or grandfather had been under-age. It has become a badge of courage, even for those who also feel sorrow about their relative's experiences in war or afterwards.

I can understand that emotion, although I did not write this book to immortalise the under-aged soldiers. They were brave young men but not saints. They had all the same foibles and weaknesses as the older men. I suspect they had an increased desire for risk and adventure, or they would not have been there. That combination of factors made them attractive to recruiters, who admired their pluck. One could also call it lack of fear or judgement. Young men will always be available for war. Older heads should know better than to exploit that. I'd be happy if this book made one or two sixteen-year-olds think twice in the future.

CHAPTER ONE

THE LOTTERY

Patriotism and a boat trip ... Recruitment numbers took off after the
fall of France, and with the prospect of fighting overseas.

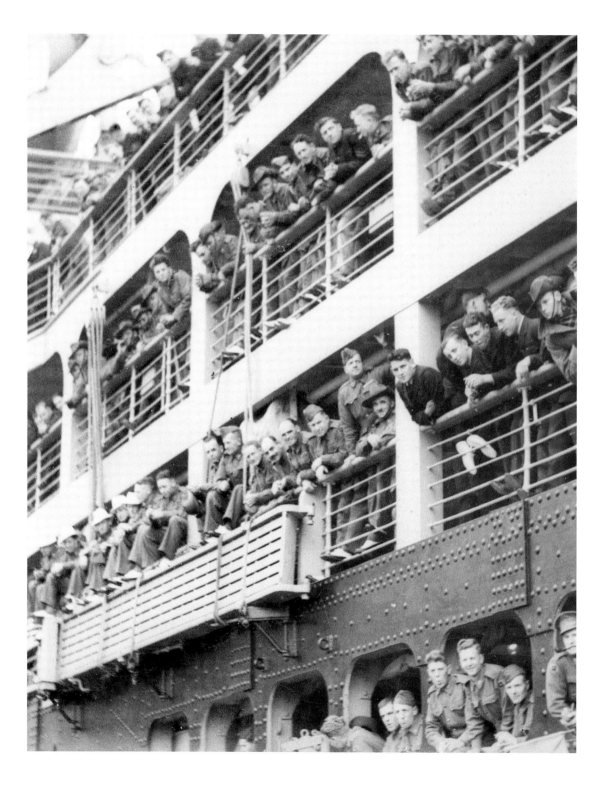

In the two decades that followed the First World War, successive Australian governments prepared for the next one by slashing defence spending and reducing the size of the armed forces. The Labor Party followed a 'never again' mindset, even as the government's own experts warned that a war was coming with Japan.

In 1929, the new Scullin Labor government cancelled the compulsory cadet training scheme by which boys aged fourteen to eighteen were supposed to be given basic training. Was that a sign of regret that the young had been allowed to participate too freely in the last war? Not at all. Labor remained ferociously opposed to conscription and the cadet scheme was a costly and inefficient way of militarising the young. It was never popular.

In other countries, Germany in particular, the opposite was true. Hitler created structures to train and indoctrinate boys and girls in his cult of war. His Hitler Youth movement had 8.8 million members at war's outset. Japan methodically created generations so devoted to the Emperor and the martial glory of Japan that they would carry out any order without question. Brutality was a benchmark for the 'good' Japanese soldier.

Frederick Crane, who was taken prisoner on Ambon Island, recalled in an interview for the Australians at War Film Archive that Japanese officers bashed

> Australia made an effort between the wars to exclude the under-aged from the enlistment process: birth certificates or identity cards were to be sighted and the attestation form actually asked for a date of birth. None of these new measures was effective if the recruiting officer decided to ignore them, as plenty did.

their own young soldiers: 'kids of fourteen, fifteen, sixteen, or seventeen years old in the army, and they'd be bashed up'. On Crete, Australian soldiers were astonished at the tender age of some of the elite German paratroopers. A German panzer unit, the 12th SS Division 'Hitlerjugend', earned a reputation for cruelty in France in 1944. It was almost wholly composed of sixteen- and seventeen-year-olds from the Hitler Youth.

As in the First World War, under-age boys fought in the British, French, Russian and American armed forces. No-one knows how many. In most cases, the official age of entry was never below seventeen, but these boys found various ways to join. Calvin Graham was twelve when he joined the US Navy after Pearl Harbor. When he was found out and discharged, he joined the US Marines at seventeen.

Australia made an effort between the wars to exclude the under-aged from the enlistment process: birth certificates or identity cards were to be sighted and the attestation form actually asked for a date of birth. None of these new measures was effective if the recruiting officer decided

to ignore them, as plenty did. Many of the recruitment officers were First World War veterans. They often abetted the young men, perhaps from a sense of sentimentality or solidarity. There was in some of these older men a tacit belief that these boys would be protected: 'We'll find something for you to do,' a recruiter said to one of the boys in these pages.

Australia and New Zealand were among the first nations to declare war, issuing proclamations on 3 September, the same day as Britain and France. Robert Menzies did not consult anyone about going to war – neither the parliament, nor the people. He just assumed the obligation: Britain was at war, so we were at war. Membership of the British Empire demanded it, even if the constitution did not. John Curtin, the leader of the opposition, reminded Menzies four days later in parliament that the government was responsible to parliament and that 'defence of the country is not a one-man job'.

Some, perhaps most, of the people agreed with Menzies but not all. Irish Catholics did not owe blind allegiance to the Crown. Much of the Labor left condemned war as a capitalist plot. The Communist Party of Australia fuelled this position, until Menzies banned the party in 1940, albeit briefly.

For the Empire-minded, it was simple: if we were to benefit from Britain's protection, then we had to do our bit when the Mother Country was attacked. Our whole defence policy was based on the assumption that the British navy would protect us in war, through the stronghold at Singapore. Some in high places in Canberra already knew that Britain's promises were shaky on Singapore, but they kept quiet. In any case, thousands of men, many too young and too old, were keen to go to war.

Note those words: a war to go to, not necessarily one that came to them. While the government dithered about sending a force overseas, some of these keen ones withheld their names. For some, it was 'no ticket, no sign', at least while there was no direct threat to Australia. Going overseas was part of the attraction – and not just anywhere overseas. They wanted to shoot at Germans, in Europe.

For an Englishman, dying in a foreign field was a poetic tragedy, because of the distance from home. But many Australians longed for the foreign field on which to prove themselves, if not actually to die.

Australian enthusiasm for both world wars was intrinsically linked to our sense of isolation. Joining the fight connected us to the rest of British humanity – 'the white race' as politicians then called it, or 'the British-speaking peoples', as John Curtin clumsily dubbed it. And if there was one thing this war was already about, it was race.

As Germany persecuted Jews, Poles, Czechs, Gypsies and the rest, Japan persecuted the Chinese, and would soon assert its 'natural' hegemony over the rest of South Asia. That hegemony was founded in a sense of racial superiority, but it was to be found on all sides. British disdain for their European neighbours went back centuries.

Australian soldiers – many of whom had never met a foreigner – had an acute

For an Englishman, dying in a foreign field was a poetic tragedy, because of the distance from home. But many Australians longed for the foreign field on which to prove themselves, if not actually to die.

(and to contemporary ears, jarring) understanding of it. Their letters and diaries are full of descriptions of the 'national characteristics' of the other 'races' they encountered, most of them disparaging generalisations. The Egyptians were filthy 'wogs', the Jews grasping 'Hebes', the Italians lazy and cowardly 'Eye-ties', the Germans bloodthirsty 'Jerries and Hermans' although good fighters. The British were weedy and hopeless 'chooms' – which seems to be an approximation of a northern English pronunciation of 'chum' – who were all right for a pint and a punch-up, but lacked the spirit to tell an officer what for, which the Australians counted as part of their right as volunteers. Things were bound to end in tears when all these groups got together in the western desert of Libya … but, first, a man had to get there.

The government finally decided in late November to send the 6th Division abroad, in January. Recruitment fell away after they sailed, then picked up again in February when the government announced a 7th Division would be raised. By March, 100,000 men had volunteered to serve overseas. This was equivalent to one in six of the men aged from twenty to twenty-nine, but the figure is deceptive: 68,000 of them applied for the air force, the more romantic option; the AIF received only 22,000 applications.

For men who had just come through the Depression, soldiering was an attractive option, now that it would mean getting on a boat. The army paid six shillings a day and board when serving overseas. The problem was you never knew where the troopship would take you. Enlisting was something of a lottery – and one of the prizes was that you might die.

For an under-age boy, the choices to enlist were complex and changing. The different services had different age

For the first time, women could enlist and do war work: **ELSIE MYRA (JUDY) RICHARDS** of Newcastle making anti-tank shells in September 1942.

requirements and different rates of pay. It appears they had different standards of proof too: the navy and air force were more likely to insist on seeing a birth certificate. Army recruiters were more hit-and-miss.

To join the AIF in 1939, you had to be between twenty and thirty-five, unless you had a parent's written permission to go at nineteen. In 1940, the maximum age was raised to forty; the minimum dropped to nineteen in September 1941 and eighteen in April 1943. This repeated the pattern of the First World War, where the authorities kept reducing the age to keep up with the rate of casualties.

The reasoning was somewhat different this time: before April 1943, the AIF was losing too many recruits to the Royal Australian Navy (RAN) and Royal Australian Air Force (RAAF) which were open to eighteen-year-olds. Boys of eighteen could also enter the militia, the part-time home defence force, a year before they could join the AIF. By lowering the AIF minimum to eighteen in 1943, the government levelled the playing field – although in practice, the navy and air force were still harder to crack.

The British navy had for centuries taken children as recruits. The youngest member of Admiral Nelson's crew in the Battle of Trafalgar was ten years old. The Australian navy did not quite follow suit. It set up training schools for boys aged fourteen to eighteen, after which they could enter the full service, signing on for seven years. A small number of seventeen-year-olds got into the RAAF, but their standards remained the highest of all the services. You would have to wait years and be among the best and the brightest to become a fly-boy.

If you had barely finished school, had dirt under your fingernails and could not afford a haircut, the only real choice was the army. That is where the vast majority of under-age boys found a place – the 'PBI', as it was sometimes called: 'the poor bloody infantry'. Even so, some of them had tragically short experience of it.

Tasman Frank Hite came from a large family in Wynyard, near Burnie in Tasmania (hence the proud first name). He had a brother in the navy, another in the air force and two in the AIF, one of whom became a prisoner of war. Tasman was the fifth of six sons, with one sister, Lesley.

Before the war, Tasman worked at Barnard's cream factory in Wynyard. He enlisted in the militia on 4 January 1940, and was sent to the 6th Garrison battalion, guarding Fort Direction, on a peninsula overlooking the entrance to the Derwent River south of Hobart. On Monday night, 4 March, Private Hite was in a tent with eight or nine other soldiers, one of whom was holding a loaded .303 rifle. As Hite bent down, the gun accidentally discharged, killing him almost instantly. He was seventeen. He had been in the army for two months and never even left the island.

Tasman Hite may have been the first under-age Australian soldier to die in the Second World War. He is buried in Wynyard cemetery.

A few months later, in Port Phillip Bay, near Melbourne, Ordinary Seaman Frank Rupert Hack stepped onto the mine-sweeper HMAS *Goorangai*, a converted trawler, for his first day at sea. He had been preparing for this life for some time, as a Sea Scout, then a Sea Cadet, before entering the naval reserve. He was finally given his chance because another sailor had been seasick the previous day. As the *Goorangai* patrolled near the heads around 8.30pm on 20 November, an interstate passenger liner entering the bay under full blackout ploughed into her side, sinking the tiny *Goorangai*. All twenty-four crew and officers on board died, including Frank Hack, aged seventeen, of South Yarra.

The passenger ship's captain was

> As Hite bent down, the gun accidentally discharged, killing him almost instantly. He was seventeen. He had been in the army for two months and never even left the island.

charged over the accident. Evidence at the coronial inquiry stated that the side lights of the *Goorangai* could be difficult to see, a result of her conversion from a trawler. Only six bodies were recovered; none was identified as Ordinary Seaman Hack.

Leonard Michael Barnes typifies the experience of boys who were determined to overcome all obstacles to serve. Neither the Australian navy nor the merchant navy wanted him. He had no identity card, so he contrived to get one by convincing a justice of the peace that he was eighteen and had been fruit-picking for two years. Once he had that ID, he tried the air force but they said he had poor eyesight.

He had one card left to play. The fake ID made him eligible for the militia – indeed, he was required to register as an eighteen-year-old. He left his home in Howitt Street, North Melbourne, on 11 January 1943, telling his mother he was going fruit-picking. Instead, he filled out his papers for the militia, giving his date of birth as 3 January 1925 (his real birthdate was 5 February 1929). At Caulfield on 18 January, they measured him and checked his vitals. He weighed 130 pounds (59 kilograms) and stood five feet five inches tall (165 centimetres). His eyes were hazel, his hair brown; his chest X-ray was clear and his eyesight was good enough for the army. The doctor recorded him as having slightly flat feet and 'hammer toes' but these did not worry him.

'And how old are you, my boy?' no-one asked.

If he had told the truth, he would have said he was thirteen years, eight months and twenty-one days old. Many later claimed to be the youngest man in the army, but at this point, Leonard Michael Barnes probably was.

On 18 January, they sent him off to a camp at Watsonia, on the north-east outskirts of Melbourne, but he had made one mistake. He gave his correct address

Youngest of the young … In January 1943, **LEN BARNES** enlisted at thirteen years and eight months – albeit briefly.

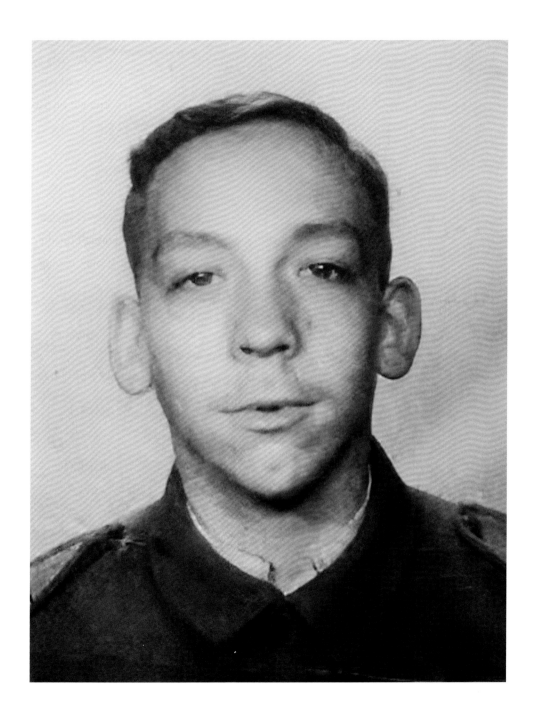

and, like a good son, allotted some of his pay to his mother, Eileen. Soon after, the army sent her a form to fill out for the allotment. She now knew that he had enlisted. Two weeks after he joined up, his father found him 'smoking his pipe in his tent', according to one of the many news reports that followed. Leonard's excellent army adventure lasted twenty-four days. It's worth noting that he was not foiled by the army, but his own sense of duty to his mother. Others in this book of similarly tender age were craftier, and able to stay in much longer.

As in the earlier war, the newspapers could not get enough of these boys. The media played their part in driving recruitment by treating under-age boys as heroes, boys with pluck and spunk, and

'a fine example to the older men'.

On Sunday, 19 September 1943, the *Brisbane Truth* carried a cracker yarn on page ten.

'Surely nowhere else in the world is there a boy, who at the same age, has tasted the full savour of life in the manner of Thomas Arthur Sullivan, of South Brisbane. He went a'soldiering at the age of thirteen, when he joined an army which was fighting its country's battles; he married at the age of fifteen; and now, at the age of sixteen, he is the father of a three-week old baby!'

The report said that Sullivan had been soldiering for two years when he told the army his real age. It gave his date of birth as 24 July 1927. He had followed an older brother, James, who had served

> The war brought misery to a lot of young women, in the form of unwanted pregnancies and unhappy love affairs, but it also brought liberation of a sort. Women were finally admitted to the armed services, and to jobs in support of the war effort.

with distinction in Papua in 1942, receiving a commendation from General Douglas MacArthur himself.

Tom Sullivan told *Truth* that he enlisted in the militia in December 1941, then transferred to the AIF in September 1942. It helped that he was 'a giant of a lad', six feet tall and 'built in proportion'.

Five years later, in 1948, Sullivan sued for divorce, on the grounds of his wife's adultery. According to his counsel, he was anxious to marry a new sweetheart once his divorce came through. The case was uncontested. This time, Sullivan said he had joined the army at age fourteen, not thirteen. He had only lived with his wife for a week before returning for army duty in Townsville. After he was discharged in 1943, he went droving.

'He has certainly made a mess of things,' said his counsel, 'but he's only twenty-one.' He had grown up without parental control, his father having died when he was about seven.

'He had a mother, didn't he?' asked the judge, before granting the decree nisi.

The war brought misery to a lot of young women, in the form of unwanted pregnancies and unhappy love affairs, but it also brought liberation of a sort. Women were finally admitted to the armed services, and to jobs in support of the war effort. They had been resolutely kept out of the workforce in the First World War, but by 1941, hundreds of thousands were already in the civil workforce. It still took two years to convince the government that it needed them in war work, both to replace men who had gone to the front and to keep production of food and matériel going.

The Labor Party, newly returned to power in October 1941, was caught in an exquisite bind. In general, women were paid less than two thirds of a man's wage, but they would now be doing the same work. Labor stood for equal pay for equal work, but what was to happen when the men returned? The unions worried that the bosses would try to lower men's wages, because women had worked for less. John Curtin promised the women would have to give up the jobs that men had left.

Most of the new positions were strictly open to women of eighteen and over, but there were some quirks. In Lismore, in September 1942, a twin brother and sister of eighteen years turned up together to enlist. She was accepted by the Australian Women's Army Service. He was rejected because the AIF did not take eighteen-year-olds (as yet).

As with their brothers, a few under-age girls used elaborate tricks to get what they wanted. Hazel Dell, of Balgowlah, Sydney, was born in December 1925. In December 1942, still only sixteen, she borrowed her older sister's identity to enlist in the WRANS, the Women's Royal Australian Naval Service. She served for two years as Ena Dell at a number of bases in north Queensland.

In most states, girls as young as fifteen could enter the Women's Air Training Corps, which prepared them to join the Women's Australian Auxiliary Air Force. Thousands attended evening classes around the country, then went on to enlist. The other states took girls of fifteen, but Queensland would not take them until they were sixteen, and resisted efforts to fall into line. Mrs W Hann, the state president, explained that Queensland 'could not accept responsibility for younger girls coming into the city at night to attend lectures'. She had a point: Brisbane by then was overrun with soldiers on leave, both Australian and American.

The double standard was quite subtle: the authorities made little attempt to stop under-age boys getting into the army. They could fight and die, and did. Young ladies, on the other hand, could not go to night classes in Brisbane until sixteen, for fear of these very same soldiers.

The Depression taught a lot of men not to trust the government, or bankers, or newspapers. The social contract had taken a battering. For some of the under-aged boys, the army offered them a full belly and a warm bed, for the first time in their young lives. They were happy to take off on an adventure, because their childhoods had ended many years earlier. It says a lot about the harrowing effects of the Depression that they thought a war might be a better bet. ✤

'Daddy, where are you going?' At Mirboo in Victoria in 1943, a small boy on parade with his father.

CHAPTER TWO

THE BOXER

BOB 'HOOKER' HOLT

BOB HOLT was a pugnacious fifteen-year-old when he enlisted.

On a cold night in December 1940, seventeen-year-old Private Bob Holt became lost on the edge of the vast Libyan desert. Holt had volunteered for a hazardous mission. He and another soldier were to go out at midnight and hide themselves near the Italian wire protecting Bardia, a small town on the coast between Tobruk and Alexandria. They were to lie out there all day watching the Italian movements, then creep back to the Australian positions after dark, hopefully with valuable information. Except that Bob Holt could not even find his comrade, who was sleeping in a dusty hole nearby.

'The sentry woke me about midnight and I went across the other section's holes to pick up the fellow going with me. When I was about there, I whispered, "Are you right?"'

'No answer so I changed direction and walked a few yards. "Are you there?" Still no answer. I called to our section leader Charlie Johnston. "Are you there, Charlie?" There never was an answer. The platoon could hear me, but I couldn't hear their reply so I walked on.'

He eventually reached the Italian wire, which was strung out in two rows beside an anti-tank trench. 'I took a line on the stars and was eventually challenged by a sentry in the Royal Artillery lines. I about-turned and hit the Iti wire, then back to our lines where I ran into the 2/1st Battalion. They turned me in the right direction and, just as it was breaking day, I saw heads bobbing up from holes. It was my platoon and I was hungry and thirsty and tired after marching all night … took me quite a while to live down this experience.'

Robert Gordon Holt was one month past his seventeenth birthday when this happened. He had joined the army on 21 October 1939, fourteen months earlier, just after war broke out. He was then only fifteen but he looked older. When he and a baby-faced friend tried to get a beer at the Great Southern Hotel in Sydney, the barmaid told them that Bob was all right but his mate – who really was eighteen – would have to come back when he grew up.

Holt had been an amateur boxer in the Police Citizens Boys Clubs around

Newcastle, New South Wales. He could handle himself but his tendency to haul off and punch people, including officers, had already earned him the nickname of 'Hooker' Holt.

Bob Holt's father and two uncles had served in the first AIF in the First World War. One died at Passchendaele in Belgium. Bob had grown up listening to their tales. The second AIF was just what this pugnacious fifteen-year-old had been waiting for.

'The Second World War broke out in September 1939 and as soon as the call went out for volunteers, I hotfooted it to enlist, giving my age as twenty-one. My people protested vigorously, but upstart that I was, I informed them that if they pulled me out, I would leave home and enlist under a bodgie name. With that they bowed to the inevitable and gave me their blessing, more or less, anyhow.'

Holt went into camp in November and realised immediately that there were two types of soldier – and he didn't like the other kind. 'At this time the militiamen who had signed up for Home Defence Duties were paid eight shillings a day, whilst the men of the AIF, who had volunteered for Active Service abroad, were paid the princely sum of five shillings a day. This created quite a deal of ill-feeling and there were regular brawls in Liverpool between the two groups. Single men and small groups were often viciously attacked by gangs of twenty or more, spoiling for a fight. Liverpool was a good place to keep away from in those days.'

> Bob Holt's father and two uncles had served in the first AIF in the First World War. One died at Passchendaele in Belgium. Bob had grown up listening to their tales. The second AIF was just what this pugnacious fifteen-year-old had been waiting for.

FRANK HURLEY'S graphic photograph of Australian troops in the battle for Tobruk, January 1941.

The rift between the AIF and the militiamen was historical. The favourite taunt was for an AIF man to shout 'Choco' or 'Violet Crumble' at a militiaman. The first meant you were a chocolate soldier (melts in battle); the second meant you were yellow on the inside, like the chocolate-covered honeycomb bar. The AIF men would also sing a parody version of a popular song: 'We do most of the work and do all the killing / Scum, scum, the militia can kiss my bum.'

Not that there had been any killing yet. The first year of the war in North Africa had been relatively quiet. The Australians of the 6th Division, the first to arrive in the Middle East in January 1940, came, saw and sat down, in a succession of uncomfortable tent camps full of flies and fine sand. Apart from the food, the only danger was an occasional bomb dropped from high altitude by the Italian air force.

The eastern coast of Libya had once been a Roman province called Cyrenaica, after the ancient city of Cyrene. In the late nineteenth century, Italian colonists came to farm and trade, living uneasily beside Arab and Berber tribes. They built Italian-style garrison towns at the ports of Tobruk, Derna and Benghazi, with a magnificent road to connect them. Mussolini, the Italian dictator, now controlled Cyrenaica as well as Tripolitania on the coast further west. The major prize in Cyrenaica was

---

Aside from his youth, Bob Holt typified many of the qualities of the Australian soldier. He was generous and sentimental, but did not take kindly to discipline. He left school early but had a keen common sense. In later years he developed a love of reading that lasted the rest of his life. He was loyal but not patriotic.

Benghazi, but to get to it, the British would have to take the towns along the Libyan coast–Sidi Barrani, Bardia, then Tobruk, each more heavily fortified than the last. Tobruk had the only good harbour on the Cyrene coast before Benghazi, but it was heavily defended. And Mussolini had his own ambitions. If he could defeat the British Army of the Nile in Egypt, he could take control of the Suez Canal. That would give the Axis forces a real chance to control the entire Mediterranean. Hitler would have been well pleased.

For the British, victory in North Africa was vital. Hitler would have to think twice about invading Britain if his underbelly was open to attack through Italy, Greece, or any country on the Mediterranean.

Aside from his youth, Bob Holt typified many of the qualities of the Australian soldier. He was generous and sentimental, but did not take kindly to discipline. He left school early but had a keen common sense. In later years he developed a love of reading that lasted the rest of his life. He was loyal but not patriotic. His atti-tude toward Arabs, officers and English-men was largely contemptuous, but could quickly change if he perceived signs of humanity. He already had a strong sense of justice and a hatred of bullies. When he went ashore at Colombo in Ceylon (Sri Lanka), on the boat over, he was appalled at the poverty, reaching into his pocket for every beggar he saw until he realised he would have no money for beer if he kept going. He revelled in the irrev-erent humour of the army, which could be very black. New recruits at camp were invariably greeted with cries of 'You'll be sorry'. Camp meals would ring out with 'Who called the cook a bastard?', to which the reply was always: 'Who called the bastard a cook?'

In 1981, in his late fifties, 'Hooker' Holt published a memoir about the war called *From Ingleburn to Aitape – The Trials and Tribulations of a Front-Line Aussie Soldier*. The book is remarkable for its irreverence and humour, but above all for its frankness. Holt did not believe in self-censorship. As a portrait of a young soldier and the way that he and his comrades behaved, it is pungently honest.

'Leave to Cairo was plentiful and at the first opportunity I headed for the Berka [the red-light district] to hire a gharry [a horse-drawn carriage] to take me out to see the pyramids and other places of historical interest. As the day was hot, I called into the Egyptiana Cafe and I was undone. The beer was cold and the salted peanuts were on the house. I never did get to visit the pyramids then or at any other time as I could never make it past the Egyptiana cafe.'

His description of the Berka district is eye-watering. 'The Berka was about a mile long, with three- or four-storied brick buildings along both sides of the street. There were brothels on one side and on the other side were cafes, drinking shops and more brothels. The girls came in all shapes, sizes and colours and the going rate for a look over the shoulder was 20 ackers [about four shillings, or 80 per cent of a day's pay] … The notorious Bull Ring was an alley off the main street and it resembled a rabbit warren with girls hanging out of the windows importuning the soldiers in a dozen different languages. The whole area had a distinctive smell all of its own. It wasn't too bad in the mornings – but of an evening – whew! Drunken soldiers would urinate from the top of the stairs in some of the establishments and this would collect in the worn portions of the marble steps. Late at night soldiers wishing to visit ladies on the top floors would have to paddle and splash through pools of piss.'

He describes how most soldiers would visit the Blue Light Clinic 'for a washout' after sex. 'There was some sort of greasy salve on the end of the penis, which was covered with a piece of tissue paper.' He was always amused to see lines of soldiers walking around the streets in their loose-fitting 'Bombay bloomers' shorts, with tissue paper falling from their shorts like confetti.

He took part in 'The Battle of the Berka', the causes of which he never discovered. 'In the main it was the Australians and New Zealanders thumping the tar out of anyone who happened to be near … I was thumping one gentleman in the only place I could reach, his stomach. Someone leaned across me and punched the provost to the ground, whereupon the Red Cap [the military policeman] got up and took himself off at the gallop.'

On the way back to camp, they had another melee with Egyptian police, who were wielding belts. 'We arrived back in camp minus a lot of skin and hair, hung over and feeling sick, sore and sorry for ourselves. We were even more sorry for ourselves when we lost twenty-eight days' pay.'

Holt was in 3 Section, 10 Platoon, B Company, 2/3rd Battalion, 16th Brigade, 6th Division, AIF. A section had about ten riflemen – the smallest unit in the army, and the closest knit. They ate, slept, trained and fought together, mostly for years. His section was known as 'the Bing Boys' after two comic characters in a popular stage musical of the First World War. The name was notorious as the Bing Boys got into more trouble than any other part of the battalion, some of it serious enough that they were disbanded before the first battle at Bardia with some sent home and others jailed or redistributed or both.

Holt describes a stunt they pulled regularly, where they would volunteer for 'picquet duty' on the streets of Jerusalem or Tel Aviv. They were supposed to patrol the streets and keep other soldiers out of trouble – a bit like poachers posing as gamekeepers. Holt and his close friend Snowy Parkinson, the youngest and fastest in the section, would enter a cafe and demand bottles of spirits and then 'leg it up the street'. Their sergeant, 'Punchy'

'As the day was hot, I called into the Egyptiana Cafe and I was undone. The beer was cold and the salted peanuts were on the house. I never did get to visit the pyramids then or at any other time as I could never make it past the Egyptiana cafe.'

O'Brien, would then appear to reassure the upset cafe owner that his men would catch the thieving devils. They would set off in pursuit, meet at a predetermined spot a few streets away, and get drunk. If the cafe owner joined the pursuit, he faced being assaulted.

Holt was reassigned briefly to the 2/2nd Australian General Hospital in Gaza. He had objected to this. 'I gave myself leave and pottered around the city and the fleshpots of Jaffa until my money ran out.' Returning to the hospital, he was sentenced to fourteen days in the Jerusalem military jail – an experience he did not enjoy. Back at the hospital, his second request for a transfer was refused. This time, he says, he punched the sergeant who was charged with reforming him and this time he was sent back to his battalion.

He rejoined the 2/3rd Battalion on 18 July 1940, resuming training at a camp just outside Alexandria. 'We had previously thought we were fit and tough, but after a series of route marches and manoeuvres, we knew we were tough, and all hands were itching to have a go at the Italians.'

In December 1940 British and Indian troops retook the town of Sidi Barrani, occupied during Mussolini's half-hearted invasion of Egypt in September. The Allied forces had been hampered by lack of supplies, particularly tanks. These had now begun to arrive. They faced a much larger Italian force, well dug in at outposts along the coast, but the Italians were a demoralised force, riven with differences. Some units and commanders were entirely pro-Fascist; others were offended by the dictator's meddling in the army and his subservient relationship with Hitler. There was a third force at work in this campaign: the weather, specifically the 'Khamsin' wind that lashed both sides with extremely fine particles of sand. These could stop heavy trucks and tanks from moving for days on end. Water was so short that no-one could

BOB HOLT became a professional boxer after the war. This was taken in New Zealand around 1949.

wash. Soldiers used spit on a rag to wipe their eyes.

Finally heading west along the coast of Egypt, Holt's B Company stopped by an old cemetery as Italian bombers came over. The men dived into any hole they could find, including graves. 'Some ghoulish chappies decorated their holes with a collection of old skulls and bones which were lying around the ground in great profusion.' That night, they marched over Halfaya Pass (immediately renamed 'Hellfire' by the troops) and into positions outside Bardia. The nights were so cold that men pooled blankets and slept huddled together, although Holt found it difficult, because of the stench of some of his comrades. There was respite when his section was sent to guard a water point at a nearby fort, and Holt was able to have a bath.

Before dawn on 3 January 1941, Australian soldiers finally went into action – their first major engagement of the Second World War. 'We were dressed and equipped in under-clothes, sweaters, woollen uniforms, overcoats, leather jackets, tin hats, extra ammunition, grenades, web equipment, gas masks and pick or a shovel. On our back we had sown a patch of white cloth, so that our own troops following in the dark would recognise us …'

The 2/1st Battalion was first through the holes in the wire blasted by the engineers using 'Bangalore' torpedoes. Holt and his unit followed, passing a bunch of Libyan prisoners, 'shivering and shaking … the result of our artillery bombardment'. One of the main tasks of the engineers was to quickly fill in parts of the anti-tank trenches, so that their own tanks could enter the town. He describes seeing men 'toiling like beavers', drenched in sweat and dust, singing 'Ho Ho, we dig, dig, dig' as Italian shells rained upon them. 'To this day, I do not know if the Sappers filling in the anti-tank ditch were drunk, but they certainly sounded like it.'

Moving forward, Holt saw the results of his side's artillery bombardment – dead men strewn about the ground. Charlie Johnston, an older man from his section, told him not to look. 'Of course I immediately did and saw one of Musso's men cut in two halves and sliced down the chest, like meat in a butcher's shop. I came very close to heaving, but in the next few days we saw a lot more shocking sights and it is remarkable how blasé a man can get in a short space of time'.

The 2/3rd Battalion lost five officers and fifty-six men in the next three days. The 6th Division took more than 40,000 Italian prisoners, many of whom were shipped back to camps in Australia. Holt describes repeated almost-charges by Australian troops on Italian strongholds, which would end as soon as they began, as white flags went up. 'The Itis fought hard on occasion from behind their sangars [rock pile fences], but in the main when we got close enough to charge, out would come the white flags and they would come out with their cardboard suitcases already packed.'

The 'ratting' then began: a systematic search of all prisoners for documents that would be useful for intelligence, and the wholesale theft of anything else. Holt was an enthusiastic ratter, taking whatever he wanted from the 'perfumed and pomaded' Italian officers. 'I had pockets full of money and wedding rings, some mother-of-pearl inlaid pistols and some flash fountain pens. I had wristwatches up both arms – so many in fact that I became quite selective with the pocket watches.'

Bardia was full of dumps of Italian food and wine, so the Australians helped themselves. Many soldiers were drunk for days. 'We trained a little, swam a little, drank a lot of wine and then took off in trucks for the hundred-mile journey to Tobruk.'

Bob Holt had a long war. He went through the Australian campaigns in Greece and Syria, where he was badly wounded in the chest and leg, then returned to Australia. He served in New Guinea against the Japanese, before his discharge from the army in late 1945. His younger brother Len had enlisted at fourteen but was found out and removed from the ranks before he could leave Australia; he later served in the British Commonwealth Occupation Force in Japan, then the wars in Korea and

Vietnam. Bob Holt became a prominent boxer and trainer in Sydney in the 1950s and '60s. He married and had two sons, Robert and Steven, both of whom also boxed professionally.

'When Dad joined up he was five foot ten inches (179 centimetres) tall and 12.5 stone (80 kilograms),' according to his son Robert Emmett Holt. 'When he got out six years later, he was an inch shorter, because of the injured leg, and 8.5 stone (54 kilograms). He spent a year on crutches when he came back. He had to learn to walk again.'

Bob Junior remembers hearing that his father found it difficult to readjust when he came home. 'He did not like sleeping in a bed. He would sleep on the floor. He liked open spaces. There was a dinner at his parents' home and one of his cousins asked how he was, and he started to laugh, and that turned to tears and back to laughter. I think that was some stress-related condition. I asked him once about what it was like to lose friends in battle, and he said, "Think about what it would be like to lose a thousand of your best mates …"

'He did not do it for love of King and Country. He did not do it because he was poor. He was a young man. I think he was tough from an early age and his father had been a soldier … It was the manly thing to do and he was looking for a bit of adventure … Dad liked to fight and he did not like to be told what to do and that never changed.

'He finished up very left-of-centre in his political views, very pro-union. I just assumed as a boy that I was going to be a soldier when I got old enough, but he said, "No, you will not be a soldier, you are not going." He helped start up the Bankstown chapter of 'Save Our Sons' group, opposing the Vietnam War. He would not march on Anzac Day, because he thought it had become a glorification of war. He would wait till after the ceremonies and then join his mates.'

Robert Gordon 'Hooker' Holt died in 1983, aged sixty-nine. His ashes were sprinkled in his favourite cove at Balmain, near the wharves where he had once worked. 🞄

BOB HOLT returned to Australia after being seriously wounded in Syria.

CHAPTER THREE

THE BABIES OF TOBRUK

EDWIN RAYMOND DAYS

DOUGLAS FOSTER

JACK JENKINS

On Easter Sunday 1940, Prime Minister Robert Menzies spent the day at his retreat on Mount Macedon, just outside Melbourne. The Minister for Defence, Geoffrey Street, relaxed at his farm in Lismore, Victoria, while the Minister for Air, James Fairbairn, flew his own plane to his grazing property at Mount Elephant, in the Western District. The Nazi propaganda machine had threatened 'Easter Terror' but it never came, so most of Australia's war cabinet took the weekend off.

These were the last days of the 'Bore War', as British newspapers called it – the unexpectedly quiet period between declaration of war in September 1939 and the launch of full-scale belligerence in Europe. German submarines were sinking British and European ships, but there was very little shooting on the Maginot and Siegfried Lines, the respective fortress lines between Germany and France. German newspapers dubbed this period the 'Sitzkrieg', a pun on the already famous tactic of 'blitzkrieg'. Americans called it 'the phoney war', maintaining their distance from a war they were reluctant to join. Everyone waited for Herr Hitler, the German chancellor, to make his move.

This was not good enough for Edwin Raymond 'Teddy' Days, aged fifteen, of Goulburn Street, Yarraville, an inner-western suburb of Melbourne. He was determined to find what war there was, wherever it was. He went off to work as usual that Saturday morning as a butcher-boy, delivering meat for a local butcher, but he never came home. He disappeared without trace – no note, no letters, no hints. His family would hear nothing from him for more than a year, and even then, the contact was not made by him. Teddy did not wish to be found.

There was a certain ruthlessness about his behaviour. It was not unusual for under-aged boys to change their names or run away from home to enlist, but most registered their correct address. If anything happened to them, their family would still be informed. Not Teddy. If he had wanted to torment his parents and two sisters, this was a good way to do it.

'Eyes right' ...
**DOUGLAS
FOSTER**, at right,
during a march-
past, before leaving
Australia with the
2/17th Battalion.

His mother would say later that Teddy had 'fighting blood in his veins'. Her father, Edward Smythe, was killed at Pozières in France in the First World War. Two of her brothers also fought in that war; another was fighting in this new war. Edwin Days Senior, Teddy's father, had served in the 8th Light Horse in Palestine, Egypt and Syria. Now his son was about to experience the same heat, dust and discomfort, in many of the same places, twenty-five years later. Teddy enlisted on 6 May, about five weeks after he ran away.

He was now on the road to Tobruk, an outpost on the coast of North Africa that few Australians could have found on a map. By the war's end, the men who fought there would be almost as famous as those who had fought at Gallipoli in 1915, and for some of the same reasons. They would become immortalised as the 'Rats of Tobruk' – 20,000 Australian and 10,000 British and Indian forces, holding on grimly for nine months to the only deep-water port on the eastern coast of Libya, against the might of Hitler's Afrika Korps. A German English-language propagandist had called them 'scurrying rats' in a radio broadcast, and the men in Tobruk adopted the term with pride. They were dug into dusty holes along a 40-kilometre frontier, short of water, ammunition and food – everything except the will to fight.

Teddy had planned his Easter escape well. By leaving on the Saturday, he got a day's start on the police, who probably would not start looking for him until Monday. By then he would be over the border in New South Wales, heading for Sydney. His father placed advertisements in the papers, had messages broadcast on the radio, searched every army camp in

---

TEDDY DAYS ran away from home to enlist in March 1940. His mother said he had 'fighting blood in his veins'.

Victoria but his efforts were hampered by the lack of a recent photograph. He suspected his son had joined the army but there was no trace of anyone by that name in army records.

That's because Teddy now called himself Robert Thomas Summers. He had become a member of the new 2/13th Battalion, headquartered at Ingleburn, just outside Sydney. His papers said he was twenty-one and five months – a full five and a half years older than he was. In the photograph taken on enlistment, he scowls as if to say, 'Don't even think about asking!'

The first arrivals at the new Ingleburn camp in November 1939 had had to bring their own knife, fork and spoon, such was the army's level of preparedness. There were few designated cooks and the kitchens and meat lockers didn't have flyscreens. Drainage ditches and mess huts were still being built, so hygiene was terrible and officers had to sit on butter boxes. 'Other ranks', meaning everyone else, slept on a canvas bag called a 'palliasse', stuffed with straw. Ingleburn would have been good preparation for the Middle East, had they known that was where they were going. It was hot as an oven in summer, cold as the grave in winter, with dust and snakes and plenty of flies.

Teddy's 2/13th Battalion was part of the 7th Division, whose formation began in February 1940. The division was not complete when Adolf Hitler invaded Holland and Belgium on 10 May 1940. Churchill replaced Neville Chamberlain that day as prime minister of Great Britain. Holland surrendered after five days, Belgium on 28 May.

> His papers said he was twenty-one and five months – a full five and a half years older than he was. In the photograph taken on enlistment, he scowls as if to say, 'Don't even think about asking!'

France was soon to be overrun by the hated 'Boche'.

The news of the evacuation at Dunkirk in June 1940 rocked the Australian public. The phoney war was over. Things were now serious. Hitler had conquered most of western Europe in three weeks. On a clear day, his troops could see the white cliffs of Dover.

Many Australian men had hesitated to enlist before this point. A significant number in the unions and the Labor Party were pacifists, after bitter experience in the First World War. Others had watched as Spain tore itself apart in a civil war and Germany embraced Nazism. For these politically aware men, the threat from Fascism was real. Unlike some of their fathers, they recognised a cause worth fighting for.

Steadily, then enthusiastically, recruits began to arrive, as the government announced the formation of the 8th Division, then the 9th. By the end of July 1940, the 7th and 8th divisions were full and another 50,000 men had put their names down, enough for two more divisions. The government sus-

pended recruitment. They had neither the equipment nor the officers to cope with such numbers, nor the places to train them. Teddy Days had chosen the right time to run away from home.

Douglas Foster was sent home on his first attempt to enlist, in November 1939. He was then aged fifteen and four months and had not long left school. He was tall but still looked like a boy. He had grown up in Willoughby, just north of the Sydney Harbour Bridge. His parents operated a dairy farm on land later occupied by Channel Nine studios. Douglas had a job in the city but he ached to be in a soldier's uniform.

Six months later, in May 1940, he tried again. He went to a different recruiting office and declared that he was twenty-one – the age at which he would not need his parents' permission. He passed the medical check and was sent straight to Ingleburn, one of the youngest in a young battalion, the 2/17th. He had not told his parents, Anne and William. The

first they knew of it was when he came home in September in uniform, on pre-embarkation leave. His father had fought in the First World War, but both parents were hard to convince. He was now sixteen and two months. They made him promise he would transfer to the navy. He never did.

Jack Jenkins first presented himself on 19 April at Homebush in Sydney, but had not been required for another month. By Monday, 20 May, the newspapers were still trying to sound optimistic about the situation in France. On Tuesday, Jack walked in to Victoria Barracks in Paddington, Sydney, and took the Oath of Enlistment.

Jack Jenkins was already eighteen when he enlisted, but that was still under-age in 1940 so he lied, claiming to be twenty-one and three months old. He was an unmarried labourer from Cabra-matta, one of the outermost western suburbs of Sydney. Jack was living at

home with his parents, Violet and Joe, which must have been riotous, given that he had fourteen brothers and sisters.

The Jenkins family was close. Jack grew up sporty and active, a handy boxer and footballer. With that many brothers and sisters, there was usually enough for two teams. He was bright and outgoing, not so fond of school, but very social. Jack had left school at thirteen to start work as a baker. By 1940, he had been five years in the workforce.

The lies Jack Jenkins told on his enlistment form were pretty standard for under-age recruits. The recruitment officers could demand to see a birth certificate, or a letter of consent from a parent, but most did not. If a boy looked old enough, he was old enough. As in the First World War, the army didn't really care about the age of a recruit, just that he looked the part and was healthy. Many boys wrote 'labourer', even if they were not. Men

DOUGLAS FOSTER was sent home on his first attempt to enlist, aged fifteen. He was accepted six months later.

who worked in a 'reserved occupation' like coal mining were not allowed to enlist, so the word 'labourer' covered all tracks, including the unemployed.

The same lack of standards applied to men too old to enlist. Jack's father Joseph Jenkins was already sixty-one, and had served in the navy in the previous war, but he borrowed his eldest son's papers in order to rejoin the merchant navy. Three of Jack's brothers also enlisted.

Jack Jenkins, Douglas Foster and Teddy Days were all in camp at Ingleburn at the same time. These three under-age soldiers were all men of the 20th Brigade, 7th Division. And as far as each division was concerned, it was the best in the army. Jenkins and Foster were in the same battalion, the 2/17th. Each battalion was distinct, partly because they were mostly based on men from a particular district and/or state. The battalion colour patch, sewn onto the uniform, allowed men to distinguish one battalion or division from another on sight. Rivalry was encouraged by sporting matches – particularly football and boxing. These rivalries and loyalties had meaning, even at the level of a division (which consisted of three brigades).

By late September, most of the 7th Division, numbering almost 15,000 men, had said goodbye to loved ones during their final home leave. They knew they were going overseas, but whether it was to the Middle East or to stop a German invasion of England, they knew not. Private Summers, aka Teddy Days, had given himself one day's unofficial leave on 9 September – the first of many times he went Absent Without Leave (AWL).

The 7th Division had moved to Bathurst in August and were heading to Sydney in October by train. Rather than rely on the army's inedible packed lunches, each man in Teddy's 2/13th Battalion had contributed nine pence to a fund that would provide a pie and

---

JACK JENKINS, one of fifteen children, enlisted at eighteen, which was still under-age in 1940.

hot coffee at Mount Victoria station. Except that the train did not stop at Mount Victoria, nor any other station until they reached Lidcombe, on the outskirts of the city. By this time, tempers were high. A cry arose among the men as the train halted, aimed squarely at the officers in a forward carriage: 'What about our bloody pies?' This would become the battalion's call from then on, heard wherever they fought during the next five years. Any injustice, any disappointment, any demand for co-operation, would be met by a voice from somewhere in the ranks: 'What about our bloody pies?'

Their movement to the wharves at Darling Harbour was supposed to be a secret, but half of Sydney knew about it. Mothers, fathers, wives and sweethearts waved from vantage points along the railway tracks. The ship was officially designated HMT (for His Majesty's Transport) QX. Even though she had been given a coat of grey paint in New York earlier in the year, everyone in the battalion knew they were going to war on the *Queen Mary*.

As a troop transport, this was the jackpot. The *Queen Mary* was the second largest ship afloat and one of the most luxurious, a masterpiece of art deco finery, decorated with woods from throughout the British Empire. At her launch in 1934, she had two indoor swimming pools, a cinema, a great hall, a music studio, beauty salons, libraries, specialist shops and dog kennels. She was huge at 81,000 tons, 41 metres longer than the *Titanic*, and a good deal faster. She was so big that most ports had no wharf that could fit her, so she would anchor off, ferrying passengers ashore in small craft. Her major rival in the late 1930s was the French-built *Normandie*. These two ships competed for the 'blue riband', the unofficial record for the fastest Atlantic crossing, but the *Queen Mary* usually won. In 1939, both became troopships, along with the *Queen Elizabeth*, the *Mauretania* and the *Aquitania*. Luxury was about to go to war.

The best of *Queen Mary*'s wooden finery had been covered over or carefully removed and stored before the Australian soldiers clambered aboard,

but it was still an awe-inspiring ship –
albeit much more crowded than before.
It was built to carry 2140 passengers
in great comfort. After a refit, it could
now hold 5500 troops – some in less
comfort than others. Staterooms that
had once slept one wealthy couple now
held six or eight officers. Other ranks
went into the second- and third-class
areas, where wooden bunks had been
installed, stacked one above the other.
Officers ate first-class food, cooked by
the ship's chefs; other ranks ate what
the army cooks dished up. When the
ship put to sea, much of the food went
over the side. Seasickness has no rank.

The old *Queen* was now carrying 6500
men. The 7th Division units included
an artillery regiment, a fully equipped
mobile general hospital, an anti-tank regiment, two field companies of the Royal
Australian Engineers, a signals company,
a cash office, a mobile laundry company, a hygiene unit and officials from the
YMCA and Salvation Army. No doubt
these spiritual guardians would have been
shocked by the amount of gambling that
broke out, even before she raised anchor.

The *Queen Mary* and the *Aquitania*
left Sydney the next morning in a complete lack of secrecy, with small craft
streaming along beside them, foghorns
blaring. German diplomats could have
stood at Sydney Heads with binoculars
and watched them leave – and probably
did. With HMAS *Perth*, a light cruiser,
as escort, they sailed south, to be joined
off Melbourne by the *Mauretania*, carrying Victorian units. West Australian
troops joined at Fremantle. The convoy then headed west into the Indian
Ocean. Many of those on board would
not see Australia for two years; thousands would not see Australia again.

The luxury only lasted as far as
India. At Bombay, everything was
taken off and repacked into smaller
ships that could get through the Suez
Canal. The troops went ashore for
several days, with strict warnings not to
go near the red-light district on Grant
Road. Of course, for many, this was
their first destination, to gawk at the

girls in caged windows. A good number of the men were shocked by what they saw; others were shocked by how cheap it was. Further shocks awaited when they boarded the less comfortable ships for the onward journey. A good number of the fourteen different kinds of venereal disease came with them.

The 7th Division arrived at El Kantara, near the top of the Suez Canal, on 24 November 1940. To the east was the Sinai Desert; to the west, a narrow strip of cultivated Egyptian fields, then more desert. A few of the older men on board had guarded these stretches of canal in 1916. The great exotic cities of Cairo and Alexandria beckoned to the west. Disappointingly for the men, the trains took them east to Palestine, to camps in what we now call the Gaza Strip. The men were crammed into cattle trucks, from which the cattle had only recently departed. It was a long way from the *Queen Mary*.

At Gaza Ridge, late that night, the 7th Division went into a camp prepared by an earlier arrival, the 2/3rd Battalion. They slept in EPIP tents – a roomy British Army invention that stood for 'eight persons, Indian pattern'. These routinely held ten or even twelve men. Training began the next day with a route march, the first of many aimed at regaining the fitness lost on the boat. Private Summers celebrated by getting drunk on 30 November. He compounded this by resisting his arrest. He copped eight days' detention and rejoined his unit three days after Christmas at Kilo 89 camp.

The men had rifles but little other equipment: no mortars, Bren guns or grenades; no Bren carriers (small armoured tracked vehicles with a light machine gun mounted) and few trucks. All available weapons had gone forward to support the 6th Division, which had won great victories along the coast of Libya against Italian troops.

Worse, the Australian war cabinet, in consultation with the commander of the AIF, General Thomas Blamey, had decided to reorganise the divisions. The 20th Brigade, in which our three boys were serving, was to transfer to the newest division, the 9th, and be combined with a brigade that had been training in England and another that had not left Australia. This was beyond unpopular. Those who had joined up early were proud of their low numbers – the 6th was first among equals, the 7th not far behind. To be relegated to the 9th, with a lot of new chums, was insulting and caused bitter resentment. Brigadier Leslie Morshead, who had commanded a battalion in the previous war, now took command of a grumpy division. The men had no cohesion or loyalty, their officers barely knew each other, and they didn't have enough equipment to stage a full-scale exercise, let alone a war.

There was one bright spot, at least for Douglas Foster and Jack Jenkins. In mid-December their 2/17th Battalion was sent to garrison Port Said, an elegant British outpost. Some of the English families hosted the Australians in their homes, where they enjoyed a home-cooked meal. Australian officers could use the elegant Continental Hotel, which had a dance band.

Port Said also had a selection of brothels. Colonel John Crawford, commanding officer of the 2/17th, placed all but two out of bounds. He decided that the Constantinople and the Golden House could operate on alternate nights. He also directed his medical staff to be on duty each night at whichever was open, to provide 'compulsory prophylaxis'. This was highly unusual but remarkably effective. In six weeks of garrison duty, the battalion recorded only one new case of venereal disease – from a man who visited an out-of-bounds establishment.

By mid-January, Foster and Jenkins were back in Palestine, waiting for their war to start. The men were getting impatient. They knew the 6th Division was being sent to Greece; they hoped to go there too. They now had some of the newest weapons – Bren guns and Bren carriers – and were keen to use them. Bob Summers spent part of January 'confined to barracks' for his usual offences – being drunk and rowdy.

When the 9th Division finally moved in late February, they headed west into Egypt, not to Greece. They crossed the Suez Canal at El Kantara and rolled slowly across the Nile Delta past Alexandria, and on towards Libya. The desert made progress inland difficult, especially for tanks and trucks. Dust storms could halt an army for days on end.

The 9th Division convoy now rolled on past the evidence of the 6th Division's victories in Bardia and Tobruk. The detritus of Italy's humiliation lay all about: tanks and artillery, trucks and cars, ammunition and stores, even aeroplanes. Every fort was wrecked and looted. The new men looked in vain for any wine their brothers-in-arms had missed, but the men of the 6th were thorough. They passed thousands of fearful Italian prisoners trudging east. The Italians were surprised they had not been shot: they had heard rumours the Australians took no prisoners.

Summers had his introduction to the shooting war on 6 March 1941, en route to Benghazi, as five German Heinkel bombers attacked the convoy in which he was travelling, causing havoc. The trucks, with British drivers, quickly fanned out to create more distance, as the men ran for cover. The raid continued for thirty terrifying minutes, the battalion's ack-ack (anti-aircraft) battery firing back. The planes killed two soldiers of the 2/13th, the 9th Division's first casualties, and riddled most of the trucks with bullet holes.

The air attack was an ominous sign that the Germans had now entered the arena. General Erwin Rommel, a favourite of Hitler's, had taken charge of the new Afrika Korps in February 1941. This small force, spearheaded by a panzer tank regiment, had begun to arrive on 12 February at Tripoli, further west, but the British did not think it could be ready to fight for two months. They underestimated Rommel's resolve, partly because the British didn't know he was there. They had relied on the French for intelligence in this part of Africa.

JACK JENKINS (right) on leave in Tel Aviv in 1940. His friend is wearing 'Bombay bloomer' shorts.

The Australian 6th Division had by then occupied Benghazi, the only major city on the eastern coast of Libya. The British commander of Desert Force, General Richard O'Connor, wanted to press on towards Tripoli and drive the Italians out of Africa but Churchill stopped him; he needed troops for northern Greece. Churchill's immediate aims in North Africa had been achieved: the enemy could not easily grab the Suez Canal. Unfortunately, no-one had told Rommel.

The British soon knew that Rommel was coming, at the head of a large German and Italian column. He had superiority in the air, and his troops were backed by 150 tanks. The Allies could not match him in tanks or transport. They no longer had the resources to hold what they had won: little choice then but to fall back to Tobruk, one of the only places with good harbour and reliable water. Tobruk could not be outflanked, so long as the Royal Navy controlled the eastern Mediterranean.

This is how the Siege of Tobruk began – in disarray and disillusion, with false premises and bad intelligence.

En route to Tobruk and further west, Jack Jenkins ran into one of his friends from Cabramatta, now a soldier in the 6th Division, who was going the other way. 'He asked me what we were doing up there. He said the war up there was over and they were on their way back to go to Greece.'

The Australian commander, Thomas Blamey, was worried that the Greek campaign would be a disaster so he wanted his most experienced troops there: the 6th Division. This meant the 9th Division, which had barely fired a shot in the war so far, were now to defend Tobruk. They were largely untried, although keen.

The British commanders had doubts about them. Sir Philip Neame, General Officer Commanding of the British forces in Cyrenaica, complained to Morshead about drunken Australian soldiers celebrating after victories in Benghazi and nearby Barce. Neame singled out the 20th Brigade for: 'drunkenness, resisting military police, shooting in the streets, breaking into officers' messes and threatening and shooting at officers' mess servants, even a drunken Australian soldier has come into my own headquarters and disturbed my staff ... I am at a loss for words to express my contempt ...'

Morshead was incensed by Neame's letter and what he perceived as its 'anti-Australian attitude'.

It's doubtful the men of the 9th Division ever knew about Neame's letter; there might have been more trouble if they had. Their responses would also have been predictable and unprintable.

The 9th had been ready to fight to the west of Tobruk and south of Benghazi; they could see Italian troops and German tanks on the other side of the salt marshes but they were ordered to retreat before they could have a crack. It left a bitter taste in their sand-filled mouths.

The retreat from there to Tobruk was chaotic and exhausting. The men dubbed it the Benghazi Handicap. German planes attacked anything that moved by day, so they moved by night, without lights. There weren't enough trucks, even with a large number of scavenged Lancia and Fiat vehicles.

Sandstorms obliterated the tracks, so the trucks ran off into ditches, or gave up the ghost with dust-choked engines. Communications were poor, so headquarters barely knew where anyone was. Rommel's troops bore down on the stragglers, picking off units that stopped for breakfast or to rest. The two senior British commanders, Generals Neame and O'Connor, were captured after taking a wrong turn.

On 23 March, the 2/13th was ordered to move from Beda Fomm, close to the enemy, back to positions at Er Regima, on an escarpment overlooking an airfield east of Benghazi. Here, four Australian battalions were spread along 100 kilometres of high ground, reaching north to the sea. They had no hope of stopping Rommel's advance but the task was largely to slow the Germans down, allowing time for Allied troops to pull back to Tobruk. The 2/15th and the 2/17th, with Jenkins and Foster, were to the north of Summers in the 2/13th, along the same ridge. Late on 3 April came news that the 2/15th and the 2/17th were being withdrawn and the 2/13th was to hold the ridge, and the pass that crossed it, till they had done so.

On 4 April, the 2/13th became the first complete Australian unit to engage a German force in battle in the Second World War. The Germans outnumbered them three to one. With captured Italian weapons and signals equipment, Summers and his comrades held up the German advance for about six hours. They withdrew late in the evening towards Barce after suffering ninety-eight casualties – most of whom had become prisoners of the Germans. Over the next few days, the battalion crept back into Tobruk, exhausted and frustrated. Here, they fell on the ground and slept. This would be their home for the next ten months.

On 8 April, General Archibald Wavell, commander of all British forces in the Middle East, flew into Tobruk with Major General John Lavarack, Commander of the 7th Australian Division. Leslie Morshead, Commander of the 9th Division, was there waiting. Wavell looked at a map, put Lavarack in charge and told him to hold Tobruk for two months, to give British forces in Egypt time to regroup. He then flew back to Cairo. So began the longest siege in British military history.

Tobruk had fallen to the Allies in part because its defences were unfinished. The tank ditch that was supposed to run in a wide arc from the northern coastline to the southern was incomplete. Some parts were 3 metres deep and 6 metres wide; others were mere shallow depressions. In front of these weak spots, the Italians had placed minefields – and in front of those, lines of booby traps to catch any enemy engineers creeping forward to defuse the mines.

Behind the tank ditch was a fence, with layers of concertina wire. The Italians then built a series of concrete outposts, 128 in all, strung in two lines along that 45-kilometre arc, at a radius of about 15 kilometres from the town. Each post was blasted from the rock and identified with a letter and number. Each had two small outlying gun pits, about 15 metres from the centre.

A trench led back to the central post, where there were underground and bomb-proof sleeping quarters for up to twenty men. In the front line, the posts were spaced about 500 metres apart, and had odd numbers. In the second line, about 400 metres further back, the posts had even numbers. Thus R33 was a front line post, and R32 was some 400 metres further back, between R33 and R31.

Each post had two or three machine guns, and an anti-tank or small field gun. The field of fire was deadly, especially as there was nothing but hard flat ground in front of most of them. This was a formidable set-up, with some weaknesses. The Australians now set about improving these defences as if their lives depended on it … which they did.

On Easter Sunday, the 2/17th Battalion and the 2/13th Battalion were manning posts in the centre of the outer perimeter, beside each other. They had been there for three days, watching the enemy's forces build up around Tobruk. Douglas Foster's D Company was in R33, 4 kilometres west of the El Adem Road, which ran south from the town. Bob Summers and the 2/13th were on the other side of that road, in R37 and R53. Each battalion was thinly spread, holding posts along sectors of about 10 kilometres. That meant the 20th Brigade held most of the western

> On 4 April, the 2/13th became the first complete Australian unit to engage a German force in battle in the Second World War. The Germans outnumbered them three to one. With captured Italian weapons and signals equipment, Summers and his comrades held up the German advance for about six hours.

British troops attack during the
fall of Tobruk in April 1941.

third of Tobruk's outer defences. And they could see that this was where Rommel planned to attack.

On Good Friday, 11 April, Rommel had cut the road south to Bardia. Tobruk was now encircled, cut off except by sea. At about 4pm on Sunday, Rommel sent seventy tanks, in three waves, straight at Foster's D Company positions. They halted in front of the anti-tank ditch and opened fire on the forward posts, which at this stage had no anti-tank guns. The ditch in front of the tanks was shallow but they did not come on: it was partly a demonstration, aimed at rattling the Australians.

The tanks then moved off to the east and ran straight into a newly planted minefield, where five tanks were lost. Behind them came 700 German infantry. D Company waited until the soldiers were about 400 metres out then gave them hell, with Bren gun and rifle. This was the first action for most of these Australians, and they were impressed with the way the Germans kept coming, despite heavy artillery and machine-gun fire. The enemy hit D Company positions with mortar and machine gun in return, then concentrated themselves as night fell, about 150 metres south of post R33. An Australian patrol located them that evening and took heavy fire. Two men were killed – the 2/17th Battalion's first battle casualties.

The Germans came on again the next afternoon on a front of about 1100 metres; again they were driven back. The next morning, the forward posts could see a lot of enemy vehicles amassing opposite R33, where Douglas Foster's 16 Platoon was holding on. An enemy aeroplane flew low over the post on reconnaissance. That evening, a German sniper hit Lieutenant George Vincent, who had just come forward to relieve Lieutenant Austin Mackell, as commander of 16 Platoon. The wound was serious but not fatal. Mackell would have to stay on in R33. At 11pm, a party of between thirty and forty Germans came through the wire in front of Mackell's post. They had eight machine guns, a mortar and two small field guns. They meant to stay. Their job would be to knock out R33, thus clearing a path for the German tanks.

Mackell's men could not dislodge them with small-arms fire, so he formed a patrol to go out and rout them. Mackell was a short, reserved man of just twenty-three years, a commercial traveller from Merrylands, an outer western suburb of Sydney. Some of his men thought he looked like a schoolboy. He took with him Corporal John (Jack) Edmondson and five privates. Edmondson had been born in Wagga Wagga in October 1914, a few months after the start of the First World War. His parents later took up a dairy farm at Liverpool on the outskirts of Sydney, on which he worked before enlisting in May 1940. Many of his mates from the militia had come across to the AIF at the same time, into the 2/17th Battalion.

The five privates in the midnight raiding party were Ron Grant, a 21-year-old from Goulburn, New South Wales; Edgar (Ted) Smith, a 33-year-old English migrant; Ron 'Splinter' Williams, twenty-eight, from Sydney; Laurence (Ron) Keogh, twenty-three, from Paddington,

New South Wales; and Douglas 'Snowy' Foster, the sixteen-year-old. They had no automatic weapons, but they did have two grenades each and a bayonet. Mackell later gave his version of events to the Australian war correspondent Chester Wilmot, who reproduced it in his superb book, *Tobruk 1941*.

'The Germans were dug in about one hundred yards to the east of our post, but we headed northwards, away from it, and swung around in a three-quarter circle so as to take them in the flank. As we left the post there was spasmodic fire. Then they saw us running and seemed to turn all their guns on us.

'We didn't waste any time. After a 200-yard sprint we went to ground for breath; got up again, running till we were fifty yards from them. Then we went to ground for another breather, and as we lay there, pulled the pins out of our grenades. Apparently the Germans had been able to see us all the way, and they kept up their fire. But it had been reduced a lot because the men we'd left in the post had been firing to cover us. They did a grand job, for they drew much of the enemy fire upon themselves.

'We'd arranged with them that as we got up for the final charge, we'd shout and they would stop firing and start shouting too. The plan worked. We charged and yelled, but for a moment or two the Germans turned everything onto us. It's amazing that we weren't all hit. As we ran we threw our grenades and when they burst the German fire stopped.'

Douglas Foster spoke of these events in an interview with film-maker Brad Cone in 2003: 'About forty yards from 'em, we went to ground and had a breather. And then Mackell told us to get mobile and start yelling our heads off, to make out we was one hundred instead of seven – which we did – but I don't know how we got there, to be honest with you. We were dancing over tracer bullets there. How they didn't knock us over in the legs or somewhere, I'll never know.'

In fact, Jack Edmondson was wounded. He took a burst of machine-gun fire in the stomach and neck.

'Still he ran on,' Austin Mackell told Wilmot, 'and before the Germans could open up again we were into them.

'They left their guns and scattered. In their panic some actually ran slap into the barbed wire behind them and another party that was coming up through the gap turned and fled. We went for them with the bayonet. In spite of his wounds, Edmondson was magnificent. As the Germans scattered, he chased them and killed at least two. By this time I was in difficulties wrestling with one German on the ground while another was coming straight for me with a pistol. I called out "Jack" and from about fifteen yards away Edmondson ran to help me and bayoneted both Germans. He then went on and bayoneted at least one more.'

Douglas Foster confirmed this account: 'This whole turnout only went for about three quarters of an hour, and in that time Mackell had shoved his bayonet into a bloke and someone else had him around the legs and he screamed out for Jack to help him and Jack had been wounded. He copped what musta been a burst through his gut, because he had a hole in his back you could put your fist in. He went and rescued Mackell and killed these two blokes that Mackell was wrestling with.'

Private Jack Harris, back in post R33, was watching the raid. He too gave his account to Brad Cone in 2003: 'We could see our blokes in amongst them clubbing and thrusting. Course you couldn't see who they were but we could just see them … It was amazing to see all these blokes that had come through the wire taking off. They were screaming and running. Our blokes didn't chase them, they let 'em go … then everything went quiet and then our blokes started coming in. Douglas Foster and Edgar Smith were carrying Jack Edmondson.'

Wilmot says the Australians killed at least twelve Germans and brought back one prisoner. The priority now was to get Edmondson to an aid post, but German fire onto R33 was too intense. Later that morning, Edmondson died of his wounds.

The raid had achieved its aims, if only temporarily. At 2.15am the Germans came at R33 again with 200 men. This time, they established a bridgehead. As instructed, the Australians in the forward posts let the tanks through and waited for the infantry. The blitz-krieg tactics that had worked so well in Poland and France were now put to the test against well-trained British gunners with a detailed plan, based on the idea of defence-in-depth. The thirty-eight German tanks effective-ly rolled slowly towards an ambush. After coming 3 kilometres inside the wire, they were hit from three sides at close range, in a mighty clash of heavy weapons. As dawn broke, in confusion and dust, seven German tanks littered the field beside the El Adem Road. The Afrika Korps soldiers had been told to expect an easy victory: the 'Englanders' would surrender once they saw the tanks, as had happened in Poland and France. Now the German tanks turned and limped away to the south and east, pursued by British trucks with anti-tank guns mounted on the back. The Allies employed 'mosquito tactics': the trucks would race at the tanks at full speed.

When about 600 metres off, they would turn sharply and stop, loosing off half-a-dozen quick rounds, then withdraw.

The German tanks were vulnerable without their accompanying mobile machine gunners. These had been hit hard by the forward posts, once the tanks passed through. When the Germans then brought up heavier guns to deal with the forward posts, the Australians let them come, then sniped every member of the gun crew, one by one. British tanks had been waiting in reserve and, with the morning sun behind them, they now attacked the retreating panzers, destroying another four. The Germans made for the same gap they had come through, which was in chaos, full of wrecked and retreating vehicles as well as men on foot. The Australians in R33 and R35 gave them everything they had: Bren guns, mortars, anti-tank rifles and rifles. The German 8th Machine Gun Battalion lost 75 per cent of its men here.

When it was over, according to Wilmot, the Germans had lost 17 tanks, 12 planes, 110 men killed and 254 taken prisoner – and that was just inside the perimeter. The Allies lost two tanks and two aircraft, with twenty men killed and sixty wounded. It was a famous victory, the first loss the German army had suffered on land since the war began.

The commanders were quick to honour the achievements of their men: honours were good for morale. Jack Edmondson posthumously won the Victoria Cross (VC), the first awarded to an Australian in the Second World War. Austin Mackell and Captain John Balfe, commander of D Company, both won the Military Cross. Two others from the 2/17th won the Military Medal.

The siege of Tobruk had only just begun, but Rommel now knew it would not be a pushover. He could bypass Tobruk and make for Egypt, but without the fresh water and deep harbour his supply lines would be untenable. Tripoli, from where he had begun, was 1400 kilometres behind him; Alexandria in Egypt was another 650 kilometres ahead. The 'rats' had to be dislodged. The siege held him up for eight months. Even then, Rommel did not take Tobruk. The Allies broke out and Rommel withdrew, to fight another day. Australian infantry held Tobruk for five months and were gradually replaced from August to October by British, Polish and Czech troops. The Australian 2/13th Battalion did not leave until December – the only Australian battalion to last out the full siege.

Our three under-age boys had been impatient to find the war a year earlier. What they found that Easter weekend in Tobruk was savage and terrifying and exciting in a way they could not have anticipated. Douglas Foster was lucky to survive his 'fighting patrol'; he said later that he received a shrapnel wound to the head which made him 'a bit bomb happy'. He told another reporter the only wound he got was 'a slight concussion from the

bomb that got Edmondson', which contradicts Mackell's account, that it was a burst of machine-gun fire that hit Edmondson. Jack Jenkins said later that he saw Edmondson's body after his death, which means he was close by.

> When it was over, according to Wilmot, the Germans had lost 17 tanks, 12 planes, 110 men killed and 254 taken prisoner – and that was just inside the perimeter. The Allies lost two tanks and two aircraft, with twenty men killed and sixty wounded.

Foster's age now became an issue after an uncle in another battalion reported it. Foster was sent back to Australia in November 1941, although it appears he had a hand in his own discharge.

'I had a sort of mutual under-standing with my CO, who, I think, had guessed the truth, but knowing what I had been through, did not think I was too young to fight. Anyway when the army was told my real age, I was sent back to a base and detailed to the AAMC (Australian Army Medical Corps). But

I didn't join up for that sort of job, so I tipped my people off to apply for my discharge. I got it last Thursday.'

He told a reporter for the Sydney *Sun* in November 1941 that he wanted to go back to the war, although he was thinking about applying to the RAAF.

He explained that he was still in uniform until he could get a new suit, as he had grown since he left Australia. He could get his old job back but what was the good of it?

'Surely there's some way for a bloke to have another crack at them when all that's wrong with him is that he is not eighteen.'

This story appears to have been arranged by the army, as it starts with a quote from the Director-General of Recruiting, Lieutenant-Colonel Whitfield, admitting that he too had overstated his age in the last war.

'I wish some of our lads who are of military age had more of the patriotism, pluck, determination and love of adventure that prompted Foster when he bluffed the recruiting staff,' the colonel said. 'Although as director general of recruiting, I ought not to condone his action.'

Quite. In fact, it is hard to find a more brazen statement of the army's hypocrisy about under-age soldiers than this statement. It's close to an appeal to schoolboys: you may not be old enough, but we'll look the other way, and you'll have a grand old time!

Foster had a more solemn task. He had been asked to take Jack Edmondson's belongings back to his family. He later called it 'the worst job in the war'. Edmondson was the couple's only son.

Jack Edmondson's mother, Maud, later recalled her son in a beautiful letter to a family friend: '[It was] absolutely impossible to get him disturbed or ruffled in any way. I had never seen him in a temper in his whole but short life, a stickler for duty at all costs … He was totally unspoiled and unselfish.' The wonderful distinction (the VC) had bucked up her husband, Will, 'but I am afraid I can't even think of it. The loss seems far too great to think of. Jack and I were very dear pals.'

She mentions that she and her husband had received many letters from army brass, including General Blamey: 'Wonderful letters from a man's point of view … but only a heartbreak to me. It all seems so futile.'

With the help of Jack Edmondson's father, Douglas Foster got a job as a fitter and turner at Garden Island, where he worked until he retired in his fifties. His daughter, Gail Langham, remembers that he was injured in the Middle East when a gun fell on him. His back grew progressively worse as he got older. He spent many periods in the repatriation hospital at Concord.

Jack Jenkins went on to serve in the battle of El Alamein and in New Guinea, where his weight dropped to 59 kilograms through malaria and chronic bronchitis. He gave an interview in the mid-1990s in which he reflected on his service.

'When I enlisted as a kid I thought war was going to be a Cook's Tour. We used to sing all the Empire songs at school and salute the flag every Monday. After I'd been chased 500 miles across the desert and come under gunfire I just realised I'd been conned.'

Jack returned from New Guinea with a diagnosis of 'anxiety state', like many other men. He married soon after the war and they had three girls. He worked in a car parts factory most of his life, taking second jobs to support his family. He suffered from war-related illnesses throughout. When he became too ill to work, he received a TPI (Totally and Permanently Incapacitated) pension, says his daughter Judy. He was very proud to have been a Rat of Tobruk. He died in April 2007 at Gosford.

Teddy Days, aka Bob Summers, got out of Tobruk in September, ahead of most of his mates, because his identity had finally been discovered. There are two explanations of how this happened, printed by rival publications in Australia. The Melbourne *Herald* was first to claim the credit: they had published a photograph of the missing Teddy Days in April 1941. Australian newspapers were constantly in demand by the troops and this one got pasted to a wall in the hospital at Tobruk, where another soldier from the 2/13th recognised Days as 'Bob Summers'. The other story, much more detailed, appeared in the *Women's Weekly* in August 1941. Quoting Days's mother, the *Weekly* said that a letter from the battalion Comforts Fund had arrived at the family home in Yarraville, addressed to a Miss L Summers. They opened it in case it might have news of their missing son, and deduced that he was calling himself Summers, and that he had joined the 2/13th in Sydney. However it happened, the family had found him by late July, almost fifteen months after he'd disappeared.

Teddy Days reverted to his real name by statutory declaration on 20 September. By now, the army knew he was under-age. He did not go quietly. His record from September 1941 until his discharge in 1945 is strewn with offences and punishments. Most of them were minor, but the frequency suggests he was unhappy to be sent back to Australia. He arrived in March 1942. He turned eighteen in April and convinced the army to keep him on, despite his disciplinary record. He fought in New Guinea in 1943, then Borneo. He rejoined his mates in the 2/13th at Milne Bay in September 1943, but soon went down with malaria. He was discharged in December 1945 and returned to Melbourne, where he became a plasterer.

These three boys paid a high price for their army service. Their stories are typical for the under-age boys of this period in the war – full of pluck and daring at the start, with disillusion and disappointment to follow. None of them had an easy time after the war but that was true of the older men as well. Their comrades and superiors knew they were too young, but no-one took any action until much later. Some of them claimed to have been the youngest rat in Tobruk, but no-one really knows who was the youngest. There were too many contenders. ✦

Our three under-age boys had been impatient to find the war a year earlier. What they found that Easter weekend in Tobruk was savage and terrifying and exciting in a way they could not have anticipated.

CHAPTER FOUR

THE BULLDOG AND THE BARRISTER

The fight for civilisation: Australian soldiers take in the Acropolis in early 1941, before their move to northern Greece. Photo: George Silk.

Winston Leonard Spencer Churchill was a man steeped in war; Robert Gordon Menzies was not.

One was born a warrior, for whom the weight of casualties was an inevitable cost of battle; the other was a Melbourne barrister, timid in the face of such responsibility. Together, their judgements and clashing temperaments would be responsible for much of the disaster that was about to unfold in Greece. If Churchill had been less of a lion and Menzies more of one, the results might have been different.

Menzies sat out the First World War as a law student. He was commissioned as a second lieutenant in the Melbourne University Rifles, a militia unit, but did not volunteer for overseas service. Two of his brothers did, one claiming much later that it was a family decision to keep Robert at home. Inevitably, Menzies knew little of war when he assumed the mantle of Prime Minister of Australia in April 1939.

Churchill had spent much of his early life preparing for this very trial – as a young officer and war correspondent in the Sudan and later Boer War, as First Lord of the Admiralty in the First World War, then as a Scots Fusilier in the trenches of France in 1916. In 1940, as Hitler's armies prepared to invade Britain, Churchill took over from a broken Neville Chamberlain during Britain's 'darkest hour'. He would become Britain's saviour, an orator and strategist whose greatness matched the threat. Or if you were an under-age soldier from Subiaco, Sydenham or Scrubby Creek, he was the man who held your life in his hands.

Churchill's belief in the importance of the British Empire and of England was unassailable. His belief in the independence of the dominions, and their right to decide the fate of their own soldiers, was far less staunch. He was prepared to sacrifice them all for the sake of Britain. 'We shall fight them on the beaches …' he thundered, but a dominion soldier in a trench in Benghazi might have been entitled to ask who was 'we', exactly?

Churchill knew that generals were not always the best judges of strategy. They were hamstrung by what had come before, blind to what was coming next. The madness of the Western Front convinced him of that. If that war could not be won with frontal assault on well-entrenched lines, he reasoned, it must be won by attacking the enemy's vulnerable peripheries, thus weakening the centre. That was the idea behind Gallipoli, the failure of which caused him to resign, but not to change his views. That was still his idea when it came to Greece in 1941.

Churchill had many gifts – writer, orator, wily political strategist – but military planning was not among his greatest. He embarked too often on military campaigns for which he did not have the resources. Once he had defined an objective, he would bully his cabinet and generals into agreement, then deny them what they needed for success. When they failed, he would replace them, or resign himself, as he did after the bloody debacle of Gallipoli in 1915, for which he was largely responsible.

Hitler's successes in May and June of 1940 – taking France and the Low Countries – had been spectacular, but the tide began to turn in the autumn. The German air force, the Luftwaffe, had been badly mauled over Kent, which rallied British morale and forced Hitler to rethink the invasion. He had believed all along that the war could not be won until he defeated Stalin's huge armies in the east. Britain could wait. Churchill was now more certain that Germany could be beaten, but only when the Americans joined the fight. He concentrated every effort on persuading President Roosevelt that it was right to do so, even if it meant allowing Japan to take control in the Pacific. This was to have profound implications for Australia.

Churchill now plotted the defeat of Germany through the back door, via a

'We shall fight them on the beaches ...' he thundered, but a dominion soldier in a trench in Benghazi might have been entitled to ask who was 'we', exactly?

Diggers on donkeys heading for northern Greece in March 1941.
Photo: George Silk.

large force attacking in North Africa, Greece and the Balkans. The problem was that most of his troops on the ground were from the dominions – Australia, New Zealand, India, South Africa, Canada – and subject to the whims of their own governments. Some, like Australia, were firm that their forces should not be divided.

Greece was not yet at war with Germany but its airfields were a strategic prize for both sides. If Hitler controlled them, he could strike at the Suez Canal, lifeline of the British Empire. If Britain had them, the RAF could attack the Romanian oilfields that gave Hitler's armies most of their oil. Greece was not at all sure it wanted Churchill's protection. Hitler had taken almost everything to its north but showed few signs of wanting to invade. His hand was forced by his unruly and incompetent ally, the Italian dictator Benito Mussolini.

In late October 1940, 'Il Duce' invaded Greece through Albania, to show Hitler that he was his own man. A stubborn Greek army pushed the Italians back into Albania, humiliating Mussolini's troops.

Hitler now ordered plans be drawn up for a limited invasion of northern Greece, enough to secure the airfields and ports. These plans were later expanded to include the rest of the country.

Churchill couched the idea of a Balkan front in noble terms: Greece was a symbol of civilisation, not just a country. Its loss would be disastrous for British prestige and it would be harder to persuade Roosevelt to join the war.

Churchill had only three British divisions in the Middle East. Australia had sent three divisions, but they were under-equipped and partially trained. Even so, this small force had routed the Italians along the north African coast. In early February 1941, Churchill instructed General Archibald Wavell, the British commander-in-chief in Egypt, to halt the advance in Libya. Wavell was to leave a skeleton force to hold Benghazi and Tobruk. The rest were to be sent to Greece and Crete.

Wavell knew he didn't have enough men to hold Greece, nor enough weapons and equipment to refit those units depleted in Libya. The RAF could not match an increasingly powerful Luftwaffe in the Greek skies. Almost none of Churchill's commanders, nor his political allies in London, saw a chance of success in Greece. Everyone worried, but no-one argued.

Wavell needed agreement from the Australian and New Zealand governments for the Greek expeditionary force. He also knew that Thomas Blamey, the Australian commander-in-chief, might oppose him.

Menzies had decided before Christmas that he must go to London, to participate in Churchill's war cabinet. He offered no clear explanation to the Australian people. Indeed, he kept his private ambitions – to find a bigger role on the world stage – to himself. In mid-January, he left the country in the hands of his Country Party deputy, Arthur Fadden, an amiable Queensland accountant. Menzies arrived in Palestine on 2 February and spent considerable time with both Wavell and Blamey over the next fortnight. He would later claim, somewhat stretching credibility, that he did not discuss the Greek plan in detail with either of them. Even his own diary contradicts him.

The Australian historian David Day says Menzies knew about the Greek plan before he left Australia. On 14 January, Australia's High Commissioner in London, Stanley Bruce, warned Menzies by cable of the dangers of such an expedition.

Day argues in *The Politics of War* that it was a gross dereliction of duty when Menzies ignored those warnings 'and failed to avail himself of military counsel' in the Middle East to reach a considered judgement on the Greek expedition.

If they had agreed that the plan was foolhardy, Menzies and Blamey might have blocked the British push towards Greece, by withholding Australian troops. Day concludes that 'a disaster might have been averted'.

Others have seen a muddier plot, which largely excuses Menzies. By this theory, Wavell tricked Menzies into believing that Blamey was already on board with the Greek plan. Blamey was in Libya with his troops in the weeks before Menzies arrived, but he was back at Lake Tiberias on 2 February, when the prime minister's plane alighted in Palestine.

Blamey's aide-de-camp, Norman Carlyon, says in his biography of his boss that Blamey knew nothing of Churchill's orders to divert Australian and New Zealand troops to Greece until after Menzies had flown on to London.

After visiting the Australian troops in Libya – where he was booed – Menzies returned to Cairo late on 12 February. The next day, he visited the New Zealand Hospital at Helwan, where 200 Australian wounded were in treatment. Menzies noted in his diary that night that he had come back at 8pm to a conversation with General Wavell, who was 'clearly contemplating the possibility of a Salonika expedition.'

This is the only diary reference to any discussions between Menzies and Wavell about Greece. Menzies left the next day for the Sudan and, eventually, London.

Wavell cabled Churchill on 12 February – the day before he talked again with Menzies – that his (Wavell's) estimate of the available resources for Greece might be improved 'if the Australian government will give me certain latitude as regards use of their troops. I have already spoken to Menzies about this and he was ready to agree to what I suggest'.

Once in London, Menzies told Churchill he agreed to the Australians being sent to Greece, subject to approval from cabinet in Australia. Arthur Fadden cabled that agreement. By now, Blamey was fully briefed and plotting his own moves.

In early March, Blamey asked Sir Percy Spender, Minister for the Army, for permission to write directly to the Australian war cabinet. Fadden agreed

> For the second time in twenty-five years, Australians and New Zealanders were about to die on Mediterranean beaches to carry out one of Churchill's ambitious but ill-considered plans.

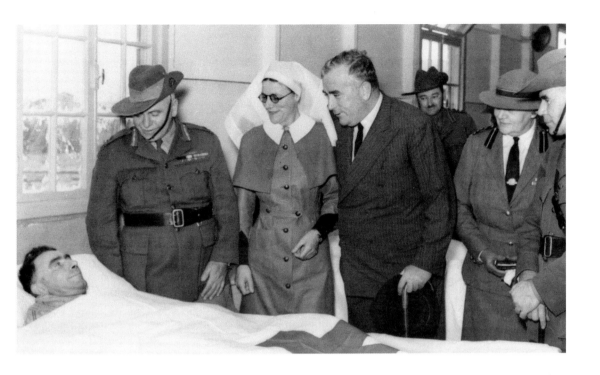

PRIME MINISTER ROBERT MENZIES (centre) visits Australian patients in the Middle East.
LIEUTENANT GENERAL THOMAS BLAMEY, commander of Australian forces in the Middle East, at left.

and Blamey detailed his serious reservations about the plan for Greece. This is curious, given that a fortnight earlier, Blamey lobbied Wavell for command of the Greek expedition, reasoning that if most of the troops were Australian, he should be in charge. Now, he was trying to distance himself from its planning. His cable alarmed the Australian cabinet, but they stood by their earlier

decision. They had little choice. Wavell appointed Sir Henry 'Jumbo' Wilson, a British officer, to command the largely Antipodean force. Blamey had successfully distanced himself from the debacle to come.

Menzies dined with Churchill at Chequers on 23 February and noted later in his diary: 'Momentous discussion later with PM about defence of Greece, largely with New Zealand and Australian troops. This kind of decision, which may mean thousands of lives, is not easy. Why does a peaceable man become a prime minister?'

Good question.

For the second time in twenty-five years, Australians and New Zealanders were about to die on Mediterranean beaches to carry out one of Churchill's ambitious but ill-considered plans. How different things might have been if Menzies had taken a more independent stance with Churchill, or if he and Blamey had acted with one purpose.

David Day is unforgiving: 'Nothing can excuse the forewarned Menzies from properly assessing the proposal while he was able to consult on the spot with Blamey...'

In this tangle of hindsight, someone is lying about what he knew and when, probably because the Greek campaign turned into such a failure. We do know that Menzies and Blamey discussed Wavell's desire for 'certain latitude'. In effect, Wavell wanted the Australian troops under his command. The Australian attitude had been that its forces should fight as a corps under Australian command, and not be split up. Menzies and Wavell discussed this at Wavell's headquarters in Cairo on 10 February. He discussed this with Blamey, who was firm that Australia's troops must stay under Australian command. Blamey had told him that if he gave the British generals an inch, they would take a mile.

It seems Menzies had been drawn into a power play between generals. Wavell treated Blamey like a lackey, but Blamey controlled the Australian troops, subject to the Australian war cabinet. Wavell attempted to get around him by going straight to Menzies. Blamey blocked him, in the characteristically blunt language above.

There is another, darker possibility. Menzies desired a position on the world stage, perhaps as a permanent member of Churchill's war cabinet. The Australian troops were his chips in the game. To withhold them from Greece would be to risk irrelevance, as well as Churchill's volcanic temper. Menzies was not about to do either.

In London, Menzies now contemplated the dangers, some of which were to his own power and prestige. He insisted in the British war cabinet that the Australian troops for Greece must be fully equipped 'on the maximum establishment scale', and that plans for an evacuation must be in place before they went, should it be needed. The reassurances he received were worthless. Menzies had committed Australia's troops with his eyes wide shut.

He was away from Australia for four months, during which the forecast disaster eventuated on the Greek front. Menzies lost the confidence of his own party; Greece helped to destroy his first term as prime minister. Others lost a lot more.

This grimy political skirmish was about much more than Greece. It was about Australia's sovereignty in time of war. Churchill regarded that sovereignty as subject to the needs of the realm. Menzies certainly did not, despite his considerable sentimental attachment to Mother England, but he was incapable of standing up to the British bulldog. Churchill's Britain-first policy was to have profound repercussions later when Japan entered the war. Australia would then face an invasion of its own, with most of its best troops away on the other side of the world, defending the British Empire. And still Churchill would oppose sending them home. A new prime minister, John Curtin, would turn to America for help, fundamentally shifting the focus of Australia's foreign policy for decades to come. In the process, he would hand full control of Australia's forces to another foreign warrior, the American general Douglas MacArthur.

CHAPTER FIVE

BOYS OF THE GOLDEN WEST

ANDY MULGRAVE

BOB FRASER

ANDY MULGRAVE grew up in Perth, then Kalamunda. His father had been wounded at Gallipoli; he met the woman he would marry in London.

This is the story of two soldiers, one who lived and one who died. Both were from Western Australia and too young to go, but each proved to be an exceptional soldier.

They fought in the same battalion, the 2/11th. Many of the soldiers in this battalion had fathers who fought in the first 11th Battalion in the First World War, before their sons were born. They too had often lied about their ages. When war came again in 1939, some of those fathers lied again, understating their years to get in. They could hardly object when their sons did the same.

Andrew Mulgrave Senior fought at Gallipoli, in the 16th Battalion, another Western Australian unit. He was there for seven days, was wounded (twice) and hurt his back when another soldier fell dead on top of him. He was invalided back to Australia, then sent to England, where he was eventually commended for his work as a staff sergeant with the Australian Army Medical Corps. In 1918, he married Fay Turner in London and returned to Perth, where he joined Foy's department store. For more than thirty years, Andrew Mulgrave was also the Foy's Father Christmas, and therefore famous. Santa's means of arrival each December was an event in Perth: conveyances included seaplane, submarine, speedboat, houseboat, charabanc (an early kind of bus) and roller skates – at which Andrew had once been a champion. It was said that even his own children did not recognise him as Santa.

The Mulgraves lived at Pearse Street, Cottesloe, near the beach. Patricia Joy was born in February 1920; her brother Andrew Robert in September 1921. Pat died at age thirteen of meningitis, bringing a sudden pall of grief to the

> Kalamunda was a small community ... These four were the first to enlist from Kalamunda district and would go to war together in the same battalion.

house. The Mulgraves moved soon after to Gooseberry Hill, known now as Kalamunda, in the hills east of Perth. Andy Junior continued to attend the Cottesloe state school, riding his bike 40 kilometres each way for a time, before switching to the Kalamunda state school.

Andy was a strong swimmer. At Kalamunda, he became a keen horserider and birdwatcher, with a large collection of birds' eggs. He was also an extraordinarily good shot. His friend Norman Aisbett, who became a well-known artist, claimed that Andy 'could take out telegraph insulators at the full gallop'.

Kalamunda was a small community. Des Beard, Jim Seiver and Colin Price – all a year or two older – were at the same school as Andy. These four were the first to enlist from Kalamunda district and would go to war together in the same battalion. There is a photograph (overleaf) of them together near the railway station on the day they left for embarkation in April 1940.

Andy Mulgrave is the slightest of the four. His tunic is too big and he looks noticeably younger. He has a high fore-head and shy smile, a cigarette in his right hand. We might imagine this as the last day of his childhood, but we would be wrong. Mulgrave had by then studied commercial art at Perth Technical College for a couple of years. He and Norm Aisbett had started a business making advertising banners by 1936, when Andy was still fifteen. He joined the militia, known as the Cameron Highlanders, at age sixteen.

By the time of the picture, Andy was eighteen and would have regarded himself as a man, although he was still too young to enlist. So were Des Beard and Jim Seiver – each added a year to his age to claim to be twenty. Only Colin Price gave his correct date of birth: he was actually twenty. One out of four was close enough for the army.

Each had joined in November 1939, within two weeks of the opening of enlistments. They were sent to Northam camp outside Perth, where Tom Louch – lawyer, sportsman and bachelor – was their new CO, as he had been in the Cameron Highlanders. He had gone ashore at Gallipoli in 1915 with the

11th Battalion. Now, at forty-five, he was at the upper age limit for his rank but he wasn't alone.

Northam camp was neither finished nor equipped. Nor were the soldiers, who lacked uniforms, weapons and boots. They were 100 kilometres from Perth, which made it harder to slip out for an evening.

The men had no rifles till just before Christmas. Louch noted sourly that when they did get to shoot, their aim was poor. He was happier in February when supplies of boots and other equipment increased, albeit temporarily.

Just before this photograph, each soldier had said goodbye to his family. A few days later, they boarded the *Nevasa*, a beaten-up old ship at Fremantle. She pulled away from the docks on 20 April. This was Adolf Hitler's birthday, an inauspicious start, but not one that most of the men would have cared about. Louch came aboard on a stretcher, suffering from pneumonia.

John Robert Fraser was on the same boat. Like Andy Mulgrave, he had lied about his age. Both had just turned eighteen.

Fraser had grown up in Mount Hawthorn, a northern suburb of Perth, four years behind his brother Tom. When their father died, their mother Emma moved to Hay Street in the city. John Robert, known to his friends as 'Bob', became an enthusiastic member of the St George's Cathedral Scouting Troop, just around the corner. In his mid-teens, he attended the Junior Technical School, where boys were prepared for apprenticeships. He also joined the militia, so it is likely that he knew Mulgrave and Des Beard before the war. He couldn't wait to enlist.

Fraser was assigned to C Company, under Captain Ralph Honner, a brilliant young officer who had been a schoolmaster, then a lawyer, in Perth. Honner had played for Claremont in the Western Australian Football League and

From left: **DES BEARD**, **JIM SEIVER**, **ANDY MULGRAVE** and **COLIN PRICE** on the day they left for the Middle East, April 1940. They were the first to enlist from Kalamunda.

served as a lieutenant in the Cameron Highlanders, so he would certainly have known Mulgrave, Beard and Fraser. Lieutenant Stan Wood, 2IC (second in charge) of D Company, had been Fraser's drawing instructor at the Junior Technical School. The 11th Battalion was like that: miners from Kalgoorlie, farmers from the south-west, men and boys from every Perth suburb. Many knew each other before enlisting.

The battalion – 816 men and 39 officers – had been reorganised twice already: it now had four rifle companies, each of three platoons, and a headquarters company comprising platoons for signals, anti-aircraft gunners, mortar and Bren gun carriers, pioneers and administration personnel. Each rifle company had three sections of about ten men. Andy Mulgrave joined 1 Platoon as a signaller: someone had already recognised his talent for precision and detail. Fraser was allocated to 14 Platoon, a good number of whom were miners from Kalgoorlie.

Conditions on the *Nevasa* were foul. The men slept in hammocks slung so tightly together that they had to crawl underneath to reach the decks. With seasickness taking its toll, this was even more hazardous. The men quickly dubbed her the 'Never-Wasser'. On 10 May, the captain informed Louch that Hitler had invaded Holland and Belgium. Louch ordered the battalion's Vickers guns brought on deck as they entered the Suez Canal, in case Italy entered the war. Her Eritrean colony bordered the western bank. The ship docked at El Kantara on 19 May, where a train was waiting to take the battalion east to their camp at Kilo 89, in Gaza.

When they left Australia, Britain was led by Neville Chamberlain. By the time they arrived at Kantara, Churchill was prime minister and a German invasion of Britain seemed imminent.

Britain and her Commonwealth allies – the dominions – now stood alone against Hitler in western Europe. The US had yet to join the war and the USSR was allied with Germany, albeit temporarily. On 10 June 1940, as expected, Italy declared war on Britain and France. In September, Italian forces in Cyrenaica (eastern Libya) advanced into Egypt to take Sidi Barrani. Their ultimate goal was to wrest the Suez Canal from British control.

Richard O'Connor, an understated British major general, spearheaded a series of British victories in the western desert between December 1940 and February 1941, pushing the Italians back more than 500 kilometres. This was where Australian units first saw action, in the campaigns at Sidi Barrani, Bardia, Tobruk, Derna and Benghazi.

Andy Mulgrave wrote to his parents on 1 February, although he wasn't quite sure of the date. 'This is the first opportunity I've had to write to you for a couple of weeks now, we have been on the go all the time and the day before yesterday, the place we have been attacking fell, and we have a few hours break. I'm writing this in a dago building on a dago table and with dago ink.

'This is quite a break for us. A nice town, green lawns and waving palm trees and the sea. We all go out on the scrounge for food and get some real good food ...'

Although he was not allowed to say, this was written from Derna. He describes being strafed by Italian planes. 'The bombers dropped their bombs (missed as usual) and all of a sudden we heard a roar and planes came howling at us, you should have seen us break evens for the wall and me with a blister too. We just got behind it and a hail of slugs spanged off the rocks. We're all getting good at dodging them now. The sky was thick with planes and then we heard a powerful roar and a flight of our most powerful fighters came whirling out of the blue and into it. Gee it was great to watch and the RAF lived up to its name.'

> The 11th Battalion was like that: miners from Kalgoorlie, farmers from the south-west, men and boys from every Perth suburb. Many knew each other before enlisting.

'The sky was thick with planes and then we heard a powerful roar and a flight of our most powerful fighters came whirling out of the blue and into it. Gee it was great to watch and the RAF lived up to its name.'

He reports the pleasure of having a hot bath and covering himself with captured talcum powder. 'We are having a good time mum and dad. We have done three big stunts now, no doubt you have read about them in the papers. This 2/11th of ours will go a long way.'

Private Bob Fraser also wrote to his mother about his experiences against the Italians. One of his letters appeared in Perth's *Daily News* in May 1941. Fraser described an incident in which Australian soldiers were tricked by Italians flying a white flag.

'When they were about 20 or 30 yards off, the Italians opened up with a machine gun and killed two and wounded three.'

The Italians were dealt with 'in no uncertain fashion', wrote the newspaper, quoting Fraser: 'They were a treacherous lot of swines, and I think they broke every rule of war ... My one regret is that I didn't make a better job of my shooting.'

Like Andy Mulgrave, Bob Fraser knew little of the grand strategy: he simply wrote about things he saw.

'After a spell at Benghazi we started on our way back to Egypt, or so we thought. Instead we were dumped in the desert miles from anywhere and told to dig in and make ourselves at home. After hacking my way through about two or three feet of rock and two or three attempts at building, I have managed to construct some sort of a shelter ... It hasn't stopped raining and blowing a gale since we got here. When it doesn't rain it blows dust storms. There was absolutely nothing to make shelters with when we came here but there was an Italian aerodrome nearby and now it has been completely stripped. Even the planes have been cut to pieces to make shelters. It looked as though there had been a war all over the 'drome.

'Well there you have my tale of woe but it is indeed surprising how cheerful the boys are. Even when things look blackest they always seem to be able to find something to laugh about and I am glad to be with them.

'I hate this racket but I wouldn't be out of it for the world. Whatever happens to us we usually find that silver lining.'

Fraser's letter is typical of a young soldier's correspondence: a combination of reassurance and bravado, and a touch of innocence. Many letters like this ended up in the newspapers because proud parents sent them in for publication. All letters were subject to army censorship, but Fraser's would have been considered good for morale.

On 12 February, the Australian Prime Minister, Robert Menzies, paid the 2/11th a visit at Tocra, 70 kilometres north of Benghazi, where they were recuperating after months of dust and deprivation. Menzies had flown in from Cairo on his way to London and was still wearing his double-breasted pinstripe suit.

He praised these ragged men for their achievements and for what they had endured. He himself had put up with a lot of hardship to visit them, he said. One later remarked that they had been living on bully beef and dog biscuits, were lousy with lice and did not have enough water to bathe, and 'that bastard said he had put up with hardship … he got howled down'. Menzies makes no mention of this in his diary. He remarks on the bad coffee and dry bread he had

for breakfast in Benghazi, then describes his visit to 'Louch's battalion': 'The visit seems to have done good'.

Private Mulgrave was impressed by the prime minister. In a letter dated 21 February, he mentioned that Menzies had congratulated the battalion on their work. 'He made a pretty good speech too.'

In fact, the battalion had done its best to conceal its threadbare condition from the prime minister. Louch noted later that 'the staff were anxious that he should not know how badly we were off for clothing, so the orders were that only the best dressed men should be in the front ranks…' This was pride as much as politics, the battalion putting on its best face.

Menzies might have benefitted more from having his eyes opened. His decisions in the next few months were often based on poor information, especially concerning the Greek campaign. His willingness to see only what he wanted to see was a dangerous flaw in wartime.

Andy Mulgrave wrote again to his parents after the 2/11th had been through the mill in Greece.

ANDY MULGRAVE became one of the youngest and most successful snipers of the war, using a captured German Mauser rifle. His Australian-issued rifle, seen here, was far less accurate.

'When we first landed in Athens some time ago, we thought it was great. The people were very sincere and the country was excellent, mountains and snow, green valleys, orchards, flowers and streams and everything was swell, much different to the dust and deserts of Libya. We thought Libya was tough, perhaps it was, but compared to what we went through in Greece, it was a picnic.'

The men sent to Greece were under-equipped, exhausted and understrength, about to fight for a country that wasn't sure it wanted them. They were also without adequate air support, artillery or even ground transport. And they were led by generals who largely did not believe the plan would work. The Royal Navy began making plans to evacuate them even before it delivered the first ill-fated men to Piraeus, the main port of Athens, in the first week of March. It would be hard to think of a worse way to send men into battle.

An advance group of the 2/11th Battalion arrived in Athens on 4 April. Hitler's forces marched across the northern Greek border from Bulgaria two days later.

By 9 April, the Greek forces in Eastern Macedonia had capitulated. Most of the 2/11th would not arrive in Greece until 12 April – too late to make a difference, except to the withdrawal.

Andy's letter continues: 'We were only near Athens for a few hours before we travelled for a couple of days through the mountains to where the German army was … The Greeks threw in the towel and we were damned lucky to get out alive.'

The assembled Allied force – largely dominion troops, with an armoured British division – could do little but hold the Germans in the mountain passes long enough to allow a fighting withdrawal. These were hard days: thousands of troops scrambling back along muddy mountain roads, without enough

> These were hard days: thousands of troops scrambling back along muddy mountain roads, without enough transport to carry them, under frequent attack by squadrons of terrifying Stuka dive-bombers.

At the same time, the Germans attacked in Libya, which meant that the 7th Australian Division could not be sent to Greece as planned. The Australians, Kiwis and Brits of 'Lustreforce' would have to hold the mountain passes of Greece without reinforcement.

transport to carry them, under frequent attack by squadrons of terrifying Stuka dive-bombers. The Luftwaffe ruled the skies. With roads too dangerous by day, trucks moved by night, without lights.

Many had not slept for days. They were cold, tired, hungry and frostbitten, and angry at having to withdraw. Over the next few days, they fought a series of delaying actions, which were doomed and costly but allowed many thousands of men to escape.

Mulgrave, Fraser and the rest of the battalion went forward to Kalabaka, 350 kilometres north of Athens, on 15 April. They were to cover the withdrawal of a British armoured brigade and block any German advance towards Larissa. They could see the dive-bombing Stukas ahead – their first sighting of these pitiless, demoralising machines – amid the area's famous mountain pillars, topped with monasteries. The men dug in on a hillside west of the town, as Greek troops and refugees streamed back down the road, having walked for days without food or rest. Shortly before the Germans arrived, the Australians

were ordered back to a line at Brallos, 160 kilometres to the south. The Greek campaign was unravelling.

In the late afternoon of 18 April, they reached the Pineios River, where New Zealand engineers had prematurely destroyed a bridge. There was another bridge further upriver, but the Stukas destroyed that before they could cross. The only thing left was an old punt, beside the first bridge. As their trucks took a long boggy detour, the men crossed in darkness in small groups. At 3am, they reboarded the trucks for Larissa. The Stukas caught them near Domokos and pinned them down for two hours, strafing and bombing. Four men were killed and eleven wounded getting back to Brallos that day.

At Brallos pass, they took up defensive positions on the 'Thermopylae line'. Those among them who had read Herodotus would have recognised the name: 7000 Greeks held up a vastly larger Persian army here in 480 BC. It was a gallant defeat, famous for the last stand of 300 Spartans. History is sometimes a cold comfort.

Tom Louch had lost the use of his left arm during one of the air attacks and was sent to Athens for medical attention. Major Ray Sandover, an English-born Perth accountant, took command of the 2/11th. Sandover was educated at Rugby School, where he captained the hockey XI, and at Bonn University, where he became fluent in German – a language he was about to need.

At the Brallos Pass on 20 April, Australian, New Zealand and British forces fanned out for their own last stand. It was one year to the day since the 2/11th Battalion had left the dock at Fremantle. Brigadier George Vasey, the Australian commander of the units at the pass, made a famous statement: 'Here we bloody well are and here we bloody well stay'.

What none of the Australians knew was that Greece was already lost. The senior British generals had met with the King of Greece and his commanders in Athens on 19 April and agreed that all British forces would be withdrawn. They would need a week to evacuate. The news did not reach Sandover till 22 April, when General Blamey outlined an evacuation plan.

Sandover's men had not slept much in four days. Some had cracked and 'gone mad with the strain', one officer wrote to his wife. The battalion was sent first to one ridge, then another, then back to the original position. By 5am on 24 April, they were astride the road, 5 kilometres north of Brallos. They dug in and waited. They were to hold the Germans back until 9.30 that night, then withdraw, but the German forces were already outflanking them. By midnight, 'Herman' had cut the road 5 kilometres south of Brallos. Bob Fraser's C Company were the last to leave their positions north of Brallos. As they waited for their allotted time to withdraw, German planes pounded them for three hellish hours. Arthur McRobbie, 26-year-old 2IC of C Company, wrote later that he thought he was finished during this attack. 'My nerves were gone to pieces and I just shook like a leaf, and for the next two hours I fought like hell to get myself into shape.'

The men escaped largely because their firing was accurate enough to delay and exhaust the advancing Germans. The

2/11th headed to Megara, a port on the Corinthian isthmus 160 kilometres further south. Royal Navy ships were waiting to pick them up.

The dive-bombers harassed them, but the men could not shoot back, in case they gave away their positions. It was frustrating, exhausting and enraging. They had come to fight, but at every turn, they were ordered to run. The straggling elements of the 2/11th came together at Megara at first light on 25 April, Anzac Day. They slept where they fell, waiting for cover of darkness.

Most of them got out that night on the *Thurland Castle* and two accompanying destroyers. They were ordered to dump backpacks and take only a rifle and what rations they could stuff in a blanket or pocket. The *Thurland Castle* was supposed to take off 1100 wounded and 80 nurses. It left with closer to 3600 men from many different units, crammed in every space. Another 300 men were left behind on the beach. When the Stukas attacked the next day, every man on the ship opened up with whatever he was carrying – Bren gun, Lewis gun, Tommy gun, anti-tank rifle or Very pistol. The planes attacked five times and were eventually driven off by the RAF, whose absence before this had been sorely felt.

The ships arrived at Souda Bay in Crete in the afternoon of 26 April. The *Thurland Castle* was too low in the water to reach the wharf so everyone had to be disembarked via barges. Other ships from other beaches took the battered Greek campaigners back to safety in Alexandria. The unlucky ones ended up in Crete.

> The dive-bombers harassed them, but the men could not shoot back, in case they gave away their positions. It was frustrating, exhausting and enraging. They had come to fight, but at every turn, they were ordered to run.

Andy Mulgrave, writing on 6 May, from Crete: 'I now understand something of the German air force. They're alright when there is no opposition coming from our air force, and they had it all their own way. For weeks, day after day, we were bombed and dive machine-gunned. They do not come over in twos or threes, nor even tens and twenties, they come over in waves of fifties, screaming dive bombers. Our battalion fought rear-guard action all the time. Being a signaller, I was out in a rifle company in the thick of it. I wouldn't be happy behind the line, though at times it's not so good. From my own experience, and I do not think I was more windy than anyone else, I thought if a man had to put up with too much dive-bombing, his nerves would crack up; it is terrifying …

'We fought the Germans in a mountain pass about a hundred miles from Athens while the rest of our brigade pulled out to safety. We had to hold them till darkness fell and then get out the best way we could. We mowed them down as quick as they came on but there were too many of 'em. The Greeks chucked it in our left flank and we were just on surrounded, and there were thousands more of the swine swarming on. One of my fellow sigs was killed and a couple more wounded. We pulled out at the last possible moment and beat a swift withdrawal. A very close shave it was too. We got out of Greece OK, bombed in and bombed out so to speak. All I possess in the world mum and dad of my personal belongings is my fountain pen, not much is it? My camera, photos, clothes, papers, everything blown up or burnt and destroyed. Such is war. All I possess is what I stand up in. Could you send me some handkerchiefs, socks, tooth-paste and brush and some stamps please, I don't possess a thing …'

Apart from the Greeks themselves, the suffering had fallen most heavily on Australian and New Zealand troops. Australia had 320 men killed, New Zealand 291, Britain 146 and another 110 lost in the RAF. Of the 13,958

taken prisoner by the Germans, almost half were British (6480). Australian prisoners amounted to 2030, another 1614 from New Zealand. Killed, wounded and taken prisoner, Australia had lost 2844 men in a month in Greece, just over 16 per cent of the number sent – the worst casualties of the war so far for Australia. The 2/11th had thirty-two men killed, the most of any Australian or New Zealand battalion. Another forty-six were wounded and thirty-nine taken prisoner. And it wasn't over yet.

Crete now became the focus of British anxieties. 'The island must be stubbornly defended,' Churchill cabled to Wavell, on 28 April. But Sandover's men had little more than the clothes they wore and the rifles they carried. Their boots were falling apart and they had no food, nor blankets enough for the cold nights.

The West Australians had been shaken by their encounter with the Germans at Brallos. They were further disheartened to know that Rommel had taken back most of the ground they'd helped win in Libya. Tobruk was now besieged.

So far, Hitler was winning in the Med-

iterranean and North Africa, although he had little interest in either. Hermann Goering, head of the Luftwaffe, had been repeatedly pushing for an airborne invasion of Crete, proclaiming his paratroopers were the best of the best and could take the island's three vital airstrips. Hitler had finally agreed on 25 April.

The 2/11th, now numbering 660 men, moved to positions overlooking Rethimno airstrip on 9 May, after marching all night. The airstrip was 2 kilometres to their right, the town about 4 kilometres to their left. To the battalion's right, 2300 poorly equipped Greek troops guarded the western end of the strip. The 2/1st, about 620 men, overlooked the eastern end. The beach, 600 metres north of the airstrip, was effectively a 12-kilometre landing zone for paratroopers, running east–west. The ground rose slowly from the shore for about 1000 metres through grapevines and small farms to terraces covered in large olive groves. Small, wooded spurs ran down to the ocean, beside deep gullies. A range of mountains loomed up 3000 metres behind their positions. The

ground nearer Perivolia was unguarded; if the paratroopers landed here, they would be relatively unopposed.

About 10am on Tuesday, 20 May, observers noted a large number of German planes towing gliders heading south-east. At 4pm, twenty fighters and bombers attacked the Rethimno strip with little effect. Then came twenty-four Junkers transports, flying parallel to the coast in groups of three, from the east. Starting at the eastern end of the airstrip, flying slow and low, they dropped waves of paratroopers until the sky seemed full of coloured 'chutes and dangling men. The sight awed the men on the ground – none had seen anything like it.

The Luftwaffe dropped 8000 elite paratroopers in the first wave on 20 May, in the biggest airborne invasion that had ever been attempted.

A storm of ground fire then followed. Some of the planes had caught fire by the time they were halfway along the beach. Ralph Honner noted how they kept their formation, as the men jumped, despite the flames. Some dropped their men in the ocean by mistake. Some paratroopers were dead before they could jump, their bodies thrown out as the planes turned back out to sea over Rethimno. The Australians brought down at least seven planes that afternoon.

> Starting at the eastern end of the airstrip, flying slow and low, they dropped waves of paratroopers until the sky seemed full of coloured 'chutes and dangling men. The sight awed the men on the ground – none had seen anything like it.

JOHN ROBERT FRASER had been an enthusiastic member of the Scouts before the war. He would distinguish himself in battle on Crete.

Hundreds of Germans died in the air, helpless against ground troops who relished the payback. It was a bloody afternoon. Similar attacks were underway against Maleme and Heraklion airstrips. These were more successful for the Germans. The 2/1st commander at Rethimno received messages asking for help he could not send; his own position was under strong attack.

Small patrols went out that night from the 2/11th to clean up the stragglers and bring in captured supplies. The battalion diary notes 'a day of heavy slaughter' for light losses – under twenty killed and wounded. Eighty-four Germans had been taken prisoner.

About half of the 1500 Germans who jumped at Rethimno died that day – but it was not quite a failure. A number of the paratroopers landed safely near Perivolia and established a stronghold. Others gained a crucial foothold at Maleme.

Many of the dead were very young, as the Australians noted in later accounts. Hundreds of wounded lay out overnight, calling for their mothers. The battalion diary noted: 'The cries of the German wounded did not make sleep easy.'

Sandover set to work translating captured documents. These included codes to be used for signalling aircraft, by laying parachutes out on the ground. The Australians used these over the next few days to fool the Germans into dropping ammunition for the weapons they had captured, and even to direct fire on their own men.

By 21 May, an estimated 400 to 500 German paratroopers were dug in at Perivolia. Two hamlets lay between the Australians and the Germans – Platanes and Cesmes. On Thursday, 22 May, B and C companies of 2/11th were told to clear the territory as far as the Platanes River, then move against Perivolia. Ralph Honner's men – who included Bob Fraser – crept into Cesmes, expecting opposition. They found only a goat that needed milking and a blind and incoherent old woman, too weak to move. They gave her food and water and left the goat tied up next to her. Platanes was also empty. B Company routed a small group of enemy from three houses on a ridge.

Perivolia was 900 metres ahead, across open ground. A frontal attack would be madness as the Germans had machine guns on the high ground at the village church. The men spread out, digging shallow pits with captured German shovels, but the German gunners had their range. The Luftwaffe came the next day with fifty planes to strafe and bomb them. This lasted five and half hours and set the country around them on fire. Honner's company withdrew that night, after three had been killed and twenty-seven wounded, replaced by A Company. Thinking they had the Australians routed, the Germans came out to attack late in the day and paid a high price.

During the night, Honner's depleted C Company – at about half strength – crawled forward with extreme care to within 120 metres of German trenches on the eastern edge of the town.

As dawn broke on the Tuesday, 27 May, two Matilda tanks that had originally been brought in to help defend Rethimno lumbered forward. One opened fire on its own men in C Company from 85 metres behind, killing one and wounding a second. The Germans now returned fire, both at the tank and at C Company. The second tank reached the first houses then exploded in flames, hit at close range by an anti-tank round. The first tank crossed the ditch in which Honner's company was hiding, advanced another 20 metres and was hit by a mortar that blew off one of its tracks. It kept firing until both guns were shot away. Its crew was still alive but could neither escape nor shoot.

Without tanks, Honner wanted to withdraw but one platoon of A Company on his left was missing. The lieutenant in charge of that company thought it may have gone forward into the first houses. Honner could not leave those men to fight alone. He sent the officer back to check: again, he could not find the men from 9 Platoon. Honner sent him back again – he came back and said he was certain his men had got through on the left. Honner now faced an agonising choice: C Company would have to cross 70 metres of open ground to silence the German machine guns. There was a well 45 metres closer to the German lines, with a low stone wall. A Bren gun at that position, just 20 metres from the Germans, could protect a charge.

Lieutenant Arthur Stoneham, commander of 14 Platoon, gave the job to Corporal Tom Willoughby, a miner from Kalgoorlie. He led his section in a dash along a low hedge, past the disabled tank, towards the well. Honner described what he saw in a letter to his wife Marjory: 'Willoughby was nearly there before he fell. Behind him, the Bren-gunner went down. The next rifleman caught up the gun in passing and went on until he was killed, and so the Bren was relayed through the section until it almost reached the well in the hands of the last runner; and he too was killed, as he went down kneeling, guarding it even in death.'

> These men of 14 Platoon did not flinch, nor hesitate. They were all experienced so they knew the risks of what they had to do. Only one man survived.

Seven more men died trying to take that gun forward: Ron White, from Pinjarra; Arthur Dowsett, from Wandering; Collin Elvy, from Narlingup; George McDermid, from Kalgoorlie; Frank Green, from North Perth; Charlie Brown, from Wembley; and Bob Fraser, the Boy Scout from Hay Street, Perth City. He was nineteen.

It is difficult now to comprehend the commitment and cohesion that such an action would have required. These men of 14 Platoon did not flinch, nor hesitate. They were all experienced so they knew the risks of what they had to do. Only one man survived. Billy Proud was stunned by a bullet that hit his helmet and knocked him back into the ditch, saving his life. Terry Oakley watched this horror unfold from inside the disabled tank, unable to do anything. He thought the fire was coming from a German sniper hidden in the tailplane of a downed Junkers, but he could not turn the tank turret to fire or warn Willoughby's men.

Honner now refused a request by Stoneham to lead another section out with another Bren. Instead he sent men to try another route; all but one of them was wounded. While this was happening, the lieutenant from A Company returned: his 'lost' men were not in the houses, but lying concealed in the ditch, near where they were supposed to be. Wes Olson, in the battalion history, tells us that Honner 'could barely contain his rage'. Captain Stan Wood, who had been Bob Fraser's drawing instructor, was killed the next day, still trying to take Perivolia.

Shortly after the original assault, two Mauser rifles with telescopic sights had been captured from dead German paratroopers. They were exceptional weapons, better than anything the Australians possessed, partly because of the superiority of their Zeiss sights. Charles Mitchell, company sergeant major, was asked to put together a sniper squad.

This was unusual in an Australian unit at that time. Snipers had played an important role in the First World War, but the British Army discounted their use afterwards, vowing that British forces would never again be drawn into static trench warfare. The Australian army blindly followed their logic. Australian units in 1941 had marksmen, some with specialised rifles, but formal sniper training did not begin again until after Crete – and partly because of what happened on Crete.

Mitchell knew that Andy Mulgrave had all the makings of a good sniper. He was reputed to be the best shot in the battalion. He had the steady hands and precision of an artist, a small build which would come in handy for fitting into tight spaces, and good concentration. He was patient, wily and keen to kill Germans. The same skills he used to watch birds and collect their eggs as a boy – stealth, observation, cunning – now helped him to become a deadly weapon, one of the first successful Australian snipers of the war.

Mitchell and Mulgrave operated as snipers for little more than a week, from around 22 to 29 May. Mitchell selected at least two other men as observers. The squad would go out before dawn to a spot which gave them good cover. They would generally not move again until dark, unless forced to. Charlie Mitchell left an account of this work in a letter to his wife, in which he says Major Sandover gave him the job: 'We have a roving commission to go where we like as long as we copped a few.'

He reports 'we had some good sport getting about ten Jerries a day that we could be sure of, but the last day wasn't so hot …'

A pencilled cross on a battalion map indicates one of the spots they operated from, about one kilometre south-east of Perivolia. The battalion diary for 24 May notes: 'The party under CSM Mitchell operated until May 29 in twin buildings … One member Pte Mulgrave scored 20 verified hits'. The diary was written days, if not weeks, later. The total number of hits grew in later reports to closer to 30.

Snipers usually vary their positions to avoid detection, but Mitchell and Mulgrave appear to have used these two buildings for a longer period. Arthur Leggett, a fellow signaller, wrote later that Andy told him they made themselves comfortable on beds on the second floor of these buildings and spent the day sniping from the beds, until a couple of Stukas came over and destroyed the buildings they had been using. Leggett and his comrades thought that Mulgrave and Mitchell were probably dead, until Andy wandered in after twilight. Leggett reports him as saying: 'It was close today … Bloody hell, it was close.'

Charlie Mitchell's letter indicates they were sometimes outside, hiding under grapevines. He refers to the Germans as 'he' and 'his'.

'We had crawled to a position covering the place where his Junker planes came each day and dropped stores and supplies to him. As they came out to collect them we got four; he must have got a wireless set the previous day as very soon after four Messerschmicts [sic] came over and sprayed the vineyard we were in with

He was patient, wily and keen to kill Germans. The same skills he used to watch birds and collect their eggs as a boy – stealth, observation, cunning – now helped him to become a deadly weapon …

M.G. [machine gun] fire. The bullets were clipping leaves of the vines we were under and that's no kid-stakes. Anyway we crawled to a peasant hut and got inside; while there we got two more Jerries who came out to the supplies, firing from the windows and soon after a Stuka bomber came over and dropped four bombs. His third and fourth bomb just straddling the hut, but blew the roof in on top of us. We had to dig ourselves out of the debris luckily nobody was much hurt. We decided it was too close so shifted our possy; while crossing an open field we saw a flock of fighters coming our way so we ran like hell for a house just beating his bullets. He sprayed the joint, some coming in the windows, a couple of shots puncturing a large earthenware crock full of olive oil alongside which one of my snipers was lying. By the time we noticed what had happened he was lying in a pool of oil. We were chased everywhere that day, one raid in the afternoon caught me up a mulberry tree having a feed. I came down quicker than I went up.'

He mentions 'one young chap who was with me all through the Crete snip-ing was only about nineteen years … His father is Foy and Gibson's Father Xmas every year … Andy Mulgrave was the boy's name. He was a whizzer. If you are in Foy's and can speak to the old chap, I knew him in the shop, he is a very nice man, you can tell him young Andy was a crackerjack with the rifle and gamer than Ned Kelly.'

Andy Mulgrave who lived to return to Australia and marry, left no written record of his time as a sniper, but he did tell his son Leigh about some of his experiences. Leigh was then a teenager. 'He said he was holed up in a chimney of a dwelling with a view of Germans moving in and out of trenches. He was aiming at tunic buttons, about 900 yards away (820 metres). He would start at the end of a trench and hit numbers 1, 3 and 5, and the rest would evacuate when the pattern was realised. Eventually planes were sent over to bomb him. He said he was there for three days and ran out of water and had to collect his own urine.'

Charlie Mitchell and Andy Mulgrave both received the Military Medal for these exploits – although four years apart.

Mitchell's award was gazetted in December 1941, Mulgrave's not until 1946. In his 1946 citation, Brigadier Sandover says that 'Mulgrave alone scored nineteen kills witnessed by our own men, and a further eleven confirmed by local Greeks. The amazing accuracy and persistence of his marksmanship was a most potent factor in keeping the Greek auxiliaries in the field with us … Far younger in appearance [and fact] than his army age, this boy's calmness, courage and deadly ability as a killer had a moral effect, which it is hard to overestimate, both on the battalion and on our Greek helpers, at a time when such inspiration was badly needed.'

In those words, Sandover concedes that he knew Mulgrave was under-age. He uses an interesting term: the boy had an 'army age' – a fictional one that nobody questioned.

Snipers made every man feel like a hunted animal. It was a visceral and per-

> Snipers made every man feel like a hunted animal. It was a visceral and personal form of soldiering …

sonal form of soldiering, for which most men were physically and mentally unfit. The sniper has to carry the death of each man he kills but Andy Mulgrave appears to have been untroubled by that aspect. He was young and, by now, hardened by war. Like most soldiers, he knew it was him or them, and every one of theirs he killed might save one of his. His son Leigh says he rarely spoke of it.

Andy Mulgrave survived Crete – although his war had a long way to go. Bob Fraser did not, killed by a German sniper. Fraser is buried at a Commonwealth War Graves Cemetery in Souda Bay, shaded by olive trees. He was one of fifty-six men from the 2/11th Battalion who never left the island.

CHAPTER SIX

THE GREAT ESCAPER

ANDY MULGRAVE

ANDY MULGRAVE in the desert, some time before his capture on
Crete at the end of June 1941.

The battle for Crete was lost in the first twenty-four hours, when the Germans took Maleme airstrip. They could then land all the troops and supplies they needed and bring tanks by sea. It took another ten days for the British forces to concede, at a cost of many lives. British 'prestige' had taken another battering.

The West Australians never did take Perivolia but nor did the Germans take Rethimno airstrip from them. The Australians were short of food, ammunition and, especially, information. There was little radio contact between battle zones, so Colonel Ian Campbell, commanding the troops at Rethimno, did not know that Maleme was lost. He suspected, correctly, that German reinforcements had arrived in Perivolia on 29 May from Souda Bay, and he knew that another German force was approaching from Heraklion in the east. The next morning, he told his commanders to surrender. Sandover, commander of the 2/11th, was incensed; he told his men they could follow the order or walk across the mountains to the south side of the island,

where the navy might rescue them. It was 'every man for himself'.

Andy Mulgrave took to the hills with hundreds of others, including Charlie Mitchell, Ralph Honner and Ray Sandover – his superiors. These officers all made it off Crete in makeshift vessels borrowed, bought or salvaged from the beaches on the southern shore. Mulgrave did not. He was captured, along with 542 other men from his unit.

The campaign to hold Crete cost the British forces almost 16,000 men, of whom 4000 were killed or wounded, half of them from the Royal Navy. The burden on land fell hardest on the New Zealanders, who had 671 men killed. The British Army lost 612 men, the Royal Marines and RAF another 185. Australian battalions lost 274 men killed, 507 wounded and 3102 taken prisoner. German losses were similar – about 4000 men killed. *Australia in the War of 1939–45*, the official history, does not guess at how many Greeks died, but it was at least 500 of the 10,000 men in uniform.

Andy Mulgrave's battalion had almost ceased to exist. It had the worst casualties of any Australian unit, just as it had in the Greek mainland campaign.

Mulgrave wrote an affidavit after the war documenting his experiences as a prisoner. He said he was taken prisoner on 28 June, which means that he spent nearly a month at large before capture. He must have been hiding in the mountains with the help of the Cretans, but he left no details of these adventures.

The Germans shipped him out of Crete on 29 June to Salonika, where he spent a few days at Salonika POW camp 1, then camp 2. He said he twice attempted to escape camp 2. The first attempt was about 9pm on 3 August, 'by crawling under the wire of the camp'. The second was six days later, through the camp sewer. 'On each occasion I was detected and fired upon by the guards and forced to abandon the attempt.'

This second attempt involved so many prisoners that the sewer pipe became jammed. The men had to turn back, by which time the guards had discovered the plot, and were clubbing each man as he emerged, stinking, from the manhole.

The Salonika camps were shocking places, riddled with lice and vermin. Most of the men soon had dysentery. Each morning, those who had died from starvation or illness were carried out on stretchers. The prisoners believed the

> The Salonika camps were shocking places, riddled with lice and vermin. Most of the men soon had dysentery. Each morning, those who had died from starvation or illness were carried out on stretchers. The prisoners believed the maltreatment was deliberate, an attempt to break their spirits before sending them to Germany.

maltreatment was deliberate, an attempt to break their spirits before sending them to Germany.

Mulgrave boarded a train on 10 August. The journey took seven days. Arthur Leggett, from the same signals platoon, left a searing description of his trip.

The men were marched to the train at night and separated into groups of forty, to be loaded onto cattle wagons fresh with horse dung. Each man was given two small loaves of 'ersatz bread' and a tin of meatloaf. That was to last the whole journey. There were no toilet stops: men with dysentery had to tear up a corner of a shirt and place it on the floor. When they had relieved themselves, they would gather up the four corners of cloth and try to force the bundle through a small window covered with barbed wire. When some of the excrement hit the guards in the next car, the guards would bash every man in the carriage, one by one. The only food stop was in Belgrade, where the Red Cross gave them bread and soup. As they pushed the prisoners back into the wagons, the guards called them 'English swine'. Leggett resented this: 'We were bloody Australians'.

Mulgrave's own account says he arrived in Germany about 17 August 1941, at Stalag XIII-C at Hammelburg, Bavaria. This was a large camp in a former training barracks, 80 kilometres east of Frankfurt. When this shipment of 1000 Australians arrived at the camp, even the camp commander was shocked by their condition. He had food brought to the platform, to fortify the men for the walk to the camp.

The camp housed many French, Belgian and Dutch prisoners, taken the previous year. Serbs had recently arrived from the fighting in the Balkans. After ten days, Mulgrave was sent to Hausen labour camp; on 9 October, he was moved to 'Stockhein' labour camp. There is nowhere called Stockhein in Germany now. There are two towns called Stockheim – one 80 kilometres west of Hammelburg, the other 115 kilometres east of Hammelburg. Stalag XIII-C had many smaller camps under its administration so it is possible that Mulgrave was in a camp at either of the Stockheims.

Here, he was housed on the second floor of an old factory with fifty other prisoners. He and another prisoner, Private Charles Fish of the 2/3rd Battalion, decided to escape.

'Every evening about 2030 hours the guards used to remove our boots and trousers and lock them in a spare room with the food supply. Pte Fish and I had managed to steal a rope from one of the farms in the area and also to fashion a key to fit the door of the spare room.

'After the guards had left us that night [26 February 1942], we managed to unlock the spare room, dressed ourselves and took a quantity of food. We tied the rope to a stanchion in that room and lowered ourselves about thirty feet to the ground below and made a break into the surrounding woods. We were not detected and no alarm was given. We remained at liberty for about fourteen days heading in the direction of the Swiss border and when recaptured we had travelled about 200 kilometres and were then about 110 kilometres from the Swiss border. We used to hide during the daylight and travelled at night, but one morning at daylight we found ourselves in open country and were surrounded by members of the German Landwache [paramilitary rural guards].'

After three days in cells at Schweinfurt, they were returned to Stockhein, where they were beaten by the guards.

'I was held by two German guards whose surnames I do not know but whose Christian names were Karl and Heinrich, whilst a third German guard named Anton Bucher belted me in the face with the butt of his rifle. When they let me go I staggered from the room and as I came out of the door was hit across the face by another guard. The guard who hit me with the rifle butt was given three weeks' detention as punishment and I have since heard that he was killed on the Russian front. As a result of the beating up that I received I spent eleven days in bed with my face and mouth bruised and lacerated and although I asked to see a doctor the only medical attention I got was from other prisoners of war. As soon as I was fit I was sent in chains to solitary confinement at Fladungen Tower which is about twelve miles from Stockhein.'

'We tied the rope to a stanchion in that room and lowered ourselves about thirty feet to the ground below and made a break into the surrounding woods. We were not detected and no alarm was given.'

Wherever he was, Mulgrave had a gift for causing trouble. He was shifted to a new camp in August after taking 'a leading part' in organising a strike at Stockhein. He and another striker, Sapper McQuarrie of the 2/1st Engineers, lasted a week at Urspringen Camp before escaping on 22 August.

'The guard used to sleep in a small building detached from the main barrack and while some of the other prisoners of war distracted his attention, Sapper McQuarrie and I escaped through the door and got away undetected into the scrub. We took with us food from Red Cross parcels ...'

Again, they travelled by night and hid by day, heading for Switzerland. They lasted a week before a party of police and armed civilians recaptured them. This time they were sent to Straf Company 362 in the Rhon mountains, to work in a stone quarry. The Straf units were penal groups for Wehrmacht offenders – that is, German military personnel. They were often given the most dirty and dangerous jobs, like clearing minefields, as punishment. It is unusual

that an escaped prisoner of war would be sent to one.

'We were working in pairs and we had to break and load fifteen tons per pair per day. I was there about five or six weeks and early in November 1943 was returned to Urspringen Camp and went to hospital for about three months on 14 November 1943. On discharge from hospital I was returned to Urspringen Camp but very soon afterwards I was again admitted to hospital for a further two months.'

Some of these dates and figures do not add up. For two men to lift that amount of rock per day (13,600 kilograms) is superhuman, unless they had access to machinery. Even if they worked a twelve-hour day, they would have to cut and lift more than 1100 kilograms per hour. There is a full year missing from Mulgrave's account, between his first escape from Urspringen in August 1942 and his six weeks breaking rocks in the quarry, ending in November 1943. He wrote this account in November 1945 in Perth, two years later. It is detailed but not complete. Given the state of his health during and after the war, some level of confusion is understandable.

In April 1944, he was sent to a camp at Grosswenkheim. Sapper Alec McQuarrie was already there. Mulgrave stayed at this camp for almost a year. In March 1945, he and Syd Cant, another West Australian from the 2/11th Battalion, escaped 'by breaking down the door with an axe'.

'We escaped undetected and got to a small village called Kleinwenkheim, about three miles (five kilometres) away. Cant and I split up that night and I have since heard that Cant was recaptured the same night. I contacted two German girls from this village whose names were Therese Stapf and Hildrud Stapf who lived at house number seventeen, Kleinwenkheim. They were sisters, Therese being the elder about twenty-two or twenty-three years of age, and Hildrud about eighteen or nineteen years of age. They led me to a safe hiding place in a barn in that village and kept me hidden and supplied with food for about eight days. When I received word that Sapper McQuarrie was hiding in Grosswenkheim I went to see him one night about 2230 hours.'

Mulgrave wrote that he stayed with McQuarrie for several days, during which they were hidden and supplied with food by two other German girls, Hedwig and Rosalie Schlenbach, of house number 37, Grosswenkheim.

Was there a network of sympathetic young Bavarian women helping escaped prisoners? The risks to themselves and their families would have been great. And how did the men know how to

> Mulgrave was fluent in German: when other prisoners disdained the language of the guards, Mulgrave threw himself into its study. He wanted to be able to pass for a German when he escaped.

find them? The most likely answer is that some prisoners had prior contact as labourers on farms.

By this time, Mulgrave was fluent in German: when other prisoners disdained the language of the guards, Mulgrave threw himself into its study. He wanted to be able to pass for a German when he escaped. Many Germans knew that the war was coming to an end. Indeed, by the end of April, Hitler was dead and Nazi authority was crumbling. The American 3rd Army crossed the Rhine on 22 March 1945, 130 kilometres from Hammelburg; the Russians were advancing on Berlin from the east. Perhaps these young women felt that the chances of them getting caught were much reduced. Whatever their motives, they saved the lives of Mulgrave and McQuarrie. And Mulgrave was to discover they weren't the only ones.

Mulgrave continues: 'After several days with McQuarrie, I returned to [Kleinwenkheim] one night and on my way back I found an empty German staff car and the guard being some distance away from it, I took from it an eight-millimetre automatic revolver and a pair of binoculars. I also destroyed a number of maps and documents which I found in the car, put sand in the petrol tank and cut all the wires of the engine of the car. I then went back to my hiding place in the barn at Kleinwenkheim.'

Mulgrave names other people who helped him in Kleinwenkheim. A woman named Ida Rink, whose husband was a prisoner of war in America, and her daughter Julitta provided food and cigarettes.

The American forces arrived on 8 April 1945, he wrote.

'I travelled with them on their armoured vehicle all that afternoon. I captured three German soldiers hiding in the cellar of a house in Grosswenkheim and handed them over to the Americans and also contacted Sapper McQuarrie. About 2115 hours that night I saw a German staff car containing three officers in the main street of Kleinwenkheim. I decided to try and capture them but when the car came level with me I found six more in the back and immediately afterwards a light German armoured vehicle pulled up behind the car with another twelve Germans and Gestapo men. Although in the ensuing fight, I did manage to shoot one of the German officers, I was properly beaten up and left for dead lying in the street …

'An old German woman named Amelie Schlenbach of house number 25 Kleinwenkheim found me lying in the street that night, carried me into her house and attended to my wounds and the next day a number of Germans came to her house and surrendered to me. I took about fifteen of them up to Grosswenkheim and handed them over to the American forces.'

He then lists three other soldiers who had been hiding in Grosswenkheim at that time: Lance Corporal Scott of the Australian 7th Division Provosts; Private Les Creati of the 2/7th Battalion; and an Englishman, Staff Sergeant Tom Jones of 'a Leicestershire Regiment'.

He concludes the affidavit by saying he then made his way to the headquarters of the US Third Army at Bad Kissingen. His record shows that he was repatriated home to Australia via England in May and June. This affidavit was made in Perth in November 1945 and co-signed by Major Hubert Stables, of the Australian Army Legal Corps. The affidavit may have been made to justify Mulgrave's claim to certain medals but there are inconsistencies in Mulgrave's accounts of his time as a POW.

In 1949, he wrote to the army to support his claim to a decoration, the France and Germany Star.

'I was in Bad Neustadt-Schweinfurt area for three or four weeks after my escape in end of Feb, early March meeting up with an American Tank Corps at Kleinwenkheim on approx March 27th. I travelled with them for three or four days and took active part in mopping up arrangements, also receiving a face wound at Seubrigshausen, where we combined with another tank brigade from the 7th Army making a combined team from the 3rd and 7th Army. Further mopping up operations went on till April 7th. I then left the tanks and made my way back to a place called Kleinwenkheim when [*sic*] several weeks previous I had hidden a few of my belongings in a barn.

It was in this village that I encountered a car full of German officers (I thought there were only three of them) and tried to get them. In the ensuing battle (it was dark) they were joined by another crowd on a light armoured fighting vehicle. In the confusion, several of them were killed, the rest got away leaving me for dead with a bad head wound, the roots of my tongue were half torn away, and several small superficial wounds. I would certainly have bled to death if a German girl had not found me and helped me five hours later. This incident occurred I think on April 9th 1945 …'

What to make of these discrepancies? Different dates, more than one German killed in his final skirmish, and a whole episode of three or four days with an American Tank Corps that he fails to mention in the original affidavit. The old woman Schlenbach has become a young girl who rescued him.

Mulgrave seems to be struggling with his own memory in this letter from 1949. He concludes by writing: 'You must understand that I am somewhat hazy about exact dates. Escaping, being

ANDY MULGRAVE was a difficult man to hold. He escaped a number of times from camps in Germany.

hunted, and travelling at nights, and the subsequent whirl of events made things very confusing …'

Given what he had been through, it would be remarkable if Mulgrave came back without some form of stress disorder. Post-traumatic stress disorder (PTSD) often has an impact on memory. Perhaps it is also accurate to see it as the other way around: the memories these men carried took an inevitable toll.

There is one powerful testimonial in-favour of his accounts: in 1986, the local historian in the village of Kleinwenkheim invited Andy and his wife Shirley to return to Germany for the village's 1200th anniversary. They credited him with stopping the Americans from destroying their village.

The *West Australian* newspaper carried a feature about Mulgrave's war in May 1986 which quotes a letter from Herr Wendelin Volk, who was writing the history of the village: 'In the last days of the World War, you left a message to the US Army on a piece of paper. This message saved our village a great disaster ...'

The article confirms that Mulgrave worked on a farm at Kleinwenkheim, and was friendly with the farmer and his family. He had written a message for the mayor, asking the Americans not to punish the villagers. The article presents a third interpretation of the clash between Mulgrave and the Germans in the car, in which Andy says he produced a Beretta pistol he had been hiding in his water bottle since North Africa. After the Germans left him for dead in the street, he was nursed back to health by a fifteen-year-old girl called Uulitta.

'She looked after me for a week. By this time the US Army tanks had gone through. The mayor handed the senior officer my letter and told him there were no SS in Kleinwenkheim. If there had been, the village would have been blasted out of existence'.

Herr Volk had married the mayor's daughter. 'Before he died my father in law gave me that valuable paper ... What you did must not be forgotten.'

> In 1986, the local historian in the village of Kleinwenkheim invited Andy and his wife Shirley to return to Germany for the village's 1200th anniversary. They credited him with stopping the Americans from destroying their village.

Andy and Shirley loved their visit to Germany. He told the *West Australian* interviewer that that was the one place in Germany that had happy memories for him. He had tried otherwise to forget the war.

Mulgrave was by then sixty-five years old. He had become a legend in Perth as an authority on fishing. Anglers used to line up in a sports store where he worked to get his advice. Until this visit to Germany, he had rarely spoken about the war. His son Leigh says that the visit had a profound effect on him. He was much more willing to talk about the war when he returned.

Leigh still has a number of metal boxes and a cigarette lighter that his father engraved by hand while in the camps. Andy became a skilled jeweller on his return to Perth.

All four of the men in the pre-embarkation picture taken in 1940 survived the war. In 1993, they returned to Kalamunda to recreate it, and were featured in the local paper.

Andy Mulgrave was the first of the four to go. He died in August 1999, in Perth, aged seventy-eight. By any account, he had an extraordinary war: a decorated soldier, a deadly sniper, a five-time escaper, a survivor of the prison camps, 'saviour' of a German town. And under-age soldier.

CHAPTER SEVEN

MISSING PERSONS

GLEN DEREK SCOTT
AKA ALLAN STUART

By the time he enlisted in late 1939, **GLEN DEREK SCOTT** had become
'ALLAN STUART'. He hitchhiked 750km from western Queensland to join up.

In January 1940 the Queensland Police Gazette listed Glen Derek Scott as a missing person.

Glen turned seventeen in November 1938. Around that time, he ran away from the family farm at Cooroy, north of Brisbane. He and his father Gordon had been at loggerheads for years. It may have had something to do with Glen being forced to leave school at twelve. He was a good student and a keen reader. He was ready to go to high school in Nambour when Gordon insisted he work on the dairy farm. It was 1933 and the Depression was ripping through the country.

It may also have had something to do with Gordon's war injuries. Gordon Roy Scott served at Gallipoli in 1915. He injured his spine in France in 1917 and was sent back to England for treatment, but the injury remained. He was given morphine for the pain and, like many soldiers, became addicted to the drug.

When war came, Glen was looking after horses near Cunnamulla. He had been gone for at least a year and may already have dumped his real name, to cover his tracks. He immediately set out to hitchhike the 750 kilometres to Brisbane, where he signed up as 'Allan Stuart'. He was not yet eighteen, but he claimed to be twenty-one. He did not tell his parents what he was doing. By the time the Police Gazette listed him in January 1940, he was at Ingleburn camp in New South Wales, learning how to become a soldier in the 2/1st Anti-Tank Regiment, Royal Australian Artillery (RAA).

The RAA was behind Britain's Royal Artillery in both equipment and thinking, but Australia's military planners had recognised that modern artillery had to be mobile and mechanised. Trucks and

He signed up as 'Allan Stuart'. He was not yet eighteen, but he claimed to be twenty-one. He did not tell his parents what he was doing.

tractors were crucial; so were motorcycle despatch riders, for communications. Private Stuart fancied himself for two-wheeled duty.

The regiment left Australia in May 1940, just as Hitler was overrunning France and the Low Countries. The ship could not enter the Suez Canal, for fear of Italian air attack. They went via Cape Town to Scotland – a long way from the Australians already in the Middle East. Worse, the regiment was then broken up, to be used as infantry in case of an invasion of Britain. They had no guns: these were to have been issued by the British on arrival in the Middle East.

They trained at Tidworth and Colchester in England. In September 1940, the regiment was re-formed for its original purpose. Stuart's unit, now issued with guns and transport, set out for Egypt in November. 'Allan Stuart' was now a Despatch Rider – a 'Don R' in army slang, 'Don' being the signaller's designation for the letter 'D'. It was a year since he had enlisted, but now he had a motorbike to show for it.

He also had a sweetheart. While at Ingleburn, outside Sydney, his duties included patrolling Liverpool Station, where men returning from leave would often have difficulties – walking a straight line being a common one. He noticed three soldiers chatting up a young woman as she left the train. He saw them off, then began to chat her up himself. Her name was Weipa Mayer. Her parents had been Christian missionaries in Far North Queensland, where she was born. They now lived at Guildford and were heavily involved in the charity-run canteen at the camp. She invited him for Sunday lunch. When he left for the war, they wrote to each other. Some of his letters and a diary he kept briefly in 1942 are still in the family.

In a letter dated 24 November 1940, he explained that he was on a ship heading for Cape Town, where he planned to post the letter. (This long route to Egypt was to avoid submarines in the Mediterranean.)

He writes: 'Well it is great to be back in shorts again after six months in the cold. We didn't see the sun for the last three weeks we were in England … We

PRIVATE 'STUART' met **WEIPA MAYER** at a Sydney railway station in late 1940. For the first few years of their romance, she had no idea of his real name.

have a lot of English troops on with us at present and they are the dirtiest mob of soldiers we have ever met and that is saying something. About three days out we struck some rather rough sea and 50% of the Tommies were sea sick. Strange to say I was not. They were sick all over the ship, in the corridors, everywhere so we haven't much time for them … It looks like we will be spending Christmas on this "tub" so that will not be so hot from our point of view. This will be the second one spent in the army.'

Five months later, he had seen war up close, in Greece. His unit was at Vevi Pass, near the Yugoslavian border. He later wrote about some of his adventures: being arrested by English troops who thought he was a spy; being blown off his motorbike by a blast from a 25-pound gun; being fired upon by German Stuka aeroplanes, then bombed by high-level Dorniers and Heinkels, followed by machine-gun strafing from Messerschmitts. He went through four motorbikes in the retreat – the third one had its tank and head blown off.

'A piece of shrapnel landed in my leg as I landed nearby. I pulled it out and applied a field dressing. Next day found another bike and continued convoy duties.'

He got out of mainland Greece on the HMS *Coventry*, at about 4am on

> He later wrote about some of his adventures: being arrested by English troops who thought he was a spy, being blown off his motorbike by a blast from a 25-pound gun; being fired upon by German Stuka aeroplanes, then bombed by high-level Dorniers and Heinkels, followed by machine-gun strafing from Messerschmitts.

26 April. The ship was strafed continually during the twelve-hour run to Crete. His unit was lucky: they were evacuated to Egypt after three weeks, before the German invasion of Crete. He travelled on a Greek coastal boat that usually carried goats and sheep 'and smelled like it'. They had no water, only Carnation milk.

On 15 May 1941, he wrote to Weipa from a camp in Palestine. He signs the letter 'Stewy', still pretending to be Allan Stuart. It's not clear that Weipa even knew his real name yet. Even if she had, 'Stewy' had to stick to his fake name in letters, all of which were subject to reading by army censors.

'Well I suppose you are wondering what happened to me as I haven't written for over six weeks but no doubt you have received my cable by this or at least I hope so. Well, I suppose you have read all about our affair in Greece so there is very little I can say about it. I was one of the lucky ones and got out very lightly although I thought Mrs Stuart's little boy's number was called out several times …'

Arriving at their old camp in Palestine, he had received his mail. 'There were six [letters] waiting here from you and two parcels. They were great sweetheart. You have no idea how well these were appreciated you see, we have nothing left after our Greece affair. All our kit bags were destroyed.'

> 'There were six [letters] waiting here from you and two parcels. They were great sweetheart. You have no idea how well these were appreciated you see, we have nothing left after our Greece affair. All our kit bags were destroyed.'

In July 1941, he went north to Syria, for the brief campaign against the Vichy French, who still had colonial control of Lebanon and Syria. The Free French, with British help, routed Vichy forces who were now under German control.

GLEN SCOTT'S diary contains some lively stories of his adventures as a despatch rider – known as a 'Don R' – in Palestine and Syria.

Allan fought in the battle for Damascus, then at Palmyra and Baalbek. 'Temperature was in the vicinity of 130 degrees F and never any shortage of snipers who didn't seem to like us'.

He began writing a diary on 1 January 1942, at Baalbek. By now, the men were living in freezing Nissan huts, or eight-person EPIP tents. Their only distractions seem to have been beer and local brandy, and rumours about where they would go next. The following excerpts give a vivid picture of a soldier's daily life – the boredom, isolation and discomfort, as well as the humour and comradeship. The casual racism is of its time. Most of the soldiers used these terms: Palestinians and Arabs were 'wogs', Jews were 'Yids', Egyptians were 'Farouks'. The British were 'Poms' and 'Tommies', the Germans 'Huns', 'Jerries' or 'Hans'. 'Wogging' became a term for trading or selling wares.

31 December – What a time ... Passed out rather early in the night ... New Year resolution – no more excessive drinking and be home for the next New Year celebrations, I wonder!

6 January – Started up the bike for the first time in over a week. Had a row with O'Hea over being taken off fire piquet [guard watch] to go out to clear a road of snow. Had to walk over four miles to get there through snow – feet wet through and frozen ... No mail from Weipa yet! Below freezing point last night ... 2 sergeants put their false teeth in water when they went to bed and they froze overnight. Had to put them over the primus to thaw them in the morning.

9 January – ... B1 and B4 [Batteries 1 and 4] went into Beirut to get some more French 105mm guns. This is the second trip our battery has made for these guns. British captured these guns in the Syrian campaign and gave them to the Free French and now the Free French are selling them to us for a 1/2 million Francs each. Just like the British ... MPs rounding up all the AIF personnel in Beirut cleaning the town out. Some have been there since Greece and Crete.

10 January – ... No mail from Weipa today. Snow still thawing slowly. Brom

(Bromley) got drunk and wanted to fight everybody. He ran down the AIF to the lowest degree reckoned we were the lowest things that God ever put breath into. Nobody got to sleep till after one o'clock. I thought somebody was going to dong him at one stage. Fought the stove and knocked the chimney over. What a man!

13 January – … Rumoured that we are going to Burma, overland. It is definite that we are going to move somewhere but heaven knows where. Hope we do go to Burma it would be a wonderful trip.

19 January – … the showers are going down at the creek now so we are going to have a shower on our way home tomorrow afternoon if we go out. This will be the first for over a fortnight. Had a haircut tonight by Bill Mackee.

21 January – … cold as hell here today … Our movement orders were cancelled today. Some say we will be here till after Easter. Hope not …

24 January – … Japs took Solomon Islands by the wireless also bombed Rabaul with 100 seaplanes. The reds have driven a wedge into the Huns army 70 miles wide – good work – Australia is threatened with invasion. Hans driven back in the desert. Our 8th division is surrounded in Malaya.

25 January – Had day in bed. Tinea better. Movement order cancelled. Tommie advance guard busy … Had to go and stack picks and shovels up into heaps so that they could be counted and handed over to the Poms … Sold our mats to the Tommies they were bought out of our regimental funds. Snowed on the mountains last night – learnt to play 500 tonight. First time I played cards in my life … Japs claim to have annihilated the 8th Divvie in Malaya.

27 January – stopped in bed all day had the flu … Got our movement orders tonight at 5:30. First stop is Haifa over 200 miles the next is in the Gaza area. From there I don't know where …

Back from hell: members of the 2/1st Anti-Tank Regiment in Egypt after their escape from Crete in May 1941. Standing from left: **RAY SHEPHERD, DARCY EVANS, RON 'SPLINTER' COLLINS, KEN FOOTE, GLEN 'STEWIE' SCOTT, EDDIE BOYD, TOM ROBERTS.** Squatting: **JOHNNIE MERRELL, BILL 'SOL' MADDEN, LAURIE RUBUCK** and ... **SMALL.**

28 January – what a turn last night. Bob Barnet came home first or should I say was carried home. Crosby wasn't much better. Bob skinned all his face on the road but that was only a preliminary to the real event. At 5:10 this morning Price and Gimmel arrived with the Pommies gunner, Jim, who was much the worse for wear as he had fallen in every muddy puddle according to Pricie and by the look of him, I quite believe it. He went home after he knocked down the chimney on Bark (poor stove) and Bdr Leo who was the life of the party if it can be called that, they eventually got to bed at 25 to 6 ... moving early tomorrow.

29 January – reveille 400 hours. Raining like hell and cold with it ... Evans just about wrecked my bike and also knocked over a Tommy soldier. Hit Haifa about 20.40 hours and tried to buy tea at a Church Cafe but they sold out. Had tea at the Barracks and slept in the back of the truck with Sgt Shephard. Quite warm after Syria.

30 January –... Lord Haw-Haw [British nickname for a German propaganda broadcaster] said we were going back to Aussie, that we were going to swim through 7th Division blood and that the Yank Navy would be convoying us home and they would supply the 'stookers' [German Stuka planes].

31 January – Had good sleep last night. Reveille 6:45. Went to RHP for tinea where they put the blue tinea paint on. Nearly made me exit through the roof. Christ it burnt ...

6 February – on light duties all day but didn't go out of the tent hardly. Have got acute tonsillitis and if the Sydney Harbour Bridge was nearer I think I would go jump over it the present way I feel. The battery going out on manoeuvres tonight after tea, one good thing about being sick – I can't go... Got a letter from Weipa today dated 4/1/42.

10 February – ... Battery went on a 12-mile route march tonight. I didn't go as I still have tinea. O'Hea said I am playing it well but still it is true.

11 February – ... Rumoured that Singapore has fallen not confirmed yet.

13 February – ... Beer in the canteen tonight. Guess there will be a few stories around. Brom is on it again and he is arguing pretty well at present. Singapore is counter-attacking I believe and the 7th Divvie has landed in Bombay. I think we might go there too...

14 February – ... The two up had a good run last night. One chap won £100 and another tossed 14 heads and pulled out with 80 quid ...

16 February – ... Saw old Mick Dow he is still bomb happy from Greece. Churchill announced last night that Singapore had fallen but by the way the papers have been reading it looks as if it fell nearly a week ago.

18 February – cleared up the camp this morning and took the rubbish out to the dump behind Julis Village. When we got there, there were wogs galore so didn't miss the opportunity of selling the best of the rubbish. Made 500 mills, sold an old EPIP tent fly for 400 mills and another bit of a tent for 100 mills and didn't do too bad...

19 February – Reveille at five o'clock but was held up and didn't move till just before daylight – very slow convoy this morning as it was raining off and on all the time... Darwin was bombed yesterday had two raids 78 [Japanese planes] in the first and 21 in the second. And they only got 4 out of the whole lot. Still not bad for a beginner. A Sig DR hit a camel yesterday morning. Killed the camel and hurt his head.

20 February – Reveille at 6 this morning hope to hit Suez tonight ... Had two big halts along the road before we crossed the Suez Canal to let a boat pass through ...

26 February – Pay day today. No parades as there is a beautiful dust storm blowing – been blowing all night most of the tents blew down last night and were buried beneath about 18 inches of sand ... It was still blowing this morning so

there was no parade and still none this afternoon. Nobody seems to be worrying about it either...

27 February – had quite an easy day today. Everybody seems to be drunk and Johnno and Bruce were out in the water cart most of the day and they are drunk as fools. Samie brought some fish up here for our dinner today and they were quite good – they must have been caught in the bitter salt lake. They were only small but quite good. Maintenance was meant to be done all day but nobody seemed to do much but drink beer ... I lost about 400 mills at the dice tonight. Another brawl in the canteen throwing bottles in the end.

3 March – had an air raid last night – a beaut lasted nearly an hour. Bombs were coming down like raindrops. The warning went out at 3 o'clock and the first bombs were dropped for 4.15 – three, one after another. They hit a drome about ten miles down, dropped about 65 on the runway and hit four Vickers-Wellington bombers. Killed four

officers and three sergeants with a few wogs. They say it was meant for the Pool about two miles from here. No Ack-Ack went up on searchlights. Some say they were intercepted on the way home and also Wellington bombers followed them home. Some of them did a little machine gunning. Told today we might be going in a few days' time so had to get all our washing out of the laundry ...

5 March – didn't get up till late this morning and had to go to regimental parade at 9 for a short arm inspection [medical check of the private parts for sexually transmitted infections] – Dalton conducted it – I think he likes that sort of thing.

6 March – heard that Java had been evacuated and that Rangoon had fallen. Things don't look so hot, do they? Supposed to be going aboard late this afternoon or early in the morning but apparently something has gone wrong with the plans as it looks like we'll be here for a few days. Some big ships in port.

18 March – Well one month today since we left Khassa. Sand storm blew most of the night and when I woke up I was covered in sand and it was still blowing pretty strong. Eggs for breakfast as per usual. They say that the Wogs are on strike on the docks and that is the hold up now. Once the guards fired three shots over their heads meaning to frighten them but they went for their lives and they took a bit of coaxing back again. We were sitting in one truck just before tea and orders came through that we had to stand by, ready to move. About 10 minutes later they brought down our stickers – red ones – got to the docks at Tewfik – just after a hail storm passed. All the roads were covered with water. One of the ships broke loose and the wire rope snapped and killed three wogs, also a truck got away and took a Tommie's arm off. We got aboard about 11 and went to sleep at 12. We are going on a Dutch boat.

When he went aboard, and for some weeks en route, 'Allan Stuart' had no certainty about where they were going. The mail bags destined for Adelaide and Melbourne gave him hope. The constant watch for submarines gave him anxiety. He was on the *Serooskerk*, a pre-First World War icebreaker that seldom went a day without it breaking down. It eventually docked at Adelaide, where he disembarked. His section was sent to Beaudesert in Queensland, separated from the rest of his unit, and transferred to the 113th Light Anti-Aircraft Regiment. He applied for a transfer back to his old unit. When it was refused, he tried to stow away on the ship taking his mates to New Guinea. The CO charged him with being AWL, rather than the more serious offence of desertion. He had two tours of New Guinea, both unhappy experiences. He caught malaria and lost a lot of friends but survived.

He had told the army his real name in April 1943, six months after he finally turned twenty-one. He and Weipa married in October 1944. Their first son, Stuart, was born while Glen was in New

Guinea. Glen was discharged in October 1945 and the family settled near Weipa's parents in Guildford, where they had another son, Colin. In 1949, Glen and Weipa took up a poultry farm near his parents at The Summit, outside Stanthorpe. Glen worked a range of hard physical jobs – cane cutting up north, clearing land further west. His daughter Roxane, born 1958, remembers him as strict, with a short fuse, but a loving father when he wasn't drinking.

'If I had to put a name to it I would say Dad had PTSD but it didn't really manifest to me until the late 1960s when his drinking did increase. He had a will of iron and would go for periods without touching a drop but then would have a few months of regular drinking. He always went to work and kept up all that needed to be done so basically a functioning alcoholic. I have never known what the trigger was ...'

He became the projectionist at the Summit Hall, devoured the Russian novelists, and became an avid bird-watcher. He encouraged his children to wear his medals in the Anzac Day march, but he did not attend. Late in life, he reconnected with men from his old unit. In the 1990s, he would go down to Brisbane for Anzac Day, to attend the Greek dawn service, followed by a lunch hosted by the Greek consul. Roxane says he never forgot the kindness of the Greek people. He died in January 2008, aged eighty-six.

Glen Scott's life was marked by war, just as his father's life had been. The bitterness between them was made worse by war. Both came back damaged and both families suffered because of it. This was far from rare. So many of the under-age soldiers went to war because their fathers had done so. In that sense, the wounds became hereditary.

The boy becomes a man ... **GLEN SCOTT**, photographed on his return to Australia, after service in the Middle East.

CHAPTER EIGHT

THE BEST OF FRIENDS

FRANK HAYES AND NORM MOLONY

JOHN FRANCIS HAYES, shortly after he enlisted. He reversed the order of his given names and lied about his age.

War brings out the worst in some men; in others, the best. Frank Hayes and Norm Molony became best friends in primary school in North Melbourne. The friendship would carry them through some dark times and places.

John Francis (Frank) Hayes was born in Seymour, 104 kilometres north of Melbourne. His father, Robert, had worked as a rabbit trapper, wheat lumper and shearer, before joining the railways. In 1921, Robert had just passed the train driver's exams when he fell while stepping off a train. He lost a foot. John Francis was born in January 1922, while his father was still recuperating.

By the early 1930s, the family was living at 51 Miller Street, West Melbourne, just north of the docks. Robert was now a carriage upholsterer at the Newport railway workshops. John Francis attended St Mary's Catholic School in Howard Street, North Melbourne. That's where he met Norman Francis Molony, the youngest of nine children.

Norm was two years younger, but streetwise. The Molonys lived at 2 Fink Street, Kensington, in a small timber 'shotgun' house. At the time, no-one lived in Kensington by choice: it was dirty and polluted, dominated by an abattoir and cattle sale yards, dating back to the 1850s. 'Kenso' smelled of cow shit and tallow. Families here were often large and Catholic, and they were poorer than ever during the Depression. Vincent Molony, Norm's son, says his father grew up straight but tough. 'He never got into any trouble with the police, but he had a reputation as a street fighter. He could look after himself.'

Norm and Frank were mad about motorcycles. At age fourteen, Frank left school to work at Beers, a paper varnishing factory. Norm would come to his house on the weekend to tinker with motorbikes.

There is a photograph of Frank and his older brother Teddy and two mates on their bikes. Frank has his hair swept back with hair oil – a handsome young man with a confident air and Robert Mitchum–style broken nose.

Norm already had a sweetheart. Lenora Agnes (Leni) Fry had grown up in

The Hayes boys were keen motorcyclists before the war. **FRANK** is at right in leather jacket, with **F DUNNE**. **TEDDY HAYES** is behind **EDDIE RITCHIE** on the left.

a neighbouring street in Kensington. She and Norm started going out just before the war, when she was fifteen and Norm was sixteen.

Around this time, Frank met Kathleen Mary Backman at a Coles staff dance in the upstairs ballroom at Flinders Street Station. Kath was one of seventeen children. She was sixteen, already working

at the Yarra Falls textile factory.

Frank's older brother was the first to go to war. Teddy enlisted on 9 May 1940. He was posted to the 2/7th Battalion, a Victorian unit that was part of the newly formed 6th Division, the first to fight in the Middle East. Their youngest sister Monica, born 1931, remembers going to Station Pier to wave him goodbye, in September 1940. Frank called out to his brother from the wharf: 'I'll see you over there'.

Frank was now eighteen, but his father wouldn't sign the enlistment papers. Frank told him he would go anyway. In the end, he waited six months. He went to the recruiting office at Royal Park in Melbourne in March 1941. He reversed the order of his first names, becoming Francis John, and claiming to be a 'fruit preserver'. No-one asked for proof of age, but he added eighteen months – claiming to be twenty and seven months – which was still underage, without a parent's consent. He gave his mother as next of kin, and the correct address, making no attempt to cover his tracks.

> Norm Molony had enlisted in July 1940, eight months earlier. His parents were shocked, given that he was still only sixteen, but he was very determined.

His parents were upset that both their sons were going to war. Robert and Susannah had already buried three of their seven children, and Susannah had lost two brothers in the First World War.

Norm Molony had enlisted in July 1940, eight months earlier. His parents were shocked, given that he was still only sixteen, but he was very determined. Vincent, his son, thinks he was motivated in part by a sense of injustice. Norm did not like thugs and bullies, and Hitler was both. Another factor was the sense of excitement.

'What he told me is that he wanted to go because there were others around him going. He thought it would be a big adventure …'

NORM MOLONY, aged sixteen, around the time he enlisted in July 1940. Frank called him 'boof' and Norm used the same nickname for Frank.

Norm entered training at Darley camp at Bacchus Marsh, just west of Melbourne. He went AWL twice in the next six months – standard misbehaviour for an Australian volunteer recruit. At the end of November he was posted to the 2/29th Battalion at Bonegilla, near Albury, then to the 2/24th at Bathurst in May, where he went AWL again. By June, Norm was back at Darley camp, now a reinforcement to the 2/23rd Battalion. Frank Hayes, recently enlisted, was already there. The two girls, Kath and Leni, had become close friends. They took the train to Darley to farewell the boys, who would soon be going overseas. On 28 June 1941, Frank and Norm sailed together from Sydney on the *Queen Mary*, arriving late July in the Middle East. By late August, they were in Tobruk.

The 2/23rd, known as 'Albury's Own', had sailed for the Middle East the previous November and trained in Palestine. In March 1941, reassigned to the 9th Division, they were sent to Libya to relieve the 6th Division. They arrived in Tobruk on 17 March, just as Erwin Rommel, the new commander of the Afrika Korps, began his campaign to push the British back to Suez. The 2/23rd would spend the next seven months besieged in Tobruk, with the sea at their backs and Rommel's tanks at their front.

British and Australian naval vessels, operating after dark at great risk, kept Tobruk supplied. Thirty thousand men, most of them Australian, held Rommel at bay with commitment and ingenuity.

The 2/23rd Battalion had lost 163 men in one day in May, before Frank and Norm arrived. On the night of 30 August, 528 shells rained down, introducing them to some of the hard lessons of siege warfare.

The 2/23rd was withdrawn from Tobruk in October, after its baptism of fire. They had been shelled, strafed and starved for seven months. They had had little water, too many fleas, and a lot of dysentery. Their casualties were

The eve of battle … **'KID' MOLONY** and a pal enjoy a recreational beverage in December 1941.

the highest of all 9th Division units at Tobruk: 78 men dead, 150 wounded.

Even so, Churchill had wanted to keep them in Tobruk, lest their relief disrupt his plans for an offensive against Rommel. The new Australian Prime Minister, John Curtin, had insisted they be withdrawn. The exhausted men of the 2/23rd went back to Julis camp in Palestine to regroup.

With the Americans now in the war after the Japanese attack on Pearl Harbor, the Australians in the Middle East hoped they might soon be going home to defend Australia. That changed when Tobruk, now garrisoned by South Africans, fell on 21 June 1942.

The British had lost a series of armoured battles across the western desert. Rommel's depleted force of Italians and Germans was now advancing along the coast of Egypt towards Alexandria. General Claude Auchinleck had succeeded Archibald Wavell in July 1941 as Commander-in-Chief of the British forces in the Middle East. After the fall of Tobruk, he took personal command of the British Eighth Army. By July 1942, he had largely lost the confidence of the ever-hectoring Churchill and most of the dominion commanders.

Auchinleck decided to make his stand at El Alamein, a desolate train stop on the coast 110 kilometres west of Alexandria. If they could not hold Rommel there, the panzers would be within easy reach of Cairo and the Suez Canal. The 2/23rd Battalion, on garrison duties in Syria, rushed back to join the rest of the baggy-trousered British force – most of whom were not born in Britain

> The 2/23rd was withdrawn from Tobruk in October, after its baptism of fire. They had been shelled, strafed and starved for seven months. They had had little water, too many fleas, and a lot of dysentery.

but India, South Africa, Australia and New Zealand.

Norm Molony was known as 'Kid' in the battalion, for obvious reasons. On the morning of 16 July, C Company was sent up through a railway cutting to take a German defensive position known as East Point 24, on the flanks of Tel el Eisa, a high point west of the railway.

B Company was then to pass through C Company and take West Point 24, further over on the same ridge. Each would be accompanied by two or three British tanks.

For Frank in C Company and Norm in B Company, it was yet another dirty job. They had lost many comrades already this way. It took C Company about an hour to subdue East Point 24, despite heavy fire from enemy machine guns and mortars. B Company, under Captain Keith Neuendorf, passed through their ranks about 6.30am on their way to attack West Point 24. They came under increasingly heavy fire, taking many casualties.

Neuendorf led them forward. His twin brother had been taken prisoner at Tobruk. As Keith Neuendorf reached for the contact button on the back of one of the British tanks, his hand was shot off. He gave the lace from his boot to his runner to tie a tourniquet around his lower arm. He then borrowed a Beretta pistol from one of his lieutenants, since he could no longer shoot a rifle. Neuendorf kept his men close behind the advancing tanks, as they went forward. They took the German post by 7.45am, wondering what they had gained: one lieutenant later described it as 'just a mound of sand', maybe six feet high. German positions further out could see them clearly. They kept firing and shelling. Neuendorf had now been wounded a second time.

> Norman 'Kid' Molony fell back into the trench, unconscious. He woke up surrounded by German soldiers, telling him to get up.

'Kid' Molony was beside the captain as he went forward again to guide the tanks onto the German positions. After the war, Molony told his son about this day: Neuendorf had told Norm to get up out of a trench and follow. 'Grab the Bren, Kid,' he yelled. Neuendorf was then caught in a rain of German shells and killed instantly. Norman 'Kid' Molony fell back into the trench, unconscious. He woke up surrounded by German soldiers telling him to get up. He had a gaping wound in his right shoulder, caused by a piece of shrapnel.

While he was unconscious, Stukas had bombed both posts.

The battalion held on for several hours, against increasing odds. At 11.30am, Lieutenant-Colonel Bernard Evans, commanding the 2/23rd, ordered a withdrawal. The positions were not worth defending, he reasoned, as they were overlooked by the enemy. Of the 200 men who took part, six officers were killed and ninety men were wounded. 'Kid' Molony was among the missing.

Giving up positions so hard-won did not sit well with the exhausted men of the 2/23rd. Soon after, eight men refused an order to go back and occupy a post at the railway cutting. They were arrested and court-martialled. A number were sent back to Australia to serve long sentences. While awaiting their courts martial, they were told the charges would be dropped if they rejoined the fight, and some did. Refusing to fight was rare in the AIF battalions, which were made up of volunteers. It was unheard of in the highly disciplined 2/23rd. Worse was to come.

Six days later, they were ordered to retake some of the same ground, in concert with further attacks on their flanks. The 9th Division commander, Lieutenant-General Leslie Morshead, objected strongly to the attack, but it went ahead anyway.

FRANK HAYES, at rear on right, with a group of other escaped prisoners in Switzerland in 1943 or 1944. More than 400 Australian prisoners escaped over the Alps to Switzerland – including Norm and Frank.

In the 2/23rd, most of the men had not slept for days. About 90 reinforcements had arrived; some died in their first action, before their officers even knew their names. On that day, 22 July, another eleven officers and forty-three non-commissioned officers (NCOs) were killed, wounded or missing. In the space of a week, the battalion had lost 270 other ranks killed or wounded, and nineteen officers. Fifty men were still missing. Lieutenant-Colonel Evans notes in the battalion diary that every company commander had been killed, and their replacements had all become casualties. 'The battle fields are still being searched by night, and many dead being buried … The number of missing is being steadily reduced as bodies are found.'

One of the missing was Frank Hayes. He had been captured attacking East Point 24 on Tel el Eisa, in the same area as his mate, Norm Molony.

At least 2000 Australians were taken prisoner in the desert war in 1941 and '42. Even if captured by Germans, they were handed over to the Italians, as this was still their territory. Both Norm and Frank were sent by train to a camp at Benghazi. The prisoners sometimes waited months to be shipped to Italy, and the journey was risky. The *Nino Bixio* was torpedoed by a British submarine, HMS *Turbulent*, on 17 August. The ship carried 3200 Allied prisoners; 336 died that day, even though the ship did not sink.

Norm was sent across in August to a military hospital at Caserta, near Naples. He was treated by Italian nuns, whose cruelty he never forgot. 'They changed his attitudes to the Catholic faith he had been brought up in,' says his son Vincent Molony. 'I remember him saying these nuns were bloody tyrants … If an Italian officer came to inspect the prisoners, the nuns would have the soldiers, no matter how ill, stand at the end of their beds, to attention. Dad recalled some of the nuns slapping the men across the feet with canes to get them out of bed. He hated that … He said there were about forty men being treated and many of them died there, from dysentery.'

Norm survived the dysentery. He was sent eventually to Campo 57 at Grupignano, 15 kilometres from Udine, in the north-east corner of Italy. Frank arrived there in November. The old mates were together again.

By the end of 1942, Campo 57 housed almost 4000 Australian and New Zealand prisoners, nearly all captured in North Africa. They usually arrived in bad condition, after long train journeys from southern Italy. Many were malnourished and sick from months in the harsh holding camps at Benghazi. Campo 57 was newly built, with magnificent views of the Austrian mountains. The wooden huts were double-lined, fifty men to a hut, some with a central stove for warmth – except there was rarely any fuel. Food was bad, medicine was short and the camp was run by a short, fat Fascist named Vittorio Calcaterra, who prided himself on his cruelty. He boasted that his camp was escape-proof, until nineteen Australians and New Zealanders escaped through a tunnel in October 1942. They were recaptured, but the escape cheered the inmates.

Calcaterra retaliated with more cruelty. The Italian camps may not have been as bad as those in Germany or Thailand and Burma, but that was not for want of trying on his part. Red Cross parcels kept many of these men alive.

In April 1943, Hayes and Molony were sent to Campo 106 – a central camp supplying twenty-five smaller camps around Vercelli, near Milan. This was the heart of Italy's rice-growing area, north of the Po River. The prisoners worked on local farms, replacing the men drafted for war – some of whom

> Norm … was sent eventually to Campo 57 at Grupignano, 15 kilometres from Udine, in the north-east corner of Italy. Frank arrived there in November. The old mates were together again.

were already in POW camps in Australia. Much of the produce went straight to Germany, and the prisoners knew that. Naturally, they did everything they could to taint the bags of rice and corn: adding excrement, dirt, whatever they could find. Some of the farmers were kind, forming friendships that outlasted the war; others became locked in daily power struggles with men who were experienced industrial campaigners. Strikes were common. Some men even fraternised with the young women drafted from the cities to work in the fields.

By 1943, Italy was suffering serious food shortages. The farmers had little for themselves, but many shared what they could. Some prisoners got stronger working in the fields, others got weaker with illness. Frank Hayes struggled with malaria for three months, with no treatment from his captors. When Italy capitulated in mid-1943, Frank could barely walk.

The king sacked Mussolini, who was imprisoned in Abruzzo. Hitler moved quickly to take full control of Italy, to meet the advancing Allies, who had landed in Sicily. The prisoners at Campo 106 now had a difficult choice. The guards warned that it would be dangerous to escape, as German troops were flooding the country. The guards then took off, leaving the gates open. British intelligence sent messages telling them to stay put, until they could be rescued. Hundreds of prisoners decided to take their chances.

Frank and Norm joined a group heading south, to link up with the Allies.

> Frank was so weak that Norm carried him on his back. After the war they used to tease each other about who carried whom, but it seems clear that Frank was in worse shape. The point is, neither would leave the other behind.

Frank was so weak that Norm carried him on his back. After the war they used to tease each other about who carried whom, but it seems clear that Frank was in worse shape. The point is, neither would leave the other behind.

Many years later, Frank wrote an account of this journey for the battalion newsletter. It begins in September 1943, after Mussolini had been imprisoned:

'When we woke up next morning there was not a guard to be seen. The only one there was an officer in charge. He spoke good English and told us the Germans were coming to take us to Germany. There were about forty of us and we all shot through. Norm and I left together.

'We headed down south for the Po River but we only travelled about five miles when we met some of the boys on their way back. They said there was no way of crossing the river as it was lousy with Jerries. So we decided that the only thing to do was to head north for the Italian Alps. We travelled for about two weeks I think on foot, mostly sticking to the bush or walking in the stony river to avoid tracker dogs. We slept at night in the farmers' barns. We met a few Partisans on the way, they were a bloodthirsty bunch. They were blowing up trains, convoys and Jerry troop barracks.

'When we got to the foothills we saw a monument of Bert Hinkler, he must have crashed thereabouts. Then further on we came to a nice village named Casa del Bosco, named after St John del Bosco. I was full of malaria and a nun from the church gave me an injection and I was not too bad after that. She was only in her early twenties and spoke good English. We stayed at an American lady's house with her daughter and young grandson. The daughter told me that her husband was taken prisoner at Tobruk and was in a prison camp in Australia. While we were travelling we saw plenty of Jerries. We were in civilian clothes. I believe they caught some of our blokes in civvies and shot them.

'After we left del Bosco we took to the mountains where we met two contro bandits [smugglers]. They used to smuggle things across the Swiss border and bring

The shoes of some of the Australian prisoners of war after they had walked across the Alps into Switzerland.

back Swiss watches. They showed us the way to go to Switzerland and pointed out Mt Moro to us. It was a 5000 foot mountain, so Norm and I left about 2am and started to climb. It was hard work, with the effects of malaria and not much food. I think we lived mostly on cheese.

'Halfway up the mountain we struck a small goat farm. The little Iti farmer didn't seem to trust us, he thought we were Jerries. He had second thoughts however and was okay after that.

'He said, "Are you hungry?" He had some beef stew cooking. I asked him how he got his beef and he said it fell down a cliff and broke its neck, then gave me a wink. The Jerries took all the food off the civilians. If they had caught him killing one of his animals he would have been shot. We stayed the night with him and his wife and daughter, then left early the next morning and started to climb Mt Moro again. I reckoned that we should reach the top about sunset. We were about three quarters of the way up when the mist came down real thick. We could not see the ground in front of us or even our hands. I was leading but we were walking blind. I must have veered off to the left a bit and suddenly I was walking on flat rock. I took about four steps and was about to take another when I looked down, there was a break in the mist and I found myself looking down about 2000 feet into a valley. If I had taken that extra step I wouldn't be writing these notes. Now that was one of the times I came close to death. We sat for about fifteen minutes and the mist cleared. When I looked up towards the border it was only a few hundred feet away.

'We made it just as the sun was setting. That was when Norm and I saw the most beautiful sight we were ever likely to see. Next to Mt Moro was Mt Rosa, it was covered with snow, the sunset was full on it, and it was blood red. I will never forget it as long as I live. When we reached the border there was a stone like a headstone with "I" on one side for Italy and "S" for Switzerland on the other. You can imagine how we felt when we saw it.

'After a while we continued on and went down the Saas-Fee Valley where we ran into the Swiss border guards. They told us they had been waiting for us, they had their glasses trained on us all day.

'We slept in their hotel that night and the next day they took us down to a place called Staldon [Stalden] where we had a hot dinner of blood sausage and sauerkraut. From Staldon they put us on a train for a place called Visp. We stayed there for a day then another train to a camp at a village called Wald. The camp was full of Poms, Poles, South Africans and Aussies.'

Norm and Frank arrived in Switzerland on 3 October 1943. A steady stream of POWs was making the journey over the same pass: twenty-two others arrived the same day. Some had local guides for part of the journey, but the

Germans had warned that they would shoot anyone who helped an escaping prisoner. Many of the prisoners would not have made it without help from sympathetic civilians.

Frank did not tell all of the story. Vincent Molony says his father told him the old farmer gave them two tablets. He told them to wait until they felt they could not go on, then take one each. Norm said the effect was like a heat explosion. They never knew what they had taken, but it did the trick.

None of these men knew if they would be interned in Switzerland. The welcome was very warm: cocoa and soup, beer and tea, showers and medical attention, new clothes and boots. Interrogators took their names and details but it sometimes took months for the families in Australia to hear that their loved ones were safe.

By late 1943, several thousand escaped servicemen had arrived from Germany and Italy, but they could not go home. Switzerland was surrounded by German troops. More than 400 Australians and 100 New Zealanders had arrived from Italy. The Swiss sent them to ski resorts, where they could be housed in empty hotels. Norm and Frank ended up at Adelboden, in the Bernese Oberland region. The British had agreed to reimburse the Swiss for the accommodation. They also paid for 700 pairs of skis, to encourage the men to regain their fitness.

Never having skied in his life, Norm became a champion skier and Frank learned to ice-skate. Norm won many local trophies, which he sold to finance the journey home.

Both men left Switzerland on 23 September 1944, after the Nazis had been pushed out of France and Italy. They arrived at Melbourne via Suez and Bombay on 17 November 1944. Both were sick, particularly Frank, whose malaria had never disappeared. He spent much of the next six months in military hospitals. Norm and he were in Ballarat Hospital together for some weeks.

Frank and Kath married at a registry office in late 1945. They had two children and Frank bought a motorcycle with sidecar, to carry them all. Kath had a tattoo on her arm, the result of a wartime dare with some girlfriends. It

NORM and **FRANK** learned winter sports in Switzerland. Norm won several trophies for downhill racing. He pawned his trophies to pay for food on the journey home in late 1944.

said: 'Darling Frank'. Her parents were furious when they saw it.

Frank worked as a wool sorter, then at the Borthwicks Abattoir, where he remained until he retired. He loved golf, football, boxing, racing and billiards. 'He was a gentle, kind and loving family man,' recalled Nicole Chambers, his granddaughter.

'I would quite often sit as a child looking at all his amazing photos from the war and with group shots of him and other soldiers and he would point to the others in the photo saying, "He's dead, he's dead and he's dead." So many of those that were his friends in the photos were casualties of war.'

Norm's brother Jack joined the 39th

Battalion and died on the Kokoda track in New Guinea. Norm and Leni married at the Holy Rosary church in Kensington in July 1945 and had three children. Norm trained for two years as a painter and decorator, as part of his war settlement. He worked for thirty-two years for the Post-Master General's department. On weekends, he doubled as a bagman for a local SP (starting price) bookie, but never got caught by the police.

The shrapnel in his shoulder was still there. It worked its way out one night shortly after the family had moved to East Coburg. 'Dad rolled over and awoke in agony with a piece of metal exiting his skin, the size of a ten cent piece, under the right shoulderblade,' says Vincent Molony. It was removed at Heidelberg Repatriation Hospital – eleven years after the war had ended.

Vincent says his father remained an optimist and a shrewd judge of character. 'He was of very strict opinion in some matters, but also very sensitive and compassionate in others.'

As older men, Frank and Norm would meet once a fortnight for lunch, on a Wednesday, alternating between Frank and Kath's war service home in Sunshine, and Norm and Leni's home in East Coburg, about 15 kilometres to the north.

> As older men, Frank and Norm would meet once a fortnight for lunch, on a Wednesday.

Kath and Leni took turns to prepare a simple lunch, but it was served separately. The two women would chat in the kitchen while the two men ate in the dining room, with a couple of bottles of Victoria Bitter beside them. The one thing they never ate was rice.

Frank's granddaughter Nicole, still a child at the time, eventually understood the reason.

'Frank had asked my nana, Kath, to never cook rice for him, he could not stand it, as I think that was all he ate while in the camp. He told me that he was delegated to work as a cook in camp. They would make huge pots of stew that were fed to the prisoners and, prior to serving, they would have to fish out drowned rats that had made their way into the pots. So I think that's why he survived on rice only. He knew better than to eat the stew … After lunch we would go down to the RSL club and the ladies would play bingo and the men would go off somewhere in the RSL club. I don't know what they did, just my memories of them happily going off together.'

It's easy to imagine that men who had known starvation would enjoy the ritual of a good lunch, but the lunches were not really about food or even beer, another thing they dreamed about as prisoners. They were about a friendship that had withstood the greatest tests.

These two men had seen the worst that men can do – both in battle and in captivity. Friendship saved them. They owed their survival to each other. In that sense, they had also seen the best that men can do.

Norm Molony died on 16 July 1993, fifty-one years to the day after he was taken prisoner at El Alamein. He was sixty-nine years old. That could be regarded as an early death, but Norm didn't see it that way. He'd been diagnosed with lung cancer. 'He had no regrets,' his son Vincent says. 'He said, "I've had fifty years longer than all my mates …"'

Norm was buried on a bleak, stormy day, at Warrandyte Cemetery in Melbourne. Frank was there to say goodbye to the man who'd carried him on his back. He missed his chance to square up: he was too frail to be a pallbearer. Frank died four years later, in May 1997, aged seventy-five. ✿

CHAPTER NINE

NO PRISONERS, NO WOUNDED

TOM JIGGINS

A studio portrait of **THOMAS JIGGINS**, around 1941. The tropical uniform suggests this may have been taken in Singapore. He was using his brother's name.

In August 1934, when Tom Jiggins was nine, he won a prize at the Leeton Intermediate High School 'annual frolic' for dressing up as an 'Indian'. His brother Freddie, five years older, was in charge of the school vegetable garden.

The local paper, the *Murrumbidgee Irrigator*, left no stone unturned in its pursuit of such news, but it failed to report a more significant event a year later, when their mother abandoned them.

Alice Jiggins, nee Blatch, was a troubled woman. She had run away to Sydney in 1916, aged fourteen and a half, with a soldier who was thirty-five. They were arrested and Alice was eventually sent back to Barellan, a small New South Wales wheatbelt town north of Leeton, where her family had a farm. At eighteen, she married Fredrick Jiggins, an English migrant fifteen years her senior. He was a kindly, gentle man, a farm labourer, but the relationship was stormy. Fredrick did not drink, but Alice drank with commitment.

At first they farmed at Barellan. Then they moved to Cow Shed Hill on the outskirts of Leeton.

ALICE BLATCH married Tom's father, Fredrick Jiggins, just after the First World War, when she was eighteen. Their marriage was turbulent.

'It was a bit of a muck-up family,' says Anne Forrest, daughter of Valerie Jiggins, the second of the five children. She remembers her mother telling her that Alice would send Betty, the youngest child, to walk into Leeton along the railway lines. Betty had to wait outside the pub for someone to come out, then ask them to buy a bottle for her mother. Betty was about seven.

Alice finally left the family home late in 1935, taking up with a local blacksmith, Ted Watkins. They moved to Victoria, leaving the Jiggins' household in turmoil.

Soon after his mother left, Freddie and a friend decided they would try their luck in Sydney. Fred was now sixteen and keen to find a job. They rode their bicycles to Sydney, doing odd jobs for food. Fred found a job with a nursery in Turramurra. A couple who had lost a son in a motorcycle accident took him in. He worked with them for the next four and a half years.

While Freddie was having his David Copperfield adventure, his brother Tom was miserable in Leeton. In the space of a year, he'd lost his mother, then the older brother he looked up to. Tom was tall and rangy. Other kids picked on him at school because of his height, so he learned boxing. They stopped picking on him when it became clear he could knock them into next Tuesday.

For Tom, like many of the under-age soldiers, the war was an opportunity.

His height was now an advantage. The family had moved to Griffith, but it was still a small town. On his first attempt to enlist, someone recognised him and sent him home. He worked up a new plan: he would become his older brother.

In late June 1940, at the age of fifteen and five months, he took the train to Wagga Wagga and signed the enlistment papers as Frederick William Jiggins, aged twenty. His brother's birthday was 18 May 1920, but he put down 1 May 1920. The family story is that he had borrowed a document owned by his brother as proof of age but it's unlikely to have been a birth certificate, given that he put down the wrong date. The army didn't notice that he was not Freddie Junior, or that he was six years below the required age. The recruiters were busy filling up a new battalion of country boys from the Riverina and the Monaro. On his forms, they noted his green eyes and dark hair and the scars on his eyelid and arms.

All soldiers were photographed at enlistment. Tom's photograph, taken on 28 June at Wagga Wagga, shows a boy with short back and sides and a defiant scowl. He does not look happy, even if he was where he wanted to be. They sent him up the line to Wallgrove camp, halfway between Sydney and the Blue Mountains. He was now a member of the 2/19th Battalion, part of the new 8th Division.

For seven months, Tom Jiggins learned the soldiering life. This was longer than most soldiers trained in Australia, but it was partly because the government wasn't sure where to send him.

When he enlisted in mid-1940, Britain was under threat of invasion. Seven months later, the world had changed. British planes had defeated the Luftwaffe in the Battle of Britain, from July to September 1940. That was one of Churchill's few victories in the year after Dunkirk.

The burden of the campaigns in the Middle East fell heaviest on the dominion forces. This did not go unnoticed in Australia, where the stench of failure weakened Robert Menzies's position. By October 1941, Labor's John Curtin was prime minister, although he was reluctant to govern, because he didn't have a majority in both houses.

Curtin's main external concern was Japan. Australia's foreign policy since the 1920s had been based more on hope than belief. Australia hoped that Britain would protect her from Japan's increasing belligerence by stationing a large naval fleet at Singapore. Britain promised to do so, but never made good. So the fulcrum of British power in the Far East was a naval base at Singapore that had no fleet – 'an empty garage' said Curtin's deputy, Frank Forde. Britain promised to send a fleet when and if Singapore (or Australia) was threatened.

In late 1940, senior British and dominion commanders met in Singapore to consider the state of readiness. They concluded that they would need an additional 534 modern aircraft in Malaya and Burma to meet any Japanese attack. They had eighty-eight, of which only forty-eight could be classed as modern. The RAAF had eighty-two aircraft, of which only forty-two were modern. It would need an additional 270.

Australia advised Britain that they were reluctant to send troops to Malaya under these circumstances, but they did it anyway. The 22nd Brigade of the new 8th Division – almost 6000 men – sailed in February 1941 to defend Malaya. This was Tom Jiggins's outfit.

In December 1940, Churchill had advised Menzies that it was now 'quite impossible for our fleet to leave the Mediterranean … without throwing away irretrievably all that has been gained there'. He added reassuringly that it was understood that 'if Australia is seriously threatened by invasion we should not hesitate to compromise or sacrifice the Mediterranean position for the sake of our kith and kin'.

In late October 1941, Britain decided to send three 'capital ships' (the navy's most important warships) to Singapore. One of these, the aircraft carrier *Indomitable*, ran aground a week later in Jamaica, so had to be scratched. That left the battlecruiser HMS *Repulse* and the battleship HMS *Prince of Wales*. The Admiralty objected to either one going, but Churchill had his way. They arrived in Singapore on 2 December 1941, to wave the flag. Churchill had no intention of keeping them there. They were to reassure Singapore, frighten the Japanese, then withdraw to patrol the Indian Ocean. Churchill could not countenance the loss of India, under any circumstances. It would signal the end of the British Empire, not to mention the flow of Indian troops to the war in Europe.

Churchill held fast to three ideas: that Germany must be defeated first, ahead of any other conflict; that Britain could not do that without the United States joining the European war; and that the Middle East and India were more important to British interests than Singapore or Hong Kong. It is not hard to agree with his analysis, except if you are the Australian (or New Zealand) prime minister. Churchill repeatedly reassured the Antipodean governments that Japan had neither the desire nor the capacity to invade them. In any case, he would give three months' notice of any impending attack.

Even Curtin wanted to believe him. The Labor Party, in opposition, had expressed severe doubts about the 'imperial defence' policy, but Curtin was slow to believe that Britain would abandon its promises to Australia. He did not immediately call for the return of the 100,000 troops still in the Middle East, nor the 8th Division, most of which was now in Malaya.

That state of denial changed on 7 December 1941, when the Japanese attacked Pearl Harbor, devastating the American Pacific fleet. They bombed Malaya, Singapore, Hong Kong, the Philippines, Guam and Wake Island on the same day – an awesome display of military power and planning. A couple of hours before they attacked Pearl Harbor, Japanese troops landed at Singora (now Songkhla) on the east coast of Thailand and at Kota Bharu, just inside Malaya. Indian units fought hard to stop the Kota Bharu landings, but were quickly overcome. Almost half of the 110 Allied planes in northern Malaya were knocked out on the first day.

The Japanese landed 125,000 men to take Malaya. In almost every respect, the Allied commanders underestimated them, partly through a sense of racial superiority. British and Australian officers told their men that the Japanese were an inferior force: small of stature, short-sighted and buck-toothed. Even now, faced with evidence of Japan's readiness for war, they preferred not to believe it. They said the impenetrable Malayan jungle would stop them; their planes could not fly at night; and they would not attack during the monsoon.

The Japanese simply split their forces and travelled down the coastal roads and paths on either side of the peninsula, as British intelligence had warned they would. The British blew bridges and

> Tom Jiggins was about to play his part in world affairs, fighting for a stronghold that was anything but, in a campaign that had almost no chance of success.

airfields. Japanese engineers repaired them within hours. Their infantry travelled on cheap Japanese bicycles – 6000 per division. They could ford rivers with their bicycles in tow, and ride village paths to outflank Allied forces waiting along the roads. They could live on rice and forage for long periods, until their supply lines caught up. They were experienced, disciplined and hardened by years of fighting in China.

The Japanese had their own sense of superiority, and a culture of martial brutality and absolute obedience. They saw themselves as the rightful rulers of east Asia, not the British or Americans. They called it 'the great East Asia Co-prosperity Sphere', although the Chinese found it hard to see the shared prosperity. The massacres at Nanjing in December and January of 1937–38 left somewhere between 40,000 and 300,000 dead Chinese, both civilian and military. To believe that Singapore was impregnable, as Churchill told himself, took a wilful blindness.

On 10 December, the *Repulse* and the *Prince of Wales*, sent out to interdict Japanese troopships, were sunk by Japanese torpedo planes. Churchill received the news in bed in London the next morning. He was horrified, not simply for the 845 men lost, but because he realised there were now no British or American capital ships in the Indian or Pacific oceans, except for what was left at Pearl Harbor. He had predicted 'heavy forfeits' would come in a war with Japan – and at least in that prediction, he was right.

Britain and the US immediately declared war on Japan. Australia did too, without consulting Britain. This had never happened before. It was a sign of Australia's growing independence, and of increased frustration with the limits of empire.

Tom Jiggins was about to play his part in world affairs, fighting for a stronghold that was anything but, in a campaign that had almost no chance of success. One can only hope he did not understand the many betrayals that put him there.

Private Jiggins had arrived in Singapore aboard the *Queen Mary*, on 18 February

1941. He was not always an exemplary soldier. He was fined for missing a parade on 6 April. Three weeks later, he was charged with 'conduct to the prejudice of good order', for using offensive language to an officer, and fined ten shillings. He copped ten days detention in June, after he got drunk and missed another parade. Then on 17 August he went AWL for two days.

In January 1942, the army discovered that he was using his brother's identity. The real Frederick William Jiggins had enlisted in Griffith in July 1941 and was posted to an artillery unit. With unusual efficiency, the army realised there could not be two men with the same particulars. With the truth uncovered, the army should have ordered Tom Jiggins home. He was still only sixteen. Instead, they asked him if he would like to move to his older brother's unit, the 2/4th Light Anti-Aircraft Regiment. Tom said no, he would prefer to stay with his friends in the 2/19th. The army amended its records, he reverted to his real name, Thomas Arthur Jiggins, but no-one bothered about his age.

By New Year, the 2/19th had been at Jemaluang village, 125 kilometres north of Singapore island, for almost a month. They were dug in to meet any Japanese force coming down the east coast. They had evacuated the village then burned it, to create a better field of fire, to no purpose. The enemy had not shown up.

Meanwhile, a force of 12,640 men from the elite Imperial Guards Division – Emperor Hirohito's own troops – was moving swiftly down the west coast. Japan now controlled two thirds of the peninsula. They expected to be in Singapore within a month, in time to celebrate Japan's Foundation Day, 11 February.

On 10 January, Major General Gordon Bennett, outspoken commander of the 8th Division AIF, was given command of Westforce, a combined Australian, Indian and British force. His job was to hold the Japanese at a line from the coastal village of Muar, 180 kilometres north-east of Singapore, to Gemas, 100 kilometres to the north. Gemas was on the main trunk road south to Singapore. The road from Muar ran through Bakri and Parit Sulong to meet the main road at Yong Peng,

65 kilometres from Muar. This was to be the decisive stand.

Bennett favoured an aggressive strategy, in personal relations as well as battle. He got on with almost no-one. He wanted his men thrown in against the Japanese on the west coast, rather than sitting in holes waiting for action on the east coast. On 14 January, the 2/30th Battalion had spectacular success with an ambush of the Japanese 5th Division near Gemas, killing and wounding more than 1000 enemy and knocking out a number of tanks.

Bennett sent the 45th Indian Brigade to hold Muar. Most of these Indian soldiers were aged seventeen or eighteen, and had seen no action. They were poorly trained and had been expecting to go to the Middle East where most of their (British) officers had gone, before Japan entered the war. Their replacements, also British, could not yet speak Urdu, the primary language of command in the Indian Army.

The Japanese began bombing the Indians at Muar on 11 January, and kept it up for four days. The river here was 400 metres wide. There was no bridge,

only a ferry. The Japanese sent one part of their force down the coast in small landing craft, bypassing Muar. They sent another battalion upriver to cross where it was narrower. The Allies had removed all suitable boats from the north side of the river; the Japanese sent men across in canoes, who towed barges back to the north bank for their troops. This force then attacked Muar from behind.

An Australian artillery battery stopped a small flotilla of sampans crammed with Japanese as they tried to come into the port at Muar, but others landed further south, near Batu Pahat. The Indians at Muar were routed late on 16 January, with many casualties. Lieutenant-Colonel Charles Anderson, commander of the 2/19th, who won the Victoria Cross in this battle, later called the use of these Indian troops 'a crime'.

Bennett thought Muar had been taken by 200 Japanese so he now ordered an understrength 2/29th Battalion to retake Muar through Bakri, about 5 kilometres east. They arrived late on 17 January. Bennett told them they would have to hold the Bakri road for a week to allow time for the rest of Westforce to pull back from Gemas, if necessary. He was still hoping to defeat the Japanese in both places. Bennett's superior, Lieutenant-General Arthur Percival, General Officer Commanding the British Forces in Malaya, now ordered Jiggins's 2/19th across from Jemaluang.

Westforce was up against large and well-equipped Japanese forces at Gemas and Muar. The enemy was well-organised, well-drilled and methodical. Fresh British units were sent to guard the roads further south. These men had arrived in Singapore only four days earlier. They hadn't even recovered their fitness after the long sea journey.

Early on 18 January, the 2/29th was in place about 3 kilometres west of Bakri, with a number of guns from the 2/4th Anti-Tank Regiment in readiness. Five light Japanese tanks came down the road, straight into these guns. The tanks were smashed, one by one. Three more followed and met the same fate. Lieutenant Ben Hackney, a farmer from Bathurst, later described the sound of the ammu-

nition igniting in the burning tanks. This was the 2/29th's baptism of fire and their finest hour, but the tide was turning. The Japanese opened up with machine guns and sniper fire from the trees in the rubber plantations, mortally wounding Lieutenant-Colonel John Charles Robertson, the 2/29th's commander. Grimly, the battalion held on to the road.

The 700 men of the 2/19th, with Private Jiggins in C Company, reached Bakri that morning. They moved quickly into positions on the small roads leading south to the coast, and west to Muar. By midday, the enemy had set up a roadblock between them and the 2/29th, further up the road. A company went forward and cleared it. By 5pm, the Japanese were shelling the 2/19th.

Percival now knew that his forces were facing the Imperial Guards Division, and that a party of them had landed further down the coast. They were already attacking the new British units. Bennett ordered a fighting withdrawal that afternoon from Gemas, to a new line 40 kilometres north of Yong Peng. Percival then gave the command of the remaining

Muar forces to General Sir Lewis Heath, whose III Indian Corps had been holding the eastern side of Johore. Everything was unwinding fast.

The Battle of Muar was savage and bloody for both sides. The Japanese had not encountered such determined opposition since they landed in Malaya. General Takuma Nishimura, commander of the Imperial Guards Division, wrote that this battle was 'severe and sanguinary'. His superior, Lieutenant-General Tomoyuki Yamashita, said later that it was the hardest battle of the Malayan campaign.

Early on 19 January, the Japanese suffered an estimated 140 dead in a botched attack on battalion. The Australians lost ten men dead and fifteen wounded. Charles 'Chick' Warden was in B Company on this day. He was from Enfield in Sydney and had been sixteen when he enlisted, a year older than Jiggins. He wrote a private account that is extensively quoted by journalist Ian Ward in his book *Snaring the Other Tiger*, published in 1996.

Warden's account says there were 'nasty incidents' following the morning attack, when some of the assumed-dead enemy jumped up and started throwing grenades. Thereafter, wrote Warden, the bayonet was to be used. 'In brief the order was: take no prisoners, leave no wounded.'

Neither the battalion war diary nor the official history, *Australia in the War of 1939–45*, mentions these orders – hardly surprising – although the official history documents several cases in that specific fight of Japanese pretending to be dead, then launching attacks. Chick Warden believed the order came from his battalion commander.

As this fight was happening, another 400 to 500 Japanese attacked the 2/19th transport column, which had been sent back to a 'safer' position on the road from Bakri to Parit Sulong. This would

> ## 'In brief the order was: take no prisoners, leave no wounded.'

have cut off the escape route of both the Australian battalions and what was left of the Indians, who were down to 200 men. About 150 men of the 2/19th fought a desperate action here for about eight hours to halt this attack.

At 10am that morning, a Japanese plane dropped a bomb on the house serving as headquarters of the 45th Indian Brigade, killing most of the officers. Charles Anderson, as senior officer in the field, took charge of a brigade that 'had practically ceased to exist', says the official history.

The wounded were many. Sixteen-year-old Tom Jiggins was one of them, hit in the arm and leg earlier that day.

The Japanese now renewed their attacks on the 2/19th, but were again driven off. Anderson decided to move his men back to the other side of Bakri. Jiggins's C Company was the last out of Bakri at about midnight. After an epic journey, during which they were fired upon by their own side, the remnants of the 2/29th – seven officers and 190 men –

had arrived back inside the 2/19th perimeter, with the 200 remaining Indians.

The wounded were many. Sixteen-year-old Tom Jiggins was one of them, hit in the arm and leg earlier that day. They were patched up and loaded into trucks, but to get out, Anderson would have to smash through a Japanese roadblock between his position and the transport column.

He did not yet know it, but the Japanese would soon control the bridge at Parit Sulong. A detachment of the new British troops sent to guard it, the 6th Norfolks, had abandoned it early on 20 January, in search of food and safety. This sealed the fate of the men still at Bakri. Any retreat would have to cross that bridge.

Anderson ordered the withdrawal of his column early the same morning, but they hit stubborn Japanese resistance at the first roadblock. This is where 'Waltzing

Matilda' became a battle song. Lieutenant FG Beverley, an orchardist from Griffith, led his men into a rapid and vocal assault on the roadblock, forcing the Japanese to withdraw. Anderson followed, using the grenades he habitually carried, to knock out two machine-gun posts.

Where the 2/19th trucks had been, they found a scene of devastation with dead from both sides strewn along the road – the aftermath of the transport column's desperate fight the previous day. Beverley pressed on, reaching another roadblock that was defended by six machine guns. The Japanese were now attacking the rear of Anderson's column and shelling the trucks as they crawled forward. At the front of the column, Anderson's men fought with rifles, bayonets and axes. Wounded in the trucks were strafed by Japanese planes and hit by small-arms fire.

Chick Warden describes these attacks in some detail: after the Japanese were routed at each roadblock, the wounded Japanese were bayoneted where they lay, he says. He estimated that hundreds died in each fight. He does not say how many were killed after being wounded.

At midnight, an Indian soldier returned from the road ahead and told Anderson that the Japanese now occupied the bridge at Parit Sulong. The column limped forward, pursued by Japanese tanks. Anderson had no choice but to try to force his way through. He received a message during the night that General Bennett was sending help. No help came; instead, Japanese planes bombed the column the next morning as it reached the outskirts of Parit Sulong. Anderson's men fought on.

At 5pm on 21 January, running out of ammunition, with his men not having eaten for two days, Anderson agreed to ask the Japanese to allow two ambulances through, with the worst of the wounded. The Japanese commander said the ambulances could only proceed if the whole column surrendered. He kept the ambulances on the bridge as a roadblock. Anderson refused, still hoping for relief. It never came, and at 9am, Anderson ordered the destruction of all guns and transport, and for every man to get out as best he could, across country through the swamplands. Anderson trusted that the wounded would be cared for by the Japanese, as required by the conventions of war. He had no choice, as they could not be carried to safety.

Ben Hackney of the 2/29th, wounded in several places, was one of approximately 150 men taken prisoner by the Japanese. Nearly all of them were wounded. They had kept up sporadic firing for six hours, to allow their comrades to slip away to the east. Those who got away faced a 50-kilometre walk to Yong Peng across rivers and swamp, plantations and rice paddies. Only about 130 men made it out from the 2/29th Battalion, and 271 from the 2/19th, of whom 50 were wounded.

Back at Parit Sulong, the wounded were forced to assemble just north of the bridge at a low building about 30 metres by 7 metres. This had been used as sleeping quarters by Indian road builders. Many of the wounded could not walk; the Japanese soldiers kicked and bashed them with rifle butts. The killing started immediately. Those who could not move were either bayoneted or shot, many of them thrown in the river. The prisoners

were then stripped down to boots and socks and made to sit in a tight circle. Of these men, 110 were Australian, 35 Indian. There were six Australian officers, including Ben Hackney and Captain Rewi Snelling, Tom Jiggins's commanding officer, who had wounds to both legs.

Passing Japanese soldiers now took out their frustrations on the helpless wounded – repeating the kicking and beating or prodding them with swords and bayonets. Some men died of wounds; others died from beatings, on top of wounds. All were desperate for water and medical attention. None was given.

Ben Hackney saw an English-speaking European dressed in a British uniform. He concluded that the man was probably a German adviser. This man supervised the search of the clothing, which was then returned to the wounded, without their wallets and other valuables.

Hackney watched a group of senior officers arrive in staff cars, preceded by tanks. The most senior officer inspected the wounded and spoke briefly to the officer in charge, then drove on. Some

Japanese press arrived and took pictures of their officers pretending to give water to the prisoners. After they left, the six Australian officers were tied together with ropes strung around their wrists which were then tightened around their throats, restricting breathing. The other ranks were tied together, with more bashings, and tethered to the group of officers. Snelling and Hackney could not walk, so they were beaten and kicked again, then cut free from the other officers and left on the ground, a little apart. Snelling may have been dead already. Hackney had shrapnel in his back and right leg, a bullet in his left leg that broke the bone, a new gaping wound above one eye and countless puncture wounds from bayonets. He watched as the rest of the prisoners were dragged away towards the river, behind the old workers' quarters, beyond his sight. Hackney was about 40 metres away on the other side of the long building, lying in his own pooling blood – and momentarily forgotten.

Around dusk, a small group of Japanese soldiers began to shoot the prisoners, with quick repeated bursts of fire. The prisoners saw it coming and cried out as they died, cursing the Japanese. Hackney heard it all. It became apparent later that some men went down without being shot, feigning death. The guards poured gasoline over the dead, the dying and the pretending, and set them on fire, living or not. A few who got clear of the fire were rounded up and shot again. This is probably how Tom Jiggins died, if he made it that far. One hopes he didn't.

Hackney crawled under one of the huts that night, and found water in an ablutions block behind the sleeping quarters. By this time, the Japanese had moved away.

> Some men died of wounds; others died from beatings, on top of wounds. All were desperate for water and medical attention. None was given.

Two other men survived the massacre: Sergeant Ron Croft, a former salesman from Richmond, Victoria; and Reginald Arthur Wharton, an eighteen-year-old from Cheltenham, Victoria. Both were from the 2/29th.

Croft was helping another soldier who had a terrible wound in the stomach, name unknown. Croft helped Hackney and this wounded man to hide in a clump of vegetation near the river. The wounded man died the next morning. Hackney insisted that Croft leave him, as he could not walk. Croft said his goodbyes and departed.

Hackney then began to drag himself through the jungle, looking for a place to hide. He did this for thirty-six days. Sometimes Malay villagers helped him and fed him for a few days, others chased him off with sticks, for fear of the Japanese. He was eventually betrayed by fearful villagers. Malay policemen took him back to Parit Sulong, and eventually he became a prisoner of the Japanese at Changi.

During the massacre, Reg Wharton had lain 'doggo', pretending to be dead.

Soldiers pierced his right lung and abdomen with a bayonet and kicked him into the swamp. That night he struggled out of the water and began to head for Singapore, with a punctured lung, and a burn under his left arm. With help from a few Chinese he met along the way, he survived for ten days, until he met up with other Australian soldiers. Patched up, he joined the fight again, but the Japanese again overran them. Wharton refused to surrender, and started to walk north, towards India. He stayed with a group of Chinese guerrillas for two months, until captured again by the Japanese. They sent him to the Burma–Thailand railroad, and still he survived.

Ron Croft may also have joined the Chinese guerrillas: he is believed to have been killed in Malaya in April 1942. By the end of the war, Wharton and Hackney were the only two living Australian witnesses to what had happened at Parit Sulong.

The massacre was neither the first nor the last committed by the Japanese in Malaya and the subsequent battle for Singapore. In that sense, it was part of a pattern, not an isolated incident.

Even so, a question hangs over the massacre: did the 'no prisoners, no wounded left behind' order contribute to the fury of the Japanese? If they had seen what the Australians had done to their wounded comrades in the previous two days, was the massacre at least in part an act of revenge? We will never know.

The Japanese lost an estimated 2000 men, but the Imperial Guards Division was a highly disciplined unit. It is difficult to believe that the massacre was not the result of a direct order. Ben Hackney certainly believed that the senior officer he had seen arrive at Parit Sulong that day had ordered the killings – but Hackney did not speak Japanese, nor could he identify the officer. General Nishimura was captured by the British at the end of the war. At Changi prison, he was photographed in the hope that Hackney would recognise him. Hackney could not.

A British war crimes court convicted Nishimura for his part in the massacre of thousands of Chinese civilians in Singapore in 1942. He had served four years of a life sentence when Britain sent him back to Japan with other war criminals, to serve the rest of their sentences on home soil. Australian authorities moved to stop this. When the ship on which he was travelling docked at Hong Kong, Australian military police took him off the ship and charged him with the Parit Sulong massacre. He was then sent to Los Negros, an island near Manus Island, where other Japanese prisoners were incarcerated under Australian command.

Nishimura was tried there in June 1950 by an Australian military court. The prosecution was based on sworn statements, with no witnesses called. Ben Hackney's account was one of those statements. Nishimura was found guilty and hanged at Manus on 11 June 1951. His body was buried at sea, as it was raining too hard to cremate his remains. The hangman, a returned serviceman, was chosen from several who had volunteered for the job.

Ian Ward argued in *Snaring the Other Tiger* that Nishimura was the wrong man, and that his trial was a miscarriage of justice. Ward relied on documents that were later shown to have been forged by a New Zealand author. That brought Ward's conclusions into question. Nishimura maintained that he ordered only that the prisoners be sent to the back areas. If that is true, the massacre would have constituted a serious breach of orders, for which there would have been documented consequences. There were none. And whether Nishimura gave the order or not, men under his command committed the crimes.

Other men in powerful positions shared some responsibility for the disaster at Muar, if not the massacre. Some have been judged harshly by history, including Bennett and Percival. Churchill stood by the decisions he made. Any consequences for him were obliterated by victory. He is remembered as the man who saved Europe, rather than the man who abandoned Singapore.

Tom Jiggins has no grave, but nor is he forgotten. There is a small park devoted to his memory in the backstreets of Griffith. Beside a children's playground, a plaque on a block of sandstone records his date of birth, his unit, and the words 'presumed killed in action at Parit Sulong, Malaya, on 22 January 1942, aged sixteen years. One of the youngest Australians to be killed in war.'

> Tom Jiggins has no grave, but nor is he forgotten. There is a small park devoted to his memory in the backstreets of Griffith.

A small park in Griffith commemorates the fate of **TOM JIGGINS**.

CHAPTER TEN

FORTUNATE SON

DENNIS MOULE

DENNIS MOULE left his home in London during the Blitz. His note to his parents said not to worry – he had gone to see the world and seek his fortune. He was fourteen.

At the age of fourteen, Dennis Moule had been bombed by the Luftwaffe in the streets of London and strafed by them in the English Channel. At fifteen, he had been shelled by a Japanese submarine off Lombok and strafed by their planes at Palembang. At sixteen, he had jumped out of three burning planes, flown by the RAAF. He was like that old joke about the man who has lost his three-legged, one-eyed dog that 'answers to the name of Lucky'.

Throughout these adventures, nobody asked him how old he was, and that was fine with him.

His Australian war record says he was born 29 October 1924 in England. He was born on 29 October but in 1926.

Dennis told me that himself. In late 2021, he was living in a nursing home on the north coast of New South Wales. He was about to turn ninety-five. His hearing and legs were dodgy, but he greeted each day with optimism, like a man who knows he is lucky to be alive. 'He's incredibly stubborn,' said his son Mick, with a certain pride. 'Only when I know I'm right,' said Dennis.

He inherited the strong will from his father, Arthur, who played saxophone and clarinet in the Chapman's Circus band, touring the length and breadth of Britain, often doing three shows a day.

By 1929 Dennis's family lived on the East Hill council estate at Wandsworth. This was a lively working-class community on a bend of the River Thames, full of newly arrived migrants and young families. Dennis won a scholarship to Wandsworth Secondary School, a step up from his older brother and sister, who attended Wandsworth Central. He didn't have long to enjoy it.

War broke out in September 1939. Arthur had been wounded at Suvla Bay, during the Gallipoli campaign in 1915. He knew the Germans had bombed London during the last war, so he moved the family to Hillingdon, on the north-west outskirts of London. Dennis and his younger sister Shirley had been evacuated for their safety to Reading, west of London. His mother, Florence, got a job as a tea lady at the recently opened Pinewood Studios, a few miles to the west. When no German bombs fell in the first year, Dennis and Shirley came back to the new home. Dennis was now thirteen. Shirley was seven and his responsibility: 'I used to have to look after her.'

The German bombing finally started in September 1940. Nowhere was safe, but Hillingdon was safer than Wandsworth, where about 1000 people died in the Blitz.

At Hillingdon, Dennis had a paper run. He remembers trying to deliver to a house that was no longer there – obliterated overnight in an air raid. He joined the Air Cadets, a volunteer youth organisation preparing boys for the Royal Air Force. He was given a uniform but his father arranged for Dennis to start as a trainee accountant.

'I didn't want to be a chartered accountant … My father wanted me to be that but I didn't want that. At all. I felt that wasn't for me … So I left home and went into London itself when the Blitz was on …

'I left a note on the table to say "Dear Mum and Dad, don't worry. I've gone to see the world and seek my fortune."'

He told no-one he was going. 'I do regret leaving my younger sister. I used to wheel her in a four-wheel pram. I didn't think about her – I only thought about myself at the time … My whole intention was to see the world.'

Dennis says he left a happy home, although he was ruthless about cutting them off, perhaps fearing they would fetch him back. That might also explain why he did not take the train. He walked the 26 kilometres to central London. About halfway there, he went into a cinema and watched a horror film. He had always loved movies.

He slept each night for the next few months in one of the many air-raid shelters, including one beneath Australia House. Strangers shared food with him. The city was full of signs for positions vacant. He got a job delivering military uniforms around the city, riding a tricycle with a large basket at the front. After the air raids, he would go up onto the roofs of buildings to look for incendiary bombs. He would take a bucket of sand or water to douse them. The bombs didn't faze him.

The cadet uniform allowed him to go into various establishments for enlisted men. He could eat a meal for a few pence or take a bath. He neither smoked nor drank.

'At one of these places, I met a young Scots fella who was already in the merchant navy, and he said why don't you go into the merchant navy? I says to him, well I can't, I'm too young. He said don't worry about that, I'll sign your parents' signature and if they accept that, you are in. He had done the same thing.'

Norway had the fourth largest merchant navy in the world but Norway was now occupied by the Nazis, cutting off access to new recruits. Dennis fronted up at the Norwegian embassy in 1941.

'In those days, they needed seamen. They didn't care. I was only five foot two when I went in. I was still growing. I can't put the blame on them – they wanted anyone they could get.'

The Norwegians sent him to Tilbury Docks, on the Thames. His first job was painting the sides of the *Leiesten*, a 6100-tonne oil tanker built in Newcastle-Upon-Tyne in 1930. The ship pulled out of Southend on 30 June to join an Atlantic convoy, but only made it as far as Gravesend, further down the Thames. Here she hit a German mine. Dennis was below decks, hanging out his washing near the engine room. The mine struck the ship aft, knocking him 2 metres into the air. None of the crew was injured, but the ship had to be towed back for repair. This would take three months, so Dennis moved onto the *Madrono*, a 5900-tonne oil tanker as old as it was slow.

Just out of Southampton, a German Heinkel plane sprayed cannon fire along the length of the ship, while Dennis was below deck. He heard the clang and clatter of the bullets striking metal. He took shelter beneath the bridge.

The ship had heavy machine guns and a 4.7-inch naval gun. The four men who operated them had no time even to get off a shot. Dennis soon learned how to work the machine guns and lug ammunition. As the youngest man on the ship, he was keen to learn. At Belfast, the *Madrono* joined an Atlantic convoy. He was heading into dangerous waters.

Britain needed one million tons of imported goods per week to survive, most of it arriving by ships from America. German U-boats sat in the Atlantic waiting for them, hunting as 'wolf packs', rather than single units. The Battle of the Atlantic raged throughout the entire war, at terrible cost. By war's end, the Allies had lost 72,000 men and 3500 ships. The Germans lost three quarters of their submarine fleet – 783 U-boats and 30,000 men. The Atlantic became a steel graveyard.

The *Madrono* could only make 10 knots in calm water. A convoy would normally travel at the speed of the slowest ship but this was too slow. It endangered the rest of the fleet. About two thirds of the way, the convoy left the *Madrono* to fend for itself. Dennis was now sitting on a ship full of oil, chugging along on a hostile sea. They were too far out for protection from the air, and too lightly armed to really defend themselves. Dennis maintains he wasn't worried, even when the waves became very large in a storm.

'I never thought about it. You were in the war, whether you lived or whether you died. That was just the way it was ... You expected things to happen. Everyone was in the war.'

A Canadian corvette came out to escort them into New York. They then sailed down the American coast to the West Indies.

'When we loaded up at Aruba they told us the ship was too slow and couldn't keep up with the convoys, that we would be left again. So they sent us through Panama Canal to New Zealand.'

> Dennis was now sitting on a ship full of oil, chugging along on a hostile sea. They were too far out for protection from the air, and too lightly armed to really defend themselves. Dennis maintains he wasn't worried, even when the waves became very large in a storm.

From Wellington they were diverted to Darwin, where Dennis formed his first impression of Australia: blowflies, beer bottles and ugly tidal flats. He arrived there just after the Japanese bombed Pearl Harbor and left before they bombed Darwin. Dennis seemed to be travelling under a lucky star. The *Leiesten* had also been torpedoed after he left it, sinking 600 kilometres east-south-east of Newfoundland, in January 1942.

The *Madrono* now made for Batavia in the Netherlands East Indies (now Indonesia), as the Japanese were closing in. Near Lombok, they sighted what appeared to be a distressed sailing vessel. The *Madrono*'s second mate recognised the trap: a Japanese submarine had hoisted a false sail to try to draw them in.

'They shelled us, but they had their own problems. If any part of their turret got the slightest damage it couldn't submerge and it would be at the mercy of our gunners, who would finish them off. When we turned around, as soon as they saw a 4.7-inch naval gun, they knew we were defensively armed, and they shoved off.'

The *Madrono* docked at Surabaya, on the eastern tip of Java, on 23 January 1942, the same day the *Leiesten* went down. Dennis was about to have another new experience. The tradition in the Norwegian merchant navy was that you didn't pay for your first tattoo or your initiation into the rites of sex. These were on the house. He waited until Calcutta to get the tattoo.

The *Madrono* sailed on to Palembang in Sumatra to load oil. Singapore had not yet fallen but the Palembang oil refineries were vital to the Japanese war plan. They attacked the Dutch airfields there on 14 February and dropped 300 paratroopers, against a similar number of Allied defenders. Another 100 paratroopers attacked the main oil refinery on the Musi river.

'We were loaded about three quarters with oil, but the Japanese were so close we had to leave. They were only about six miles away … I had gone ashore to find this crewman. He was the only other Englishman, and he liked a drink. I went off to find him. The captain warned me to get back quickly – he would not wait. When I got back, the other fella was already back on board.'

Palembang is about 70 kilometres upriver. The *Madrono* pushed off as Japanese planes roared in to attack the docks. The *Madrono* had to pick its way past burning ships on the way downriver. They were strafed again once they reached the open sea. This was one of the closest calls of Dennis's war.

Back in Melbourne in April, Dennis signed off, looking for a ship that would take him home. The *Madrono* sailed off to be captured on 4 July by the German auxiliary cruiser *Thor*, while en route to Abadan. Some of her crew spent the rest of the war in prisoner of war camps in Japan. Dennis's lucky streak was holding.

His next ship, the *Troya*, took him to Ceylon, India, and back to Perth. In India, a fortune-teller told him he would marry a girl whose name began with P in a city that started with S, and that he would live until he was eighty-four. Dennis was not superstitious, but he took comfort in the prediction.

'It made me feel good, that I was going to survive the war…'

The fortune-teller also told him he would win the lottery. As of late 2021,

After he left the merchant navy, **DENNIS** joined the RAAF. He was a popular figure with the opposite sex.

that had not happened, but Dennis was eleven years past his use-by date – a different kind of lottery.

Changing ships again in Sydney in early 1943, he sailed on the *Tricolor* to Alexandria, Mozambique, Cape Town and back to Melbourne, where he signed off for the last time.

At Winnipeg Air Training School in the winter of 1943–44, **DENNIS** learned to be a wireless man – on aeroplanes that Australia did not fly.

'I left the *Tricolor* because I wanted to get back to England. They told me that if you joined the RAAF, specifically to be a wireless-air-gunner (and I finished up a radio operator as well) then you would automatically be sent to England. But we were the first graduates to be sent back to Australia ...'

In August 1943, when he enlisted in the RAAF, he was still only sixteen. The RAAF was the most selective of any service, but expanding fast. There were seventeen Australian squadrons based in Britain, others in the Middle East, Burma and the Pacific. By 1945, Australia would have the fourth largest air force in the world.

The Empire Air Training Scheme had been set up in December 1939, to supply recruits to the Royal Air Force. The RAF estimated it would need 55,000 new personnel each year to remain at strength. More than half of these would have to come from the dominions. Initially, Australia agreed to provide 28,000 air crew over three years. Advanced training was to be done in Canada, closer to the European war. That's why Dennis ended up on the vast Canadian prairie, in the winter of 1943–44.

'I went to No 3 Wireless Training School at Winnipeg. It got to 70 below the first night we were there. We had these hats with flaps over them to protect our ears. They chose Winnipeg because it is very flat and open. You couldn't get in too much trouble in the aircraft we were trained in. They were Bristol Blenheims.'

He spent almost a year in Canada. He was trained, with typical military efficiency, on the wrong aircraft. By March 1943, the RAF already had surplus air crew in Britain so Dennis was sent back to Australia to fight the Japanese, but the RAAF was using Beauforts, not Blenheims.

An American ship took him to New Guinea. Once in Port Moresby, he waited six weeks for a ship south. He swam, surfed and fished, and watched the air raids by Japanese bombers. By April 1945, he was at 1 Operational Training Unit, in East Sale in Victoria.

'I had three crashes in the RAAF. One was at Sale. One was at Richmond in New South Wales on a training flight there … The other was in New Guinea.

'The one at Sale, we were retraining on a Beaufort. On takeoff it caught fire and it was still going along the runway when I jumped out. The fire was right throughout the aircraft. It was full of smoke. The Beauforts had something wrong with the petrol lines, so they sometimes caught fire.'

A similar thing happened on a training flight at Richmond – another fire in the plane.

By the time he was ready for active service, the war was over. Dennis was sent to New Guinea in December 1945, to Aitape on the north coast. Many Japanese soldiers were still in the jungle, unaware that the war was lost. Dennis spent many months there, helping to find them. They patrolled and dropped leaflets, urging them to surrender.

This time, a fire broke out as they were landing. The good old Beaufort!

'I thought that time that I was gone. Everything went black, because of smoke. I didn't think I'd get out. I thought this is it. I jumped out onto the wing through the gun turret, and jumped off the wing. The runway was covered with metal matting, and my legs just went out from under me.'

His head just missed being taken off by the tailplane. The plane skewed off the runway into the jungle, but the pilot and navigator were unhurt. 'They were looking back up at the engine when I found them. They had used the extinguisher to see what happened. That was the cause of my leg problems. I got spreadeagled and dislocated my leg. It was a long time healing.'

Dennis signed on for two more years in 1946. He had no more thoughts of returning to the UK.

'After the war, the RAAF gave me a course on chiropody, but that wasn't for me either. So I bought a mail run from Walgett to Quirindi. I lived at Walgett.'

On a visit to Sydney in 1951, he met Patricia Tucker. 'She was an usherette at a theatre in Pitt Street. The show was *The Red Shoes*.'

They were married in Sydney in 1952 and had two sons, Warren and Michael. Dennis believes the prophecy was right. 'I was going to marry someone whose name began with P in a big city starting with S.'

He worked a succession of jobs before taking on various businesses. He ran a guesthouse in Newtown, a service station with drive-in cafe in the Blue Mountains, and sold fishing lures in Coffs Harbour. He retired at fifty and played golf.

He had almost no contact with his English family until 1980, when he was diagnosed with melanoma and given six months to live.

'They told me to go around the world and see what you want to see and if you come back, we will throw our hats up in the air. They operated under my arm and took out a lump. I didn't know if I was going to live or die but I remembered what the fortune-teller told me that I was going to live till I was eighty-four, so I took a positive attitude.

'I went back to England as soon as I could after that. Saw my mother and father before they died. It wasn't that they had done anything wrong to me. I just didn't want to go back. Australia was my home.'

Dennis Moule did indeed see the world and make his fortune. His war was one lucky escape after another. The fortune-teller had said he would win the lottery, and in a sense, he did. He survived. ✦

An Indian fortune-teller told **DENNIS MOULE** he would live till he was eighty-four. He was ninety-four, living on the north coast of New South Wales, when this picture was taken in 2021.

CHAPTER ELEVEN

A NICE OLD BLOODY MESS

LEN LEGGETT

LEN LEGGETT was seventeen when he returned to Australia on leave in mid-1943. His sister asked him to have his portrait taken in Newcastle.

en Leggett turned ninety-five in 2021, in the midst of the pandemic. He wasn't overly concerned.

'I'm the last of the Newcastle boys,' he told me, sitting in a house he built at Wangi Wangi, on the shores of Lake Macquarie. A lot of his comrades in the 36th Battalion were from around there. 'The others are all dead .'

He could so easily have been one of the first to go. The Japanese shot at him many times in New Guinea and missed. They dropped bombs on him in Moresby harbour, sinking the ship he was unloading, but he got off in time. They threw grenades and mortars at him at Buna and Sanananda, in two of the worst battles of the war. He came through that hell, when most of his battalion became casualties. He was hospitalised ten times for malaria, and dysentery made him feel like dying.

One thing he did not have was regret or anger that the army took him when he was fifteen.

'No. The only thing I did, every time I found myself in a crunch situation especially on the Kokoda trail or track, whatever you call it, I would be sitting with my back against a tree, with my cape over me, in the dark, pissing down with rain, overnight and I would say to myself, this is a nice old bloody mess you've got yourself into [laughs]. I could have got out any day I wanted to. I could have walked up to the captain and said, "Look I've got no right being here, I'm sixteen years of age." I'd have been on the next plane home. I don't blame the army for anything. I always considered I did it to myself. The only person I blame for anything I've ever done is me.'

> They threw grenades and mortars at him at Buna and Sanananda, in two of the worst battles of the war. He came through that hell, when most of his battalion became casualties.

In another sense, he was lucky to make it to sixteen. He was the thirteenth of fourteen children – two of whom died young. By the time he arrived in the world in May 1926, his mother Vera was worn out. He has only a vague memory of her.

'My first day at school, I remember her taking me to school … I have no memory of her before that, and very little after that, because she died shortly after, aged forty-two, when I was about four and a half.'

He barely knew some of his siblings. They had moved out by the time he was born.

'I had only one younger than me, but I had sisters old enough to be my parents. Matter of fact they had children of their own … My father William was by trade a blacksmith and he worked at various pits and he used to sharpen the picks and shovels and spades and mattocks. They were all underground pits. He did whatever he could get. In those days, you are talking severe Depression. One week's work, two weeks off. In between that, he done whatever he could do. He broke in horses, went bullock driving. We were dirt poor. We were the poorest.'

The family was Irish Protestant. 'I was raised strict Church of England. My mother went to church every Sunday with my sisters and they belted us to church and Sunday school whether we wanted to go or not.' He laughs. 'Once I got in the army I had all that knocked out of me.'

Len was born at Wallsend, a western suburb of Newcastle, but the family moved to Bolton Point, on the shores of Lake Macquarie, when he was seven. His father had built a house on ten hectares of leased bushland.

'We sold vegetables all over Bolton Point. There were a couple of ladies who had lost their husbands in the pit, and they had to get their vegies first every Friday. We walked around the Point selling with a big cane basket full of peas, beans, carrots, anything you'd like to name. Those women whose husbands had got killed in the pit, they got theirs for nothing. Dad was a wonderful worker; he wasn't much of a drinker.'

Len was an outdoor kid. By eleven, he would hunt rabbits at a nearby dam with a .22 rifle, helping put food on the table. His father gave him the job because he was the best shot.

At Fassifern Primary School, he was top of the class. In 1939, he was among the first intake at a new selective school, the Newcastle Technical High School.

'I went for one year and then my father caught pneumonia and died and I had to leave school. We couldn't feed ourselves. I was fourteen … I hated giving up high school. I would have stayed at school every year I could have.'

He took a job at a joinery shop in Newcastle, hoping to be apprenticed as a carpenter. His family by now was just himself, his two nearest brothers Bill and Ron, his stepmother Grace and her daughter Ruth. By 1941, Bill had joined the air force and Len was wondering about the army.

'I was only thirteen when the war started. I am going to be very blunt… I have always made it clear it was an economic decision for me to join the army … I was working forty-eight hours a week for fifteen shillings [at the joinery]. In the army, I was getting two guineas,

which is two pounds five shillings and sixpence, all my medical, my dental, my food and my clothes. And half of that I sent home to Grace. All my army service I sent half my pay to my stepmother.

'As well, look, I would be telling a lie if I didn't say I had a hunger to go. Because I was always an outdoor type of bloke. My idea of a good weekend was a footy match or to go climb a bloody hill or climb a tree or do something in the bush. I always wanted to be in the bush. I got my share of it in New Guinea.' He laughs. 'I was fifteen and five months when I signed the papers.'

Enlistment had required both endurance and 'native cunning'.

'I went to New Lambton where the recruitment centre was … they had this old sergeant there, who was enrolling people. He was a miserable bastard of a bloke and he was about thirty-five years old, he was a real old bloke.' Len laughs. 'And he knocked me back twice. He told me to go home and grow up. He said, "Come back when you're older, son." I said, "I'm eighteen," and he said, "You're bloody not, go home."

When his eighteen-year-old next-door neighbour was called up for the militia, Len saw his way in. He sent in his registration, backdating his date of birth by two years and eight months. 'I was still fifteen when I got the letter.'

He was adamant he wanted to join the army rather than the air force.

'I loved reading about the troops in France in the First World War. Anything about that I could get my hands on, I read. From about twelve, before I went into high school.

'I loved the army from the start. I can't tell you why. I liked everything about it. I liked the regimentation. I liked the discipline but I made up my mind when I went in that I would not accept a promotion. I was offered promotion to corporal and sergeant later … but I did not want promotion because I was two years younger than I shoulda been and I would not have been able to live with myself if I had sent somebody to do something and they'd got killed.'

The 36th Battalion was made up largely of men from Sydney's inner-western suburbs: Balmain, Leichhardt, Five Dock, Haberfield and Lilyfield. The rest were from around Newcastle and the Clarence River, in northern New South Wales.

No-one asked him how old he was, except for the battalion doctor.

'He said, "Are you sure you're eighteen?" I said, "Of course I'm sure, you think I'd bloody be here if I wasn't?" I always got aggressive. "You think I'm an idiot?"'

For three months, they marched up and down the countryside around Greta. Then they marched 100 kilometres to Nelson Bay, and ran up and down the sandhills there.

'We used to have sessions where we would be addressed by this person and that person about what to expect when we were sent away overseas, but it was mainly figured on the Middle East and one night this fellow said, "Are there any questions?" And my mate Bert Lidbury said, "Yes, why are we here running up and down sandhills when everybody knows that the war has shifted home and we are going to New Guinea?" Well, three or four days later trucks turned up and took us back to Greta and then we spent the next few months running up the Watagan Mountains and cutting our way up the sides. And we said to Lidbury, "You shut your bloody mouth in future!" [laughs]. 'Albert Mortimer Lidbury. Best mate I ever had. We saved each other's life a coupla times ...'

Lidbury, born at Wallsend in 1922, was nineteen when he enlisted. He arrived at Greta a week after Len, in February 1942. They shared a love of all sports, especially soccer and cricket.

The tide of war had indeed turned closer to home. In one year, everything had changed for Australia, including the unshakeable allegiance to Britain. A bond had been broken by the British failure to adequately defend Singapore and by the appalling waste of men in Greece and Malaya. Prime Minister John Curtin made it plain that Australia now looked to America for its security, rather than Britain. The question was whether there was still time to prevent a Japanese conquest of Australia. The Australian chiefs-of-staff predicted it could come within two months. No-one was certain that the Japanese were coming, but there were plenty of portents.

By the end of March, the Japanese had taken Malaya, Singapore, the Netherlands East Indies and most of the Philippines. They had landed at Rabaul, Lae and Salamaua in New Guinea. On 19 February, just after Leggett went into camp at Greta, they bombed Darwin, killing more than 250 people. The American general Douglas MacArthur had fled the Philippines, en route to setting up his new headquarters in Melbourne.

Thomas Blamey, who had commanded the Australians in the Middle East, returned to Australia in March as Commander-in-Chief of the Australian Military Forces (AMF). MacArthur, with Australia's support, was appointed Supreme Commander of the Allied Forces in the South-West Pacific. Australia's troops were now fully under American command. A year earlier in the Middle East, Blamey had fought hard to stop British generals taking control of Australian troops, but that was before Australia was under direct threat.

What Australia didn't know was that Churchill and Franklin Roosevelt had a secret agreement to defeat Germany first. The fight against Japan was to be 'a holding war', which meant withholding American forces and matériel from Australia. The implication was that Australia was expendable.

Leggett and Lidbury now found themselves in a slit trench north of Port Stephens, their first time on active duty. They were watching the beach, in case the Japanese landed at Fingal Bay. Hundreds of other men were dug in along this coast. Len remembers long, nervous nights, punctuated by hilarity.

'Lidbury shot a cow there. It caused a helluva lot of trouble. We were on duty. You gotta understand, I was not yet sixteen, Lidbury was only nineteen, we were only kids …

'He wakes me up, and I had just gone to sleep, and he said, "There's someone here, there's an intruder." I said, "No there's not," but he said, "Look!" and coming through the trees, there were these two big eyes and the head darting around. I said to Lidbury, "Jesus, do you think they're Japs?" And he said, "I'm gonna find out."' Len laughs. 'And he's up with the rifle

and went bang and hit him right between the eyes.

'Lidbury was just frightened. We killed ourselves laughing. Oh the farmer put on a hell of an act, he wrote to his member of parliament. Lidbury and I had to give statements. Mine was simple: I just said I was asleep. The next night, Phil Maguire and I arranged a couple of the boys, and they all got out in the scrub about half past twelve, and they were all going moo, making mooing noises.'

Militia units could only fight on Australian territory, but that included Papua and New Guinea, where Australia held colonial sway over the eastern half of the island. To complicate matters, the 36th Battalion also included men who had signed up for the AIF and had been diverted as reinforcements.

The 36th Battalion moved to Port Moresby in late May 1942. Before that, there was a serious insurrection that says a lot about the attitudes of the Australian soldier in 1942. According to Len, the men had been promised two weeks' leave before embarkation. In the end, this was denied, so 400 men absented

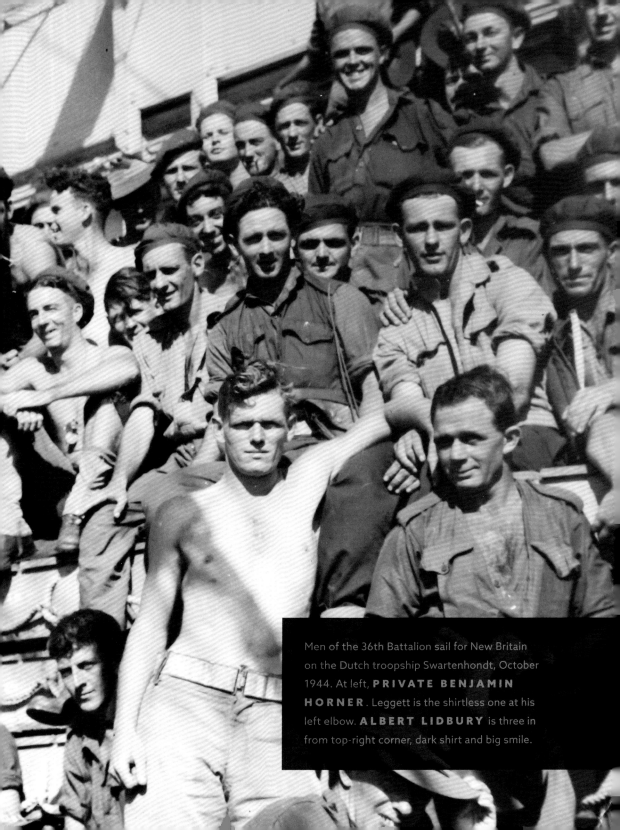

Men of the 36th Battalion sail for New Britain on the Dutch troopship Swartenhondt, October 1944. At left, **PRIVATE BENJAMIN HORNER**. Leggett is the shirtless one at his left elbow. **ALBERT LIDBURY** is three in from top-right corner, dark shirt and big smile.

themselves without leave from Greta camp. They were mostly from the inner-west of Sydney. 'They did it in secret. They left us country kids out of it.'

They sent word that they would reassemble in two weeks' time at Central Station in Sydney, ready to go to war. For these men, it was a question of fairness, not discipline. The army disagreed: they were arrested at Central. All were charged and all later exonerated. The battalion history does not mention this incident, nor the battalion diary. Most of the 400 were conscripts, not volunteers, according to Len.

In Port Moresby, the battalion was sent to a makeshift camp 26 kilometres out of the dusty, infernally hot town. There was one water tap for 900 men but it hardly mattered: it rained every afternoon, turning the road to slush. Carrying parties soon had to lug supplies the last few miles to camp as the road became impassable. Len's work for the first few weeks was unloading ships at the Moresby docks.

'At that time we had ninety-odd air raids in ninety days. We had air raids every day, sometimes twice, but you always knew before the siren went off that they were coming because the natives would run. I don't know how they knew but they bloody knew.'

The Japanese wanted Port Moresby's airfields. From there, they could control the shipping routes between the US and Australia. The first Japanese attempt to take Moresby ended in the battle of the Coral Sea, from 4 to 8 May 1942, when American and Australian ships stopped a Japanese force heading for Port Moresby. In late July, the Japanese landed another force on the beaches at Buna and Gona, on the north-eastern coast of Papua. Between them and Port Moresby lay the Owen Stanleys, a misty, jungle-covered mountain range rising to 4000 metres (13,248 feet). There were no roads, only steep and slippery jungle tracks used by the villagers. The battle for the Kokoda track would be epic for both sides.

'We were late up there because we were doing patrols elsewhere. We were sent to do fighting but it never eventuated. We reinforced [other units] on two or three occasions. We were on it for about six weeks before we went to Buna. We supervised the natives bringing in wounded and sick. The 2/14th Battalion, they were totally depleted, and we carried in their injured and their wounded and a couple of their dead. We organised the natives and we supervised and protected them … At one stage at Uberi we dragged a three-inch mortar up a thousand-foot cliff. Like everybody else, we slipped, we slithered, we bloody fell.'

For the first two months, the Japanese were unstoppable. The Australians fought a series of withering strategic withdrawals. At the end of September, as the Australians clung to the last defensible position on the track, the Japanese withdrew. The Americans had landed a month earlier at Guadalcanal in the Solomon Islands. A second Australian force had rebuffed a Japanese force at Milne Bay, on the eastern tip of Papua. The Australians now pursued the Japanese back along the track, driving them back to where they landed. What followed were some of the most brutal battles of the war.

'You have to take the Kokoda trail and the beaches fighting as one campaign. It was a continuous thing. We did most of our fighting at Sanananda, Buna and Gona. That was worse than Kokoda. On top of that you had malaria, dengue fever, blackwater fever. If you got scrub typhus, it was like being told you had pancreatic cancer. I don't know anyone who got scrub typhus who survived.'

Len had not fired his gun in anger until the battalion reached Sanananda. 'Between the Kokoda track and Sanananda we had several months around the hills of Port Moresby, at Murray Barracks. We dug pits for the defence of Port Moresby, and we

> 'At one stage at Uberi we dragged a three-inch mortar up a thousand-foot cliff. Like everybody else, we slipped, we slithered, we bloody fell.'

climbed mountains … We trained incessantly. We was as fit as mallee bulls. Seven hundred of us went to Sanananda and about six weeks later there were ninety-two of us walked out. There were seventy-three killed, I know that, and more than that were wounded.'

This battle had a profound effect on Len's life. He was still only sixteen at the time.

'I shot two blokes dead on Christmas Eve at Sanananda. I can remember that. It haunted me for ten years actually. To me, until then, it was a game … I didn't know of course that it was Christmas Eve till several months later … We didn't know what month it was at different times. We were in an ambush and I shot these two … They were on patrol.'

After the ambush, Len and his mates had to search the bodies.

'That was the worst part of it. We had to search them for the intelligence section to see where they had come from, what unit they came from, and you search them, and there is one fella there, he has a photograph of a wife and two little girls. I could never get them out of my head for ten years, that photograph. Christmas time would come, I would be sitting watching my girls unwrapping their presents and my body would be in my house at Wallsend and my head would be in Japan, wondering what happened to them kids.

'They sent me to psychiatrists after the war but I said … I never got it out of my head … I killed a couple of blokes after that but I was used to it by then. It's a terrible thing to do.'

Privates Leggett, Lidbury and Stanislaus Philip Maguire, known as Flip, were now the closest of comrades. 'We done that much together, we were better than brothers,' Len remembers.

'We were on a patrol and Lidbury was forward scout and I was second scout, at Sanananda. We were ahead of the platoon and you'd give them signals to come up and stay, and we had given a stay, and we had gone forward and Bert realised the Japs were letting us go through and they were going to get into the platoon later. He dragged me down … I crawled up to him and he said, "We're in trouble, we're in the middle of 'em"… They used to conceal themselves with cut bushes and he noticed some had withered a bit, the leaves were drooping a bit on the branches of the trees that they had covered themselves with.

'We got to where we thought we could make a run for it and we gave the platoon the signal to stay and then the signal to disappear. And so we made a run for it. I tripped arse over and he grabbed me by the scruff of the neck and dragged me from here to the other side of the road. There was bullets going everywhere.' Len laughs.

Len repaid the debt when he stopped Lidbury from going on a patrol that was heavily ambushed. The sergeant, Leslie 'Butch' Whittall, had been a wharf labourer in Balmain before the war and a gifted amateur boxer – not someone you argued with. 'I got up into the sergeant and said to him, "Look, he's been out every day for about eighteen days and he needs a bloody good rest."'

After eight months in New Guinea, the 36th Battalion returned to Australia in February 1943.

'We came back to Queensland. We got forty days leave. I was home about twenty days and I went back, because there was no-one here, I knew nobody, and I started to get a bit drunk, to get on the beer a bit, as you do on leave, so I went back to the unit.'

The battalion returned to New Guinea in August and would remain there for another eighteen months. They saw service at Wau and Bulolo, but their longest stint was on New Britain, the large island stretching east–west between the New Guinea mainland and Bougainville. Their job was to contain the Japanese forces left behind at Rabaul, more than 50,000 stranded men.

At times this became a comedy.

'We were there about seven months in New Britain at Jacquinot Bay. We patrolled up and down, up and down. I remember we were patrolling in sight of the Japs – to give them the illusion that there was a very big force of us, we would patrol along the beaches, then go inside into the jungle where we had a track cut back; we would get changed into different gear and equipment and we would come back on the beach a couple of miles further down, and we did this for weeks.'

When the war ended, Len returned to Australia, with numerous health problems, including anxiety.

'I was a classic case of post-traumatic stress disorder, so a professor told me when I was about seventy. It took him that long to tell me, I was a classic case. I would fight at the drop of a hat. Anyone I argued with, it would always finish up, "Well, get yourself out to the backyard." Fight at the drop of a hat.'

He drank heavily, like most of his mates, but he had also met a girl. Kathleen Duncan had a brother in the 36th Battalion. She had served in the Women's Air Force. They married in 1946, and had two daughters.

'I had blue moods, my wife used to call them, where I would be in myself for days at a time … whereas normally I'm an outgoing person. But my wife used to notice them. I could be working, pitching a roof and instead of thinking about the roof, I'd be thinking about something I did overseas … One year about March I realised I didn't think about Japan at Christmas … and I didn't think much of it ever since.'

Len was very active in his local RSL after the war, fighting for the rights of returned soldiers.

> 'The army did not consider malaria a war-caused disability … We fought and fought and fought through the RSL – the only thing they approved was anxiety state and skin cancers, wounded or prisoners of war. None of the other complaints.'

'That was another bone of discontent with me, the way that Veterans' Affairs treated us after we got discharged … I had malaria ten times, on and off. When I got a good job, I was earning good money, I would have a relapse of malaria and be in hospital for a week or fortnight. There was no hospital schemes in those days. I had to pay for my own hospital. I had to pay for my own doctors. There was no repatriation hospital in Newcastle.

'The army did not consider malaria a war-caused disability … We fought and fought and fought through the RSL – the only thing they approved was anxiety state and skin cancers, wounded or prisoners of war. None of the other complaints. With malaria, that didn't change till around about the 1960s. I spent twenty years fighting them.'

He also disagrees strongly that a soldier's war records can be made public while he is still alive.

'I hate that my army record is available to anyone who's got a computer. On one part of my army record it says there was a warrant issued for my arrest … When we come home the first time [from New Guinea] and we were home for about two or three months, a writ was issued for me being AWL and I was never ever AWL. I was in hospital in Brisbane with malaria and they never reported it.

'When my daughter showed me this on my record, I wrote to Veterans' Affairs and asked them to have it deleted, and I never got a letter back. I wrote twice and never got an answer. I have a good friend in Sydney, his granddaughter was twenty-five years old, loved her grandfather and admired him; so did his wife. She got his records to have a real good look at what further she could know and she finds out that he was dishonourably discharged because he got venereal disease when he was in Brisbane. He picked up with a girl, he was single, she was single, they were both over age … The family didn't know and it broke the family apart. That sort of thing should not be available. My army records should be like my medical records – private …

'I never got disillusioned with the army, I liked army life. I got disillusioned with the way we were treated after the war by Veterans' Affairs …'

Len spent ten years as a carpenter, then took a job in the architectural section of the public works department, supervising the building of high schools and hospitals around Newcastle. He took early retirement at fifty-six and started his own building company, which he ran successfully until he was seventy-two.

I asked him if he considered himself lucky.

'Oh I often thought of that, yes. I think especially of the Wallsend boys who got knocked over, well I could have been easily … how do you explain that? Okay, there's a section of you going forward, ten of you – that one there gets hit, one here gets wounded, the next one gets hit, the next one on the outside gets wounded, and I don't get a scratch. That happened once. How do you explain it? I tried to explain it to myself a million times … I started thinking about religion, I started to think, geez, what sort of a god picks this one out and picks that one out?'

The only good lasting impact for him was the friendships.

'Lidbury was like a brother, Phil was like a brother. They all went in their late eighties. I'm the last of that group …'

LEN LEGGETT, at home near Newcastle, in 2021, aged ninety-five. He calls himself 'the last of the Newcastle boys' from the 36th Battalion.

CHAPTER TWELVE

PARADISE LOST

LESLIE 'JUNIOR' EDWARDS
RONALD 'BADEN' THOMAS

LESLIE EDWARDS, aged fifteen, enlisted the day after news of the Japanese attack on Pearl Harbor reached Australia in December 1941. He wanted to rescue his older brother, who had been taken prisoner at Tobruk.

On Sunday, 7 December 1941, when Japan finally launched its war in the Pacific with co-ordinated attacks from Malaya to Pearl Harbor, it was a devastating display of military power and organisation. Most Australians slept through it.

John Curtin, who had been prime minister for only two months, had chaired a meeting of the war cabinet on the previous Friday afternoon in Melbourne. He was about to board the train back to Canberra when he received word that a Japanese fleet had been spotted near the Philippines. Curtin stayed on in Melbourne, where communications and advisers were close, but he already knew what was coming. The Japanese ambassador, Tatsuo Kawai, a close friend, had told Curtin during a private meeting in Canberra on 29 November that diplomacy had failed.

'Is it to be war?' Curtin asked.

'I'm afraid it has gone too far,' said Kawai. 'The momentum is too great.'

The Japanese timed their attack on Pearl Harbor for the Sunday to catch the maximum number of ships in port. In Melbourne, twenty-one hours ahead of Hawaii, Curtin was asleep at the Victoria Palace Hotel in Little Collins Street. He preferred this modest temperance hotel for that reason, because he no longer drank alcohol. His press pals might fill the halls with tobacco smoke but they could not drink there.

His press secretary, Don Rodgers, roused him at 6.45am with news of the attack on Pearl Harbor, picked up by short-wave radio. Word had also come through that the Japanese had landed in Malaya, two hours before they attacked Pearl Harbor.

'Well, it has come,' said Curtin. He had devoted much of his political life to pacifism. Now he was supposed to lead a country into war, knowing that it was far from ready. There was every possibility that Japan would try to invade Australia. Curtin knew there was little to stop them.

The morning newspapers were too late for Pearl Harbor, but they had caught up by the afternoon. The late edition of the Melbourne *Herald* announced that Japan had declared war on Britain and the US, with a 'treacherous' bombing at

Pearl Harbor and a simultaneous landing on the Malay peninsula. On Tuesday morning, the papers gave considerable space to Curtin's address to the nation the previous evening. 'Men and women of Australia,' he said over ABC radio. 'We are at war with Japan.'

On that Tuesday, 9 December, Leslie George Edwards presented himself to the recruiters at the Melbourne Town Hall, hoping to take advantage of the confusion. He wrote his date of birth as 26 February 1922. In fact he had been born on that date in 1926. He was not nearly twenty, as he claimed, but fifteen and nine months.

He said he was a farmhand, but gave his permanent address as Green Street, Richmond, in the heart of the inner suburbs. Two of his sisters lived in Richmond, so this was probably their address. He gave his father Frank as next of kin and his correct address: Princes Highway,

Moe, in Gippsland, east of Melbourne. If his parents did not already know that Leslie had enlisted, they soon would.

Leslie was the fourth of eight children. His father worked as a timber-getter; he had been badly injured the previous year when a truckload of logs fell on him, causing severe cuts and bruises and a broken leg.

> There was every possibility that Japan would try to invade Australia. Curtin knew there was little to stop them.

Leslie's older brother Harold went to the Middle East with the 2/23rd Battalion just before his father's accident. He was captured at Tobruk and sent to an Italian prisoner of war camp. Leslie's mother Annie received a postcard from Harold, whose nickname was 'Tiddley', at the end of November 1941, a few days before Pearl Harbor. He wrote that he was in good health, which may or may not have been true. 'I am still working during the day and that helps to pass the time more quickly than if I was doing nothing.' This was the first postcard they had received since Harold's wounding and capture some months earlier.

Leslie wanted to join up to go over and rescue Harold. That's how naive his conception of the war was.

His sister Laetitia found out that Leslie had enlisted and told her mother that she would have to go to Victoria Barracks in Melbourne to get him out. His mother said, "If Leslie wants to go to war, then let him."

The Edwards family was well-known and respected in Moe, in part because the three eldest boys had been stars of the Australian rules football club. The local newspapers often recounted their triumphs during the 1930s, when Moe made the finals for the first time in the mid-Gippsland league. The games were rough and tumble: the players would have to chip the ferns off the oval before a game. Harold, Ivan and Tom were renowned for their speed, cleverness and high marking – and their physicality. Leslie was too young to join these bloodthirsty pursuits, where serious injuries were common.

Harold was sent off to war with a 'farewell social' in November 1940.

There were dancing and gifts – a wallet inscribed with his name, and pairs of knitted socks and handkerchiefs. Leslie was next to go, in December 1941, but he left in secret. Ivan and the eldest boy Tom enlisted in 1942. Both had married before the war started: single men were expected to go first. Ivan became a gunner in the 16th Field Regiment. Tom joined the Army Service Corps. By late 1942, all four of the eldest Edwards boys were away serving, leaving just the youngest, Lionel, at home.

Leslie's training consisted of about two weeks at Darley camp. Three days after Christmas, he boarded a train for Darwin. On 9 January, he embarked for 'overseas service' as a reinforcement for the 2/21st Battalion. He was heading for Ambon, an island that almost none of his comrades in arms could have found on a map.

Ronald Keith Thomas was four months ahead of Edwards, but the same age. Thomas was already in Darwin when the Japanese attacked Pearl Harbor.

He had enlisted in August, taking the route that Les Edwards would follow: Melbourne Town Hall, Darley camp, train to Darwin. Thomas was a reinforcement rather than an original but he told even more lies to get into the army.

He was barely fifteen, but he wrote nineteen. His mother Olave Thomas was living in Scott Street, Dandenong, but Ronald did not mention her on his forms. Nor did he mention his father, Leslie Harold Thomas, who had married Olave in 1927 at Elsternwick. She was twenty, he was nineteen. Ronald, her baby, was seven months old when they married. By the time Ronald enlisted, his father was no longer living with his mother. Olave had refused to allow Ronald to join either the navy or the air force. He waited until his fifteenth birthday, in August 1940, then took the train to Melbourne to join up. He had already left home to work on a farm near Berwick, just beyond Dandenong, so Olave never knew he had gone into the army.

On his papers, Ronald wrote that his next of kin was his 'guardian', Mr Thomas Toogood, of Berwick. He also gave himself a new middle name – 'Baden'. Lord Baden-Powell, founder of the scouting movement, was one of his heroes. Thomas Toogood was probably a family friend. If something happened to Ronald, the news would eventually reach his mother via Mr Toogood, who may not even have known that Ronald had used his name. Olave Thomas received no letters from her son once he enlisted.

Why were Australian soldiers even going to Ambon, an island 1000 kilometres north of Darwin that belonged at this time to the Netherlands East Indies?

The answer was largely an accident of geology. Ambon is a small island, barely 50 kilometres from one end to the other, in what we now call the Maluku Islands of Indonesia. In shape, it's more like two islands bisected by a deep harbour, and joined at the top by a narrow sand isthmus. That harbour, 16 kilometres long, was big enough to shelter the entire Japanese fleet. On the harbour's northern

shore, there was an airstrip at Laha. From here, Japanese planes could reach Darwin – and soon would.

On the southern shore, there was a small, sleepy colonial town with a wharf and a handful of elegant colonial houses among the thatched native huts. Most of the island, on both sides, is volcanic and mountainous. The flat areas were abundantly cultivated with bananas, pineapples, sweet potato and pawpaw. The crystal waters teemed with tropical fish. When the Australians first saw it, they thought they had found paradise, a tropical heaven. Their senior officers feared that it might turn out to be more like the other place.

When the Japanese declared war, three quarters of Australia's armed forces were away in the Middle East and Europe, protecting British interests. Curtin did not immediately request their return to Australia. That suggests he was not worried about an immediate Japanese invasion. He had believed Britain's repeated prom-

ises to defend Singapore, which would protect Australia. Australian troops were already in Malaya. That was where the decisive fight against the Japanese would take place.

Australian, British and Dutch military thinkers had pondered the coming war with Japan for at least two decades. In February 1941, the Australian and Dutch governments agreed that Australia would send troops and planes to defend the islands of Ambon and Timor if the Netherlands East Indies came under Japanese attack. The Dutch knew that they would be one of the first targets, because Japan needed their rich oil reserves to prosecute the war.

The US and Britain had goaded Japan into war by cutting off their supplies of oil, after Japan moved its forces into Indochina in 1940. Franklin Roosevelt, facing a hostile congress, knew that America could not join any war unless America itself was attacked. The oil blockade – which cut off 90 per cent

---

RONALD KEITH THOMAS, barely fifteen, gave himself a new middle name, 'Baden', when he enlisted. He did not mention his mother on his forms. She never knew he had gone to war.

of Japan's oil supplies – ensured that Japan would eventually lash out. That aggression would justify America's entry into the fray. Even so, the Americans did not think the Japanese capable of such a devastating first strike. The Pearl Harbor raid destroyed almost half the US Pacific fleet. Just like Churchill, Roosevelt had underestimated the Japanese. Churchill went to sleep that Sunday night in London feeling elated by the attack on Pearl Harbor: the Americans were now in the war. A few hours later in Melbourne, John Curtin awoke to a world of woe and danger.

The Australian war cabinet met again that afternoon. One of its first decisions was to approve the movement of Australian troops to Ambon and Timor.

The 2/21st had been together for fifteen months by the time that Ron 'Baden' Thomas arrived in Darwin. The men were bored, irritable and unruly, desperate to get overseas to fight. The climate was unhealthy, mail was slow, leave to the southern states was almost impossible, the food was bad and there was a shortage of beer. The men had started to call themselves the 'lost legion', and the IAF ('in Australia forever').

> The climate was unhealthy, mail was slow, leave to the southern states was almost impossible, the food was bad and there was a shortage of beer. The men had started to call themselves the 'lost legion', and the IAF ('in Australia forever').

The orders to prepare for embarkation came through on 9 December, the day that Les Edwards enlisted in Melbourne. Two days earlier, Australia sent two flights of Hudson bombers from Darwin to Ambon, at the request of the Netherlands East Indies government.

They were to operate from Laha airstrip.

Brigadier EF Lind was in charge of the 23rd Brigade, which included the 2/21st. The other battalions were the 2/22nd and the 2/40th. Each was soon operating under a new code name: Sparrow Force, based on the 2/40th, would go to Timor. Lark Force, based on the 2/22nd, was already in New Guinea, protecting Rabaul. Gull Force, comprising the 2/21st with support units, would go to Ambon. In each case, the strategic factor was an airstrip. Whoever controlled the airstrips, controlled the war in the Pacific.

The commanding officers (COs) of Gull and Lark forces had known where they were going since May: their deployments were held back in case they 'provoked' the Japanese. The COs had grave doubts about their capacity to do what they were being asked to do. Lieutenant-Colonel Len Roach, CO of the 2/21st, had been to Ambon twice in the previous six months to reconnoitre. He and Brigadier Lind repeatedly expressed concerns to their superiors in Melbourne about the lack of resources. Both Lind and Roach had told the Chief of the General Staff, General

Vernon Sturdee, that without adequate air and naval support, anti-aircraft guns and more artillery, one battalion could not hold the island against a sizeable Japanese attack. Roach was less than diplomatic: as early as May, he wrote to his liaison in Melbourne, Major William Scott, warning him that delays in sending his force to Ambon had seriously compromised its capacity to fight. Unless they went soon, it would not be a case of 'gallant service' but of 'murder'. Six months later, they were finally embarking, but Roach had seriously damaged his own standing in Melbourne. Sturdee, in particular, referred to him as a 'squealer'. Controversially and secretly, Scott put himself forward to replace Roach.

Gull Force, with just under 1200 men, sailed for Ambon on 12 December. Most of the 861 other ranks of the 2/21st had not seen their families for ten months. Most of them would never return. Roach was right: headquarters was sending them to be murdered and the Japanese were happy to oblige. What other word should we use? Headquarters was repeatedly warned; they knew the force was inadequate and could not hold out more than a few days.

Disembarking on 17 December, the Australians moved into a new camp the Dutch had built for them on a hillside near the town of Ambon. Tan Tui camp had huts with cement floors and thatched roofs. It had no direct water to the kitchens, and the latrines were on stilts, suspended over the water. The men soon dubbed this the 'bridge of sighs'. Even so, they thought this camp far better than the hot, dusty, mosquito-infested one they had left in Darwin.

The 1200 Australians were to support 2500 Netherlands East Indies troops on the island. They were under Australian command, but they were to operate through a combined headquarters. They had to co-operate with the Dutch commander, Lieutenant-Colonel JRL Kapitz 'in all operational plans'. Most of Kapitz's troops were Indonesians, with Dutch officers. Both sides were inexperienced.

Roach kept up his complaints and demands to Melbourne. None of the things he had asked for arrived, including food.

The men were forced to ration. Worse, Melbourne rarely replied to any of his messages – the line of communications through Darwin was unreliable. Meanwhile, Major Scott had been promoted to Lieutenant-Colonel in Melbourne. He was now effectively running Gull Force.

Major General Sidney Rowell, Deputy Chief of Staff in Melbourne, signalled his disapproval to Roach on 26 December. 'Concerned at your remarks concerning ammunition and food reserves, since adequate supplies had been despatched Ambon 19/12. Additional units you asked for are not repeat not available. Your task in co-operation with the local Dutch forces is to put up the best defence possible with resources you have at your disposal.'

This message never arrived.

Privately, Roach wrote to Lieutenant-Colonel Scott on 1 January: 'I find it difficult to overcome a feeling of disgust and more than a little concern at the way we have been seemingly "dumped" at this outpost position.'

On 12 January, he wrote again to Scott: 'Is it the intention to continue the policy of allowing small forces inadequately equipped for their task, to be sacrificed, as it seems possible that this force will be overwhelmed if present enemy tactics are pursued?'

On 13 January, as Roach was signalling Melbourne that he thought his force should be immediately evacuated from Ambon, Scott was told to proceed to Ambon to take charge of Gull Force. Roach was to be relieved of his command and sent home. Scott brought a letter from Rowell which outlined the case against Roach: 'It is apparent from messages reached at Army HQ since your arrival at Ambon, and from letters written by you to Lt Col WJR Scott, that you have not the necessary confidence in your ability to conduct a resolute defence of Ambon … you have generally given the impression that you have accepted defeat as inevitable, even before being attacked …'

Roach was on the next plane home. His men were outraged: he was popular, and the animus that greeted Scott's takeover never disappeared. Japanese air raids began to intensify soon after, forcing the Australian planes to withdraw to Australia by 28 January. Two Dutch pilots, flying obsolete Brewster Buffalo fighters, took on the Japanese and were shot down. The Dutch commander reported that he had lost his air force: 'Both of them.'

Even General Sturdee knew that Roach was right, to some extent. In a memo of 14 January, Sturdee commented that the force for Ambon was sufficient to defend against an occupation 'on a light scale'. 'To provide sufficient forces to withstand a major attack is entirely beyond our means. Great value should accrue, however, if the enemy is denied the island except by the employment of overwhelming force.'

How did he think the Japanese would attack? A few canoes full of men with samurai swords? The real meaning is inherent in Sturdee's words: the Ambon force was there to delay, so that 'great value' would accrue with our Allies – the British, Dutch and especially the newcomer, the Americans. We were playing for time, and the right to sit at the top table of decision-making in the Pacific war – then and in the future.

What other choices could Sturdee have made? He might have tried to concentrate his resources in a way that gave his men more chance – perhaps on one island, not three – but to do so would have risked greater losses. He did not have the weapons or aircraft to support them: those had been denied to Australia by the British and Americans, for the war in Europe. These are the ugly mathematics of war. On Ambon, Sturdee wagered one battalion, not three. Stronger political leadership might have questioned his decisions but Curtin was not yet confident to do so. Nor did Sturdee inform the war cabinet of his own doubts about the operation.

The Japanese came in an armada of seventeen transports, five warships and five other support vessels. They were spotted en route two days out, by reconnaissance aircraft. They landed more than 5000 troops in the early hours of 31 December, on two sides of the island. They dealt swiftly with all opposition.

Many of the indigenous troops simply donned lap-laps, fading back into the villages. They had little allegiance to the Dutch, and a long history of colonial mistreatment.

The Australian forces were split between the airport at Laha on the north side of the harbour and defensive positions along the southern shore and in the mountains. Ron Thomas was at Laha; Leslie Edwards was across the water. The Dutch commander capitulated on the second day. Australian units fought on for another two days, against the odds, until Lieutenant-Colonel Scott surrendered.

The 300 or so men at Laha surrendered separately late on 2 February, after putting up fierce resistance in which around fifty Australians were killed or wounded. What happened next has never been properly explained, but every man captured at Laha died, or was executed, in the next twelve days. Their hands were bound behind their backs with wire. Over a number of days, small groups were led away to pre-dug pits and made to kneel. They were then beheaded swiftly from behind – considered a painless and honourable death by the Japanese – or stabbed with the bayonet from behind. No-one at Laha survived.

The dead included Ronald Baden Thomas, aged fifteen. His records say that he died on 2 February, so it is possible he died fighting, rather than as a result of cold-blooded execution. One can only hope that he did. It's also possible that that's a catch-all date for the massacre victims. There were no witnesses or records to consult: everyone who might have kept a record died. Ronald 'Baden' Thomas had been in the army for five months and one day.

No-one at home knew the details of the massacre until after the war. Four separate execution pits were excavated in late 1945 by Japanese prisoners, some of whom were tried for war crimes. The Australian movie *Blood Oath*, made in 1990, is loosely based on those trials at Ambon.

Even so, the trials do not explain why this group of 300 was wiped out, while 800 men on the other side of the harbour became prisoners of war, 'spared' by the imperial Japanese forces.

Those prisoners were marched back to their old camp at Tan Tui. As a POW camp, it was more than comfortable, having been improved by the Australians in their two months' residency. There were more than fifty long huts, each of which could hold seventy men, and the prisoners were not crowded. The Australian food dumps were used to feed them, so for three months, no-one starved.

The Japanese guards were even humane, at least in comparison with later. Australians regularly went under the wire at night to trade goods with the Ambonese. The Dutch male prisoners sent notes to their wives and children housed in a camp next door. Beatings were rare.

> The dead included Ronald Baden Thomas, aged fifteen. His records say that he died on 2 February, so it is possible he died fighting, rather than as a result of cold-blooded execution. One can only hope that he did.

'Some huts had less and some had more,' George Williamson, a butcher from Northcote, told an interviewer in the 1980s for the ABC radio series *Australians Under Nippon*.

'When we first went in the camp, things were that easy you could have your own little vegetable garden, you could keep your own chooks and have your own eggs and that sorta business. You could buy soap, fruit, sugar off the natives as they went through the camp. I suppose the first three months was like a holiday. There was nothin' to do. You just get up in the morning, you could play cards, or play basketball, you could play anything you like. It got that monotonous that they [the men] was asking to go out to work … So they sent 'em out to work and when the work parties started to go out it used to be a scramble to get on them, and it finished up, it was a scramble to get off them.'

The prisoners established a camp 'university', a way of sharing skills and knowledge between otherwise bored men, and made musical instruments, which they used to perform at camp concerts. Williamson built himself a guitar and performed country and western songs. The strings came from unravelling lengths of cable wire.

Things changed when the Japanese discovered that a number of prisoners had escaped in the first few weeks without being detected. Men changed positions during the 'tenko' – a head-count – to fool the Japanese who were counting prisoners. John Van Nooten, who became 2IC and adjutant of the 2/21st in camp, says they even 'promoted' men from the ranks to pose as officers, so their absence would not be noticed. This ruse went on for some time in a never-ending game of wits against the captors.

'These other ranks assumed the name, personality and everything else of an officer who had escaped, and were respected just as much by the other ranks as the true officer was. In fact, later on we lost some of those other "officers". They died and they were at that stage, although officially identified, they were buried in the name of the person they were standing in for.'

In June 1942, a new camp commander

arrived. Captain Ando Noburo was much more vicious than his predecessor. He imposed new rules to restrict entertainment and 'university' lectures and introduced spot inspections. In July, Ando discovered that the Dutch prisoners had been sending messages to their wives and children in the next camp through Ambonese villagers.

'The natives were intercepted and letters taken and all those Dutch concerned, some thirty in number, were taken up the hill as we called it, towards Japanese headquarters, some 30 to 40 yards outside our camp … Captain Ando then called forward his full guard, forty to fifty NCOs and other ranks and gave instructions … that the Dutch were to be thoroughly punished … immediately after his harangue, the Japanese broke off and collected all sorts of weapons – pick handles, star pickets, pieces of wire, cable, sticks, anything they could lay their hands on – and on a command whaled into the Dutch. I saw it. I was some 100 yards away.

'It went on for two hours or more. At the time it seemed to go on all day. There were terrible screams of agony and the Dutch eventually quietened considerably because quite a lot of them were unconscious. This I think was the first occasion in which we really realised how the Japanese could react: it was the kind of butchery for a Roman holiday, as it were, with those who were performing the acts doing so to show how good they were for the onlookers, and the onlookers egging them on further, and thoroughly enjoying it. Sadistic and quite horrifying …'

Three men were beaten to death and another eighteen or more were taken to the camp hospital with concussion, broken bones and internal injuries. Some of the men survived the bashing and the war.

One of the more enthusiastic attackers was a civilian interpreter, Ikeuchi Masakiyo, who was becoming increasingly assertive in the camp. He would become the most hated and powerful man in the camp, but he was not a soldier.

Lieutenant-Colonel Scott retained his position as CO of Gull Force, even in the camp, despite his unpopularity. He issued strict orders about what the men were to say when the Japanese tried to question them casually about their home towns, their ages, the places their units had been, what skills they had. These were confined to name, rank and next of kin. If the Japanese pressed for answers, they were to make up lies but be sure to remember which lie they had told.

John Van Nooten says, 'We all had to change our ages, because the Japanese had an idea that we in Australia had a call-up system on conscription lines and they thought that they could get to some kind of a pattern, that there may be not so many able-bodied men left behind and we would have to start using our old men, our young boys or our women, to defend the country. So ages were changed rather haphazardly – young ones were put up and older ones were put down. The Japanese could not really tell our ages anyhow, just like we couldn't tell theirs. At that stage I had just turned twenty-two, so I became an officer of thirty-six, because how could you be in charge of anything at twenty-two?'

Conditions in the camp became progressively worse as time went on and the Japanese realised they were losing the war. They refused to allow signs to be painted on the roof that would indicate it was a prison camp. They converted a couple of huts into ammunition dumps, close by the hospital and Australian officers' hut. John Van Nooten said they stored something like 250,000 pounds of high explosive inside, as well as armour-piercing shells.

'On 15 February 1942, a squadron of American Liberators flew over and blanketed the bomb dump. It was a direct hit that set it on fire. Our first thoughts were remove our hospital patients. We found that in the original bomb strike some of our officers and other ranks were badly injured, and these plus our hospital patients had to be got out of the area. Somebody timed it and tells me we had one and three quarter minutes before that dump exploded.

'Those of us who were lucky, carrying stretcher cases and had got far enough away, survived; those who didn't, were caught. On that day we lost six officers and four other ranks killed directly, and quite a large number injured, many of whom died later. Amongst them were those who we felt we could least afford to lose. We lost Johnny Hooke our adjutant,

'JUNIOR' EDWARDS (centre, front row) survived one of the worst prison camps of the war, at Ambon. This picture was a few weeks after they were liberated.

who was the only guy who had had any real experience in direct daily contact with the Japanese; we lost our doctor Peter Davidson; we lost our padre Charlie Patmore. We lost our engineering officer, another one we could ill afford, because later occasions when we had to dispose of unexploded bombs and minefields and the like, he was the only one who knew anything about it … Ninety per cent of the camp was destroyed in a huge blast that was just beyond your powers of registering. It left a hole in the ground some 350 feet long, 200 feet wide and 40 feet deep … Next door to our camp, separated by barbed wire and a road, were the Dutch women and children, and they were very badly hit … I think that was the start of the real deterioration in conditions, in food, in treatment, in the type of work parties we had to do, in punishment. In fact it was the beginning of the horror period of the prison camp life.'

In October 1942, Lieutenant-Colonel Scott and 267 of the Australian prisoners were put on a boat and transferred to Hainan Island, near China, where they saw out the war in another camp. Conditions were harsh, but about 180 of them survived, more than at Ambon. Leslie 'Junior' Edwards remained on Ambon along with 527 other Australian men and a handful of Dutch and Americans.

In the last year of the war, the Japanese kept reducing the rations until each man was surviving on the equivalent of a matchbox full of rice per day. At the same time, they increased the work parties, sometimes on pointless backbreaking tasks that the men believed were meant to grind them down. In the last months, POWs were dying at the rate of ten per day.

When the war ended, Gull Force on Ambon consisted of 121 men, including Les Edwards. Most of the men could not walk. Edwards was suffering from malnutrition and beri-beri, which required hospital treatment when he got back to Melbourne.

> Leslie 'Junior' Edwards, being so young, was to some extent protected by his comrades, who 'fathered' him. More surprisingly, according to his son Peter, the Japanese guards generally refrained from bashing him.

Leslie 'Junior' Edwards, being so young, was to some extent protected by his comrades, who 'fathered' him. More surprisingly, according to his son Peter, the Japanese guards generally refrained from bashing him.

'Dad never talked about Ambon but I heard a lot of stories about Dad from the other men. They said the Japanese never hurt the boys but when there was a beheading or a bashing, they had to stand and watch and if they didn't, they would get a crack across the back

PRIVATE HA PURVIS was photographed at an army hospital at Morotai, on 13 September 1945, to show the condition of some of the men recovered the previous day from Ambon camp.

with a stick to make sure they got the message …

'They used to lift his arms up and if he had no hair under the arms, they called him a word that means "boy" in Japanese. Dad had a baby face. There is a picture of him in uniform – he was nineteen at the end of the war and he still looks fifteen in the picture. That is when he came home because you can see colour ribbons on his uniform.'

The death rate among the Australians at Ambon was 77 per cent, higher than at any other Australian prisoner of war camp except for Sandakan on Borneo, where only 6 out of 2500 men survived. Four of the Japanese guards, including Ikeuchi, were convicted of war crimes after the war and executed.

Edwards struggled with post-war life. He married Ida and had four children, living at Mt Druitt, Sydney, but he was an alcoholic, prone to violent rages. Peter Edwards says his father terrorised the family and would disappear for years at a time. Some of his battalion mates tried to talk to him but it was more usually the police, called to the house during a drunken rage. The neighbours used to open their doors for the Edwards children when they heard him shouting. Edwards returned to Victoria in the early 1970s, after his wife divorced him, but he never mellowed. 'He got worse,' says Peter, who visited him in a dementia ward shortly before Leslie died, in December 2001.

'When he was dementing, my sister Joy used to look after him at her home and she would have to lock him in, and he would start talking about chopping the wood for the cookhouse. He was reverting to a memory of the camp, I think.

'My cousins didn't want anything to do with him. One of them said to me later, "The Edwards are a broken family." And I said, "Yeah, I coulda told you that."'

After the war, the unidentified bodies of more than three hundred men massacred at Laha were reburied at a war cemetery at Tan Tui, on Ambon.

CHAPTER THIRTEEN

HAWKS AND SPARROWS

ALAN SINCLAIR POLLOCK

KEN HICKEY

Of the many stories of woe and waste that litter the history of the Australians in the Second World War, the story of the 23rd Brigade should be the one taught in schools, the one turned into songs and poems, the one remembered by those who chant 'Lest we forget' without ever having known.

Three battalions, three tropical outposts, three disasters, within weeks of each other. Each disaster was foretold.

The three forces were dubbed Lark, Gull and Sparrow. Lark went to Rabaul, Gull to Ambon. Sparrow went to Timor, immediately after the Japanese bombed Pearl Harbor on 7 December 1941. Portugal and the Netherlands held different parts of the island.

None of these battalions was ready to fight. They didn't have enough weapons, equipment or men. They could not hope to hold for more than a few days, as they had neither air nor naval support. Worse, most of the men knew their situation was dire, as did their commanders. The generals who sent them even knew it and insisted they go – largely to demonstrate a fighting spirit to our new allies, the Dutch and the Americans. Around 4000 men of the 23rd Brigade left Australia. One third came back. It was an expensive gesture.

The mistakes in the Middle East, Greece and Crete had cost thousands of Australian lives, but they were largely British mistakes, based on British decisions. The 23rd Brigade was destroyed by Australian generals and politicians, making their own mistakes. Two of the battalion commanders warned general headquarters of what was coming; both were replaced for being defeatist. Even after the disasters played out, the generals who planned them were promoted.

> Three battalions, three tropical outposts, three disasters, within weeks of each other. Each disaster was foretold.

There were good strategic reasons to deploy forces to these islands. Each had an airfield, from which the Japanese could strike Darwin and American ships in the Pacific. So why risk annihilation of each force by sending them without proper supply or support?

Lark Force was mauled at Rabaul in a few days, beginning 22 January 1942. The Japanese captured about 160 fleeing men at Tol plantation and massacred all but six, who survived. The massacres at Ambon are covered in the previous chapter.

On Timor, the men of Sparrow Force waited, knowing they were next. Sparrow Force was built around the 2/40th Battalion, almost all Tasmanians. Its support units included the 2/1st Fortress Company and the 2/1st Heavy Battery, an artillery unit. In these, there were at least two under-aged boys – Ken Hickey and Alan Pollock.

Ken Hickey was born on 31 July 1925, but he put down 1923 when he signed up for the militia. That was on 13 January 1941. He was fifteen years and five months old. He gave his address as Denham Street, Bondi, but the family was from Mudgee. The Depression had forced them off their farm, to live for a few years in Sydney and then at Patonga Beach, north of Sydney. By 1942, the large Hickey family was back on a farm near Mudgee. Ken's father Colin had been gassed in the First World War. He suffered from the effects for some years afterwards.

Ken was the third of seven children, but the first to enlist. Older brother Don would go into the air force in late 1942.

Hickey family lore is that young Ken was sent home on his first attempt to enlist, before he turned fifteen. When he tried again, the recruiting officer said, 'Okay, I am sure we can find something for you to do.' That sounds like he knew that this boy, even though he was more than six feet tall, was under-age.

The militia sent Ken to the 33rd Fortress Engineers at North Head, overlooking

---

KEN HICKEY, from a large family at Mudgee, was turned away on his first attempt to enlist before his fifteenth birthday. In the end he joined Sparrow Force, heading for the island of Timor.

Sydney Harbour. There were large guns on both heads pointing out to sea. The Fortress Engineers maintained and operated the searchlights that supported them.

By July 1941, Ken had grown restless. He transferred to the AIF, which meant resigning from the militia and re-enlisting for overseas service. This time, he gave his date of birth as 29 June 1922, because that would mean he could claim to be nineteen years old. The timing was carefully chosen – the minimum age for enlistment had just been lowered to nineteen, but even so, anyone under twenty-one needed written consent from a parent. Again, the family story is that he wrote to his mother (known as Nan) telling her he was going to enlist and not to try to stop him, or he would just enlist under another name. He was one of many boys in both wars to use this threat.

Ken was now part of the 2/1st Fortress Engineers. The unit would soon go to Darwin to join the 2/40th Battalion, preparing for action on Timor (although their destination was still secret). Sparrow Force was coming together.

Alan Pollock's family had also been brought low by the Depression. His father had been manager at several banks in the Northern Rivers of New South Wales during the 1920s, moving to Bankstown in 1929 where he lost his job through a merger. He bought two acres of land in West Ryde, where he grew vegetables and raised chickens until he was gored by the family cow. He then worked at a local grocery. Alan attended schools at Earlwood, North Bondi and finally Randwick High, where he gained his Intermediate Certificate.

He was fourteen when war broke out. He worked for a year as a junior clerk in a solicitor's office in the city. In late 1940 he joined the Naval Cadets, a part-time feeder service for the navy, to become a semaphore signaller. In 1941, he tried to borrow a friend's birth certificate to join the navy. When that failed, he tried the militia, who took him in July, when he was just fifteen and nine months. They sent him to the Coastal Artillery at North Head, later to a radar station at

Brookvale on Sydney's north shore. Ken Hickey had departed for Darwin by the time Pollock arrived at North Head, but their paths were about to converge.

When Japan bombed Pearl Harbor, the men of Sparrow Force were already on a ship, waiting to leave Darwin Harbour for Timor. Ken Hickey was among them. Alan Pollock, still in Sydney, decided immediately to transfer to the AIF. He wrote an account of his time during the war. 'Getting parental consent was no problem,' he wrote, 'as I could sign my mother's name almost as well as she could.' His transfer took effect on 3 January. He was on a train the next day, without final leave, heading to Darwin. His mother Katie queried why he was wearing the 'Australia' badge on his shoulders. He convinced her that it was part of the uniform of the men going to Darwin.

Pollock arrived in Timor on 19 January 1942. His unit was already at Klapalima, a few kilometres east of Koepang, manning the two six-inch guns that had recently been sent from Australia. The guns had been badly

ALAN POLLOCK failed the first few times he tried to enlist. He was accepted in mid-1941, when he was still fifteen. He arrived on Timor in January 1942.

installed by the Dutch; the first task of the 2/1st Heavy Battery was to move them and cement them in position, so that they would not topple over. These guns would never be fired in anger.

Pollock recognised the futility of what they were doing. Their main reason for being there was to protect the aerodrome at Penfui, just behind them. By the time he arrived, there was hardly any air force left to speak of. The only aeroplanes coming over with monotonous regularity were Japanese, on daily bombing runs.

'During the early stage of the bombings, I wound up in Babau Hospital with dysentery and malaria, both of which were to plague me over the next two years. I ultimately returned to my unit a week before the [Japanese] paratroops landed.'

When it arrived, Sparrow Force had about 1330 other ranks and 70 officers. It had now been detached from the 23rd Brigade in Darwin and was under direct control of headquarters in Melbourne. The RAAF had sent an understrength squadron of Hudson bombers, which was soon withdrawn. Dutch soldiers were to hold the western tip of the island, south of Koepang. The Australians were to hold Penfui and north from Koepang along the coast towards Babau.

Lieutenant-Colonel William Leggatt was in command of the 2/40th Battalion, after headquarters recalled Lieutenant-Colonel JG Youl. Leggatt was a Melbourne barrister, aged forty-seven, who had seen action in France in the previous war – a decisive tactician who would become popular with his men. He too had complained to Melbourne about lack of resources. He got nowhere. He wrote to Brigadier Lind, commander of the 23rd Brigade, on 4 January to point out his difficulties: the wet season had arrived, making movement off the roads impossible; no ships had called, and he had no news about the Bren carriers and motor transport he had been promised, nor of reinforcements. Relations with the RAAF were good but they knew no more than he did. Lind already knew most of this, but he too was powerless.

Even the British were worried about Timor. General Archibald Wavell, having incurred the wrath of Churchill in the Middle East, was now commanding the joint American–British–Dutch–Australian forces in Java. He asked the Australian government to send another battalion to Timor. Wavell sent a battery of British anti-aircraft artillery from Java. The Australian war cabinet initially refused Wavell's request – they only had two battalions to protect Darwin. On 5 February, they relented. The 2/4th Pioneer Battalion would go forward from Darwin. Brigadier WC Veale would go with it to take command of Sparrow Force from Leggatt. The Americans would send an artillery battalion that had just arrived in Darwin. All of this was too little, too late. The 2/4th Pioneers were turned around and sent back to Darwin as they neared Timor, because of Japanese bombers.

On 19 February, the Japanese bombed Darwin. A Japanese convoy with one aircraft carrier, one cruiser and five destroyers was reported 110 kilometres east of the southern coast of Dutch Timor. That night, another convoy was spotted off the coast from Koepang, on the north side of the island. The Australians of Sparrow Force wrote their last letters home, knowing they had little chance. They knew that Singapore had just fallen, Ambon was gone, the RAAF had pulled out and Darwin was in flames. They wondered if

the Japanese were about to invade their homeland. 'We had many drinks with old cobbers, expecting them to be the last, and endeavoured to get a little rest before the landing,' wrote one of the 2/40th soldiers.

The Japanese landed around midnight near Dili airport, on the north coast of Portuguese Timor. The next morning, a separate Japanese force landed at the Paha River, south of Koepang, on an undefended beach. Their planes bombed the 2/1st battery at Klapalima soon after. The battery commander, Major A Wilson, was hit in the chest by shrapnel. Tom Uren, later a well-known Labor member of federal parliament, was one of the stretcher-bearers who carried him in. Wilson did not survive the wound.

In the resulting confusion, someone ordered the destruction of the six-inch guns, to stop them becoming useful to the enemy. Alan Pollock stayed behind to help destroy the breech blocks and heavy ammunition. This was an ignominious end for the guns and the unit. The Japanese had seen which way these heavy guns were pointed and brought their ships in behind them for the landing. The

2/1st Heavy Battery had had no chance to prove their mettle.

Pollock and the rest of the battery were now told to join B Company of the 2/40th Battalion. In typical understatement, Pollock says that was 'quite an experience without infantry training'. There had been too little time for the usual long route marches to increase fitness. The 2/1st was full of young men who barely knew how to shoot a rifle.

'When the demolition was complete we made great haste to catch up with our unit but ultimately constant machine-gunning from the air made this a difficult task. I eventually finished up with R Company, the battalion reinforcements, under Lieutenant John Strickland. Most of our action was supporting A Company, and this included a bayonet charge at Usau Ridge on Sunday, 22 February.'

Ken Hickey may have been beside Pollock on this day. The Fortress Engineers had been manning their searchlights at Klapalima, in support of the 2/1st Heavy Battery, since mid-December. Dysentery and malaria had ripped through his small unit, so the men were severely weakened.

Hickey was assigned to Lieutenant Gregory, as a runner and stretcher-bearer. He remembered later that one of his duties was to stand guard with a Bren gun watching for crocodiles while his comrades swam in the ocean. When they abandoned Klapalima, the 'fixed defences' men – the 2/1st Heavies and the Fortress Engineers – left on the same trucks.

The Japanese landed about 5000 men at the Paha River. Soon after, they dropped more than 300 paratroopers about 8 kilometres north-east of Babau, near where the Allies had a small hospital – little more than a casualty dressing station. This meant the Australians had enemy both in front and behind, aiming to cut them off. When Pollock's 'Heavies' abandoned Klapalima, they were directed toward Babau, straight into the path of the Japanese paratroopers. A small makeshift force of Australians – cooks and clerks, medical orderlies and patients who could shoot – held the paratroopers at Babau for several hours, taking heavy casualties. This was where Ken Hickey had his finest hour – certainly, his most lethal.

At Klapalima, west of Koepang, Australian soldiers eat their Christmas dinner, December 1941.

Hickey and Sapper Mal Livingstone had attended an anti-aircraft light machine-gun course in Darwin before they left. Livingstone was twenty-three, from Henty, a tiny farming community near Wagga. Hickey was fifteen years and almost seven months.

Defending the main road through Babau, they were now given the only light machine gun in the unit. With very little cover, Hickey and Livingstone kept firing for more than two hours, as the Japanese tried to cross the road. No-one was sure of the number they killed but the citation from 1946, awarding both of them the Military Medal, says they caused approximately seventy-five casualties. Hickey's commendation reads 'the resolute and courageous action of this soldier prevented further penetration while reserves were being brought up …'

As bold as this was, the Japanese took the village later that day. Hickey, Livingstone and what was left of the others withdrew along the road to Leggatt's main force. Babau was the only road into the mountains, from where Leggatt hoped to organise a guerrilla force.

His force attacked the town again at 5.30am on 21 February. Meanwhile, the Japanese landed another 300 paratroopers north-east of Babau. From 7am, their planes strafed the attacking Australians, many of whom had not slept for three days. After another day of harsh fighting, an Australian company outflanked the Japanese on the left and took the town. Their way was littered with dead Japanese paratroopers. Inside the town, the picture was different, but just as ugly. The Australians at the hospital, wounded as well as medical staff, had all been killed. Some had been tied to trees and had their throats cut, others were bayonetted with hands tied behind their backs. For the Sparrow Force men, this was their first sighting of the cruelty that Japanese commanders demanded of their men.

The next day, Leggatt's column tried to move further into the mountains towards Champlong, where another base had been prepared. About 1.5 kilometres past Babau, they found the Japanese dug in with a mountain gun on Usau Ridge near the Amaabi River. Leggatt gathered his commanders and outlined a plan of attack. At just after 5pm, two companies would attack the ridge while a third poured down everything it could fire on the enemy. The attack was still in progress, both sides taking heavy casualties, when Leggatt's 2IC, Lieutenant-Colonel NP Maddern, ordered R Company to charge. These men were the largely untrained reinforcements who had only recently arrived. Most of them had been in the army less than three months.

Alan Pollock had joined up with them in the retreat from Klapalima. Trained or not, they charged up the ridge and routed the remaining Japanese, killing all but one, whom they took prisoner. He escaped and got control of a machine gun, necessitating a second, and final, charge.

Pollock survived this battle through sheer dumb luck. 'A mortar exploded to my right,' he wrote. 'Fortunately a chap was between me and the mortar when we were blown off our feet. He was killed immediately and I received a piece of shrapnel in my left arm.'

Leggatt's men fought on through the Sunday, 22 February, but it was only a matter of time: they were exhausted, unsupported, low on food, water and ammunition. The 2/40th had taken more than 200 casualties. They were unable to link up with the 290 men at Champlong. Brigadier Veale led those men – 250 Australians and 40 Dutch soldiers – into the mountains to find an Australian commando unit.

Ken Hickey was taken prisoner near Usau on the Sunday, although he was reported at first as missing in action. He told his children later that he had seen a peculiar sight – a Japanese column marching up the road behind an officer with a parrot perched either on his shoulder or the hilt of his sword. He couldn't be sure which, but he was sure he saw the parrot.

Leggatt surrendered the next morning, 23 February, at Usau.

Japanese tanks towing artillery had caught up with the tail of his column during the night. He was threatened on three sides. He was given an hour to decide. His commanders told him the men were willing to fight on, but each unit had voted to surrender. A few dissenters took off into the hills.

Leggatt ordered the surrender soon after 9am. No-one told the Japanese air force, which strafed the column not once but twice, killing some of their own men, and some prisoners. This was the final idiocy – to die after surrender.

> The Australians of Sparrow Force wrote their last letters home, knowing they had little chance. They knew that Singapore had just fallen, Ambon was gone, the RAAF had pulled out and Darwin was in flames.

A rare picture of Usapa Besar camp on Timor in 1942. **SERGEANT EVAN FULLER** of 2/12th Field Ambulance hid a Leica camera in an army water bottle. The words 'walking wounded camp' are written on the back of the photograph.

The battle had taken four days, about as long as that in Ambon. The butcher's bill for Sparrow Force: 84 men killed, 132 wounded, more than 300 missing. On the Japanese side it was much higher – most of the 600 paratroopers had been killed.

Many of the Australian missing were in fact at Champlong, the headquarters that Leggatt thought had already been taken.

Some of these men escaped into the mountains and joined the Australian guerrillas. A few made it back to Australia by boat. Many died of disease and hunger.

The Japanese had taken about 900 Australians and 184 British prisoners, the latter from the ack-ack gunners sent at the last minute from Java. In the following weeks, another 119 men were brought in – either captured or surrendered. The prisoners were marched to Usapa Besar, to a former coconut plantation near where they had landed two months before. Ken Hickey and Alan Pollock were among these 1200 prisoners.

'The camp was built from scratch,' Pollock wrote. 'The engineers in particular did an incredible job with limited tools to build the huts from rough timber and atap [palm branches] for the roofing. Fortunately we were on the beach and this was our means of bathing.' Pollock notes sourly that the officers took all the available tents for their own use.

The Australian cooks did not know how to cook rice: first attempts resulted in gelatinous sludge. They soon learned, as that was nearly all they had.

'We had to bow to every Japanese guard,' wrote Pollock. 'And this caused many problems and bashings. One of the rare "decent" Japs explained that it was their way of saluting and was not to make us feel "inferior". Similarly, roll calls by huts was quite an affair with chaps running sneakily between the huts to make the numbers correct, particularly to cover the chaps outside the wire. Work parties to Koepang were rather popular as this was a means of acquiring additional food to share with your mates.'

Dysentery, malaria and beri-beri swept through the camp. Worse were the tropical ulcers that developed from even minor scratches. The Dutch doctors had some experience of these tropical conditions; the Australian doctors had none. There was tension between the two sets of doctors, as well as with the Dutch and British prisoners. A prison camp is a concentration of unhappy men.

The treatment at Usapa Besar was the best these men would experience as prisoners, although they had nothing to compare it to. There was less brutality, slightly more food. This was often true in the Japanese camps: things got worse in 1943, as they started to lose the war. There was a constant power struggle between men with nothing but their pride, and the Japanese commanders and guards, who had been trained to hold anyone who surrendered in contempt.

Luke Hickey, son of Ken, believes his father was tortured in the early weeks at Usapa Besar. As a small boy, Luke made the mistake of touching his father's feet. The reaction was instant and frightening. Luke's sister Caroline remembers the same thing happening, more than once. The Japanese sometimes used bamboo sticks to beat the soles of the feet. They were seeking useful information: how and where the Australian forces were organised; the layout of camps and towns and defences in Australia.

Hickey and Pollock must have known each other: they had been stationed together on the guns at Klapalima. In Usapa Besar, the 2/1st Heavies and the 2/1st Fortress Engineers – which had only fifty men and a few officers – had huts next to each other.

In July, a group of prisoners was sent to Java. The rest followed in September. Pollock was put on the rusting, stinking *Dai Nichi Maru* which sailed up the north coast to Dili 'where we were bombed'. Fortunately, the bombs missed.

The Allied planes had no way of knowing the ship contained prisoners. The combatant countries could not agree on a way to mark prisoner transports so they would be visible to the enemy. As a result, many thousands of prisoners died when sunk by 'friendly' submarines during the next three years. In June 1942, the *Montevideo Maru* left Rabaul for Hainan island, with more than 1000 prisoners on board – about 850 men from Lark Force

> Dysentery, malaria and beri-beri swept through the camp. Worse were the tropical ulcers that developed from even minor scratches.

and another 200 civilians. An American submarine torpedoed the unmarked ship off the Philippines. No Australians survived. That was the end of the 2/22nd Battalion and Lark Force.

The *Dai Nichi Maru* seems to have travelled under a luckier star.

'We then proceeded through the Flores Island where it was considered we were hit by a torpedo which did not explode. At this time in the war this was not uncommon,' wrote Pollock. They docked at Surabaya, its harbour full of wrecked ships, and boarded trains for the 600-kilometre journey to Batavia, the old name for Jakarta. From here they were marched to the large camp at Tandjong Priok, near the docks. They were given haircuts, which Pollock described as one of only two decent things that happened there. A haircut reduced lice and vermin. The other decent thing was their liberation, years later.

The Japanese insisted the men learn Japanese commands – eyes right, eyes left, et cetera – and how to count to ten: *ichi, ni, san, shi, go, roku, shichi, hachi, kyuu, jyuu*. On one parade the Austra-lians changed this to *ichi, ni, san, shi, go, get, stuffed* – but one of the officers understood, so this resulted in a belting. The Japanese were keen on propaganda film-making: they would set up a food banquet, film the prisoners standing by, then take the food away. This was a cruel trick to play on men suffering severe malnutrition.

Some prisoners were sent to other camps for work: Singapore and Haruku island, or worse, the Burma–Thailand railway. Pollock was sent to Makasura Camp, near Bandung, a farming camp, where the la-trine was an open drain through the centre of the camp. When it rained the latrines drained onto the gardens as fertiliser.

Hickey went to a number of different camps.

Sometimes the men unloaded ships; sometimes they grew food on farms to feed the guards. Hickey spent time making string. He celebrated his seventeenth, eighteenth and nineteenth birthdays in the camps. He told his mother afterwards that he thought he received slightly better treat-ment from the Japanese because of his age. A friend who was with him told the family that Ken once punched a guard. He was strung up by his thumbs as punishment. Hickey never spoke of this.

The Hickey family had been notified by mid-1942 that Ken was a prisoner of war. Ken's mother went to mass every day to pray for his safe return, often taking Ken's sister Molly with her. Molly remembered that when Ken came back in October 1945, she and her younger sisters were scared to touch him. He was so skinny that his ribs showed through his skin. His mother told him he need never speak of the war if he didn't want to – and he barely did. That is why the family knows very little about where he was from late '42 until after liberation in late '45 – three blank years.

Alan Pollock had by now caught amoebic dysentery. He was sent to the Dolorosa hospital for infectious diseases in Batavia, which saved him from being sent to the Burma–Thailand railway. Relapses and malaria kept him in hospital for ten months. In February 1944 he was sent to Bicycle Camp, an old Dutch barracks in the suburbs of Jakarta, where he worked in the Japanese cookhouse, until they discovered he had come from an infectious diseases hospital. The guards were mostly Koreans, and disgraced Japanese. 'The slightest incident would provoke a bashing.'

In late May, Pollock was one of 800 men selected to work in Japan. A succession of ships took them first to Singapore. A number of ships in the convoy were torpedoed and sunk before they reached Manila. From here, they sailed north on 10 June, in a convoy of fourteen ships headed for Taiwan. They ran into a typhoon and Pollock's ship broke down.

'The ship was towed into Takeo. Bear in mind that as the cookhouse was washed overboard, no-one had had any food etc. for three days. When the hatch covers were opened, the dead were put over the side.'

In Takeo Harbour, they boarded the *Tamahoka Maru*, 8000 tons, with 500 Japanese soldiers aboard and a load of sugar and rice, bound for Japan. The prisoners were crammed into the forward holds.

'The Japanese crew and guards were jubilant that we would arrive in Moji the following night but they did not bargain

KEN HICKEY and **ALAN POLLOCK** went through a series of POW camps on Java. This is Bicycle camp in September 1945, after its liberation.

on meeting the USS *Tang*, which at midnight on 24 June, fired off six torpedoes and sank four ships. Our ship took two torpedoes, one amidships and one under the forward hatch.

'My recollection of this action was a vivid orange flash, a hell of a bang, and I was sailing through the air. It subsequently turned out that everyone around me was killed. The ship literally sailed under by the bow and reports had it gone in less than five minutes.

'I have little recollection of what happened when I landed back in the fast filling hold, or how I resurfaced, but I do remember hitting my shoulder on what was part of the hatch cover, and this became my home for the next twelve hours, when I was eventually picked up'.

The Japanese sent out small vessels to rescue those in the water, while the destroyers dropped depth charges, hoping to sink the American submarine. Pollock and the other survivors landed that afternoon in Nagasaki, most of them naked. They were taken to the Mitsubishi foundry and armament factory, where there was a Dutch POW camp. Pollock noted that 212 prisoners survived the sinking, 72 of them Australian. 'There were only nine out of my unit that survived out of twenty-seven on board.'

He went to work in the blast furnace. Beatings were common, food scarce as ever. He would raid the garbage of the Japanese cookhouse for food scraps. That is how he survived the harsh winter of 1944–45.

In July 1945, he went with forty others to the coal mines at Omine near the western tip of Japan. Twenty-four Australians remained at the Nagasaki camp; two others were in another camp nearby. They were less than 2 kilometres from the blast, but all survived. When the war ended in August, American planes dropped food and medical supplies to Pollock's camp. A month later, these men boarded a train for Nagasaki, where the Americans put on a big party: marching band, hot baths, new clothes, medical treatment and good food. In Manila,

> Beatings were common, food scarce as ever. He would raid the garbage of the Japanese cookhouse for food scraps. That is how he survived the harsh winter of 1944–45.

they were debriefed for two weeks about their treatment by the Japanese. Alan had his twentieth birthday here. He arrived home by Catalina seaplane at Rose Bay in Sydney on 19 October 1945. After seeing his parents, he spent ten weeks in a military hospital at Merrylands, where he met the woman who would become his first wife.

They settled in western Sydney and had four children. Alan qualified as an accountant and eventually moved to the Central Coast, where he became a champion lawn bowler. He received a Medal of the Order of Australia in 2007 for his services to bowling. In later years, he would hold an annual party for those men of Sparrow Force living on the Central Coast. That's how his own family learned about his war experiences. He wrote a short memoir for his children and grandchildren. Alan Pollock died in 2017, aged ninety-one.

Ken Hickey returned to Mudgee and married Clare Jacklin. They had seven children. After her death, he married Beryl Halpin and they had three more children. He worked mostly as a farmer and long-haul truck driver. He died in Mudgee of a heart attack in 1987, aged sixty-two.

CHAPTER FOURTEEN

HEART OF DARKNESS

JACK BLACKMAN

REG HUNTER

By the age of eighteen, Jack Blackman had seen a lot of war. He'd been in uniform for almost fourteen months and was part of the 2/13th Battalion, who called themselves 'the Devil's Own'. He had been hit in the leg by shrapnel on two occasions and had seen many of the hotspots and hospitals in Libya, Palestine and Syria. He'd been to Bardia, Benghazi and Tobruk in Libya; Buq Buq and Mersa Matruh in Egypt; Larissa and Daphni in Greece. He'd not quite been everywhere, but of travel, he'd had his share.

John Edward 'Jack' Blackman grew up in Gunnedah. Before the war his father, Jack Percival Blackman, had moved the family to Cootamundra, a farming town in central western New South Wales, where he was a police sergeant. The two Jacks spent a lot of time out in the bush, and were very close.

Young Jack was well-built and looked older than he was, so he had no trouble enlisting in the AIF in June 1940. He signed the papers at Cootamundra and gave his father's correct name and address, which suggests he was not trying to hide his progress, although he may have kept his enlistment secret. He claimed he was twenty years and three months old, having been born 25 February 1920. It was the correct date but wrong year. He was born in 1923 so he was seventeen years and three months old. He had hazel eyes, strong features and thick dark hair.

By December of that year he was in Kilo 89 camp in Palestine, training as a signaller, a role he did not want. He transferred to the 2/13th on 30 January 1941. That year must have been something of a blur for him: he copped shrapnel in the leg on 3 March and was evacuated to the Australian General Hospital at Kantara, Egypt. No sooner had he returned to the unit than he was hit again in the leg. The wound must have been relatively minor this time as he remained with his unit.

In July, he was sent to a guard battalion at headquarters, which would have felt like a punishment. That's because his father had told the army he was under-age. While he was waiting for a boat home, he caught sandfly

fever – another hospitalisation. At least he came home in style, on the *Queen Mary*. He was discharged in Sydney at the end of October for being under-age. He was not happy about it, given that he was now eighteen years and eight months old – practically a man. Another four months and he might have been able to stay with his unit.

He was sent to a medical board two days after he got back, which declared him fit. He re-enlisted in the militia in November, but lasted only ninety-five days, during which he was charged with three offences in ten days – being AWL, breaking out of barracks and leaving his post without permission. His record before this had been exemplary.

He visited his family in Cootamundra. A press report says he brought home a tin hat marked with the names of all the places he had fought. Jack was the only son, but his two sisters had husbands in the war. Thora's husband CJ Lambert became a prisoner of the Japanese; Maxine's husband, Stanley Woodlands, was a warrant officer in the RAAF. Having tasted peace, Jack Blackman was anxious to get back to war.

The same newspaper report quoted his reasons: 'I could not content myself with being a parade ground soldier after having been through so much action and activity.'

He rejoined the AIF on 3 March 1942. This time, his third enlistment, he gave himself a birth date of 25 February 1921, and the age of twenty-one. He was still only nineteen. He enlisted in Paddington, Sydney, far from his father's protection. The army sent him to a training unit at Dubbo, then Bathurst, where the shrapnel in his leg played up. He became restless and reckless. He disappeared, AWL, from Bathurst on 7 to 15 July, then again on 21 July. This time he stayed away. The army issued a warrant for his arrest as a deserter. He

---

JOHN (JACK) BLACKMAN was the son of a Cootamundra policeman, who got him out of the army for being under-age. He rejoined the AIF in March 1942 and was sent to New Guinea.

returned after five weeks, and was sent before a district court martial.

He said he left his unit on 21 July 'because I had been left out of three drafts from Bathurst and I was very anxious to be in action again …

'I had heard that American bombers came to Brisbane to have their engines rebored, and I thought I might get back to Moresby with them. I was on the way home and at Albury I met some chaps who told me they were going to Moresby and so I went to Melbourne and tried to get on the boat, but I never had a chance. I found officers and piquets [guards] all around, so I immediately gave myself up at Melbourne to the air force police, and they took me to the gaol.

'I was brought to Sydney by the military police. When I got to Sydney, I went AWL again, and on that occasion there was a couple of chaps under escort with me and one of them belonged to the 2/14 Battalion, which is in Moresby, and he said we might get away up there, and so I went AWL again.

'I was very light on with regard to money, and I wired home to Cootamundra for some. I got a reply saying my dad had been operated on the day before and they also sent some money, so I immediately set off home to see what was wrong. That is why I went away. I had no intention of deserting. I was trying to get into action, not out of it.'

> 'I had no intention of deserting. I was trying to get into action, not out of it.'

Under cross-examination, he admitted he had been discharged for being under-age. 'I turned seventeen going over on the boat' to the Middle East, he told the court, which was not quite true. By now he must have had trouble keeping track of the lies he had told about his age.

Blackman pleaded not guilty and the court believed him, finding him guilty of a reduced charge of being AWL. He was fined one pound, which was lenient. Blackman had not been to Papua yet, although he said in his testimony that he wanted to 'get back' there. If he had been there, he might not have been in such a hurry.

A handful of Australians knew a lot about Papua and New Guinea, having worked there as administrators before the war. The rest, including most soldiers, knew almost nothing, except that the Japanese had landed on the coast of New Guinea and had taken Rabaul in the islands, where they controlled an airstrip and a good harbour.

The Australians knew they would be fighting in the jungle but not what that meant – that they would have to carry supplies because the country had few roads; that some of this would be up and down mountains covered in impenetrable tropical growth; that it rained almost every afternoon in these mountains and was cold at night; and that the place had more diseases than they'd ever heard of. Some of them caught malaria in the Middle East, but Papua and New Guinea also offered exotic forms of dysentery, plus scrub typhus, yellow fever, blackwater fever, tropical ulcers and a form of madness called 'going troppo' that seemed only to afflict white people unable to stand the heat and humidity.

The Australians also had little idea of the cultural complexity of the native peoples – they were more diverse than almost anywhere on earth, spoke close to a thousand languages and had little formal schooling after fifty years of colonial and missionary occupation. Their spiritual views were based on good and bad spirits, and in certain parts, there was almost constant warfare between tribes, which sometimes resulted in the taking of heads and the ceremonial eating of the flesh of one's victims. It was a tropical paradise if you were somewhere comfortable with a breeze, in the islands; and a tropical hell if you were toiling up a mountain in the Owen Stanley Ranges. The soldiers were about as prepared as the army itself, which sent them north in their desert-issue khaki uniforms rather than 'jungle greens', thus making them easier to see in the jungle.

The Australians knew even less of the enemy. Some had heard that the Japanese were small, short-sighted and disorganised, but anyone who read the papers knew they had conquered most of Asia and a large part of the western Pacific in the seventy days after Pearl Harbor, including the 'impregnable' fortress of Singapore. After 19 February 1942, when Japanese planes bombed Darwin, every Australian knew the Japanese were coming to take Australia. They were wrong – the Japanese never seriously considered it, because of the size of the task – but Australians had plenty of reason to think it was true. It meant that, for the first time, they would be fighting for their homeland. It was, as John Curtin said, 'the battle for Australia'.

The 2/14th Battalion was formed at Moonee Ponds in May 1940, moving quickly to Puckapunyal camp in central Victoria. It was largely composed of Victorians, who tended to be grouped by region, especially if they had come from the pre-war militia: men from Mildura and the north-east in A Company; Geelong, Prahran and Brighton boys in B Company; 'Scottish' units in C Company; and Collingwood and the 'Irish' in D Company. Those of like religion – Catholics, for instance – tended to congregate with their fellows, although this wasn't uniform. There was another unofficial category: one section was renowned for the number of under-age boys. It was so well-known that WB Russell mentions it in his post war battalion history: 'Probably the youngest of them was (VX15382) Pte Norm. Hunter of D Company, who enlisted at fifteen. In the same section – surely the youngest section in the second AIF – were his brother, (VX15196) Pte Bert Hunter (sixteen) and (VX15470) Ptes Don (Butch) McCann (sixteen), (VX15467) Laing, and (VX15463)

REG HUNTER pretended to be his brother, Stanley, to get into the army. He ended up in the 2/14th Battalion, fighting along the Kokoda Track.

SONS OF WAR

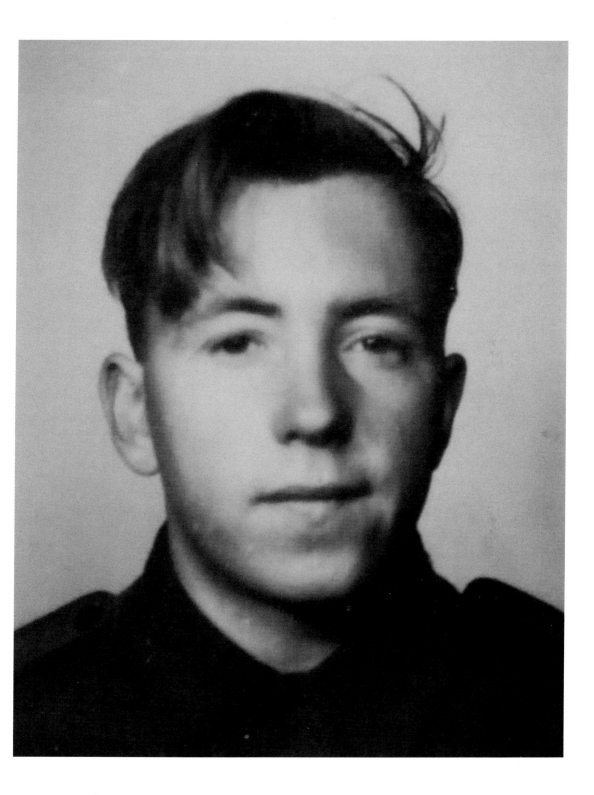

Bulman (seventeen), (VX15508) Edwards (kia), (VX23155) Williams and Hall (eighteen). Their Section Commander, (VX15273) Cpl Horrie Phefley, was aged eighteen…'

Russell lists another eight men aged sixteen or seventeen, then adds: 'There were probably many others, if appearance was any indication.'

One was Ronald Frank Woodward, known to his comrades as 'Georgie'. He used his brother's birth certificate to enlist in May 1940, aged sixteen. He did not tell his parents. He was in Syria when they found out. They notified the army, but Georgie's mates hid him from the Military Police (MP) whenever they came looking. The MPs only caught up with him after he was wounded on the Kokoda track. His parents then consented for him to stay with the battalion. He became a corporal and was one of the few who saw action in every campaign of the 2/14th Battalion.

There were also a number of men in the battalion who were fifty-five and older. One had fought in the Boer War, around 1901; others had served in the First World War. Recruiting regulations had been tightened since that war but, clearly, it didn't matter in some battalions.

> He used his brother's birth certificate to enlist in May 1940, aged sixteen. He did not tell his parents. He was in Syria when they found out.

The 2/14th sailed for the Middle East in October 1940 on the venerable Cunard liner *Aquitania*, a ship as old as some of the men she now carried. The 2/14th had their first action in Syria against French colonial troops, loyal to Vichy France, in June 1941. As French colonies, Lebanon and Syria were now allies of Germany. The 2/14th pushed along the coast and fought major engagements at Zahrani River and Damour. After the Vichy troops capitulated, the 2/14th remained as garrison troops till the end of the year.

Back in Australia, Private Reg Hunter signed his papers that July, just after the fall of France. He claimed he was one month short of twenty years of age but he was only just sixteen. He was born 19 June 1925. He borrowed his brother Stan's birth certificate and pretended to be him. It worked.

He said he was a butcher, which may have been true. His father worked a family farm at Axedale outside Bendigo. It was dry, hardscrabble country, even before the Depression. Reg and his elder brother Stanley grew up poor. Stan's daughter Rhonda says they had shoes but 'only for Sunday's church'.

Mary Jane Hunter bore six children. One died at birth, then three were taken by pneumonia in quick succession at a hospital in Melbourne. 'Family lore is that she died of a broken heart when Reg was three,' says Rhonda. The two surviving boys were sent to a children's home in Brunswick, Melbourne, at one point, because their father was often hospitalised by a serious heart condition. Both boys were athletic, playing football and cricket in the local Axedale

teams in the 1930s. In summer, they loved to swim in the Campaspe River.

The real Stanley Hunter followed his brother four months later, joining the militia on 5 November and transferring to the AIF a year later, in July 1942. Stan was sent to the 2/4th Armoured Regiment, a tank unit. So by mid-1942, there were two brothers with the same name in the AIF. Reg's chances of being found out were slim as long as his brother didn't visit him, although maybe not even then. The real Stanley was known as 'Maurie' for most of his life, a nickname picked up in childhood, after a famous Richmond footballer. For the sake of clarity, I will refer to Reg by his real name.

After two months' basic training, Reg shipped out to the Middle East at the end of November 1941. He reached his battalion (2/14th) on 30 January 1942, among a group of 180 reinforcements. On the same day, Jack Blackman had reached the 2/13th Battalion nearby, as a transfer. The 2/13th had just vacated the camp that Reg's battalion took over in Palestine. The 2/13th moved to the same

A happy **PRIVATE REG HUNTER**, safely returned from the Middle East, during jungle training in Queensland, mid-1942.

area in Syria that the 2/14th had just vacated. Such is life in the army: a frontline battalion that stays too long in one area is thought to become bored, mischievous and hard to control.

Reg arrived just in time to turn around and head back to Australia. By May, the battalion was in Queensland, doing jungle training around Yandina.

By mid-August, they were in Papua, preparing to fight the Japanese in the Owen Stanley Ranges.

The next month would see the making, and the breaking, of the 2/14th Battalion. One of its members would be awarded the Victoria Cross and others would distinguish themselves with acts of valour. It would become a graveyard for some. Of the 546 men of the 2/14th who went up the track, only 87 came out. Nearly half were battle casualties; the rest were sick or cut off behind enemy lines.

The Japanese had landed at Buna on the north-eastern coast, in the last week of July 1942. The Australians estimated the force to be about 1200 men, but it was at least three times that. Japanese intelligence advised there might be a road across the mountains out of Kokoda. They would follow it over the 2100-metre range and take Port Moresby by land, having just failed – in the battle of the Coral Sea – to take it by sea. The Japanese knew even less about the terrain than the Australians. They brought bicycles, where climbing ropes would have been more useful.

Reg Hunter was assigned to the 2/14th Battalion's C Company. The 21st Brigade assembled at the foot of the ranges in mid-August, throwing out everything they might not need, to reduce the weight in their packs. Even so, each man carried about 20.5 kilograms, plus his weapon. Up and up they went, through mud and rain and mist, past native villages made of thatch, village gardens growing *kaukau* (sweet potato) and yams. Many of the villagers had fled – afraid of being press-ganged to work as carriers for either side. The air cooled above 1000 metres, but rain showers and sweat meant that the men were always wet. Starting a fire for a billy of tea was a struggle.

The 39th Battalion, a militia unit, had gone up the track two weeks earlier. In hard fighting, the Japanese had pushed them back to Isurava, about a day's march from Kokoda, on the far side of the range. The men of the 2/14th and 2/16th arrived at Isurava at a desperate moment. From here, 1500 metres up, they could see down the valley to what had been the quiet mission of Kokoda.

Reg's C Company was the first forward, to take over 39th Battalion positions at Isurava Guesthouse, beyond Isurava. A large Japanese force was already climbing the mountains on either side, trying to outflank them. On 27 August, Japanese patrols probed the Australian lines, and vice versa, with some short sharp clashes. On 28 August, the battle erupted in full – two battalions of Japanese charged the Australian lines,

> The next month would see the making, and the breaking, of the 2/14th Battalion. One of its members would be awarded the Victoria Cross and others would distinguish themselves with acts of valour. It would become a graveyard for some.

The Kokoda Track in 1942: 100km of jungle path through impossible terrain across the Owen Stanley Ranges. The Japanese had expected to cross it on bicycles.

into the face of heavy fire. The Japanese were supported by mountain guns, heavy machine guns and mortars. First Reg's C Company, then D and B companies took the brunt of these frontal charges, which came at a huge cost to the enemy. Even the Japanese diaries of the battle confirm the severity of their casualties. The next day, the Japanese committed two more battalions to the fight.

Reg Hunter and his comrades had not slept much in four days. They had suffered many casualties. The Japanese now knew their positions, so they pounded them with mortar and mountain gun, then attacked all of the Australian positions simultaneously and continuously through the day and night of 29 August. Most of the officers and NCOs of the 2/14th were now gone – wounded or dead. The platoons had become separated and some sections were cut off. Private Bruce Kingsbury went out with a Bren gun, firing from the hip, to clear a path, inflicting many casualties before he was brought down by a sniper. For this action, Kingsbury won the Victoria Cross – the first Australian VC winner of the Papuan campaign. That night, Brigadier Arnold Potts ordered the 21st Brigade to withdraw to one mile behind Isurava, to dig in again. Thus began the 'fighting withdrawal', one of the most demanding manoeuvres an infantry force can be asked to perform.

One problem for the defending force is that it is almost impossible to make sure that no-one is left behind. The Australians were spread out across the valley, trying to stop the outflanking. Now they would have to withdraw, dig in, fight again, as their comrades withdrew through them to dig in further back. Each unit must cover the others as they leapfrogged back in withdrawal. The idea was to make the Japanese fight for every inch of territory, with a high casualty rate, as their supply lines grew longer and their men grew more exhausted. It might eventually work, but there were great risks for the defenders too.

On that Sunday afternoon, 30 August, fifty men from A and B companies were cut off from Isurava. Captain Sydney 'Ben' Buckler took charge, with Lieutenants Maurice 'Mokka' Treacy and Charles Butler – all officers of the 2/14th. The party included three men on bush stretchers, each stretcher requiring six to eight men to carry it, and three walking wounded. They moved off at dusk but quickly discovered the Japanese had occupied the track behind them.

Buckler took the men off the track, attempting to follow the Eora Creek back to their own lines. Corporal John Metson, from Sale, wounded through the ankle, refused to be carried by stretcher. Instead, he bandaged his hands and knees and crawled behind the party as they struggled through mud and tree roots, at snail's pace.

Reg Hunter was on one of the stretchers, with a shattered knee. He was now seventeen and two months old. He had been in the thick of the fighting for four days with C Company, his first action of the war. Buckler's party had little food or medical supplies but water was plentiful, from the sky.

They struggled on for four days, scavenging food from native gardens and dead soldiers. On 5 September, Buckler sent Lieutenant Treacy ahead with two men to find the battalion and return with help. Buckler would wait for six days, and if they were not back, he would make for the New Guinea coast, hoping the Australians had landed there. On 11 September, with no sign of Treacy, Buckler and his starving men set off again, this time down the mountains towards Kokoda – in effect, away from their own lines. They stayed east of the Japanese along the track, moving carefully and silently down through the undergrowth. They did this for ten days until they reached the village of Sangai, south-east of Kokoda.

Here the villagers fed them and gave them huts to sleep in. In effect, they saved their lives, at great risk to themselves, defying the Japanese threat of reprisals for assisting the enemy. Buckler now had little choice but to leave the wounded. There were fast-flowing rivers ahead that they could never cross with stretchers, and the villagers had promised to look after the five wounded men, and another two who were sick with fever. Private Tom Fletcher, B Company's

> Reg Hunter was on one of the stretchers, with a shattered knee. He was now seventeen and two months old.

Getting the wounded out from the Kokoda Track could take a week, even with eight strong men per stretcher. The 'Fuzzy Wuzzy Angels' were often pressed into service against their will, as carriers and stretcher-bearers.

medical orderly, volunteered to stay with them. Before they moved off, Buckler and his men formed up to present arms to the eight men – a moving gesture of respect, and farewell.

Buckler's journey, leading the remaining thirty-eight men back to their own lines, is one of the epic stories of the war in Papua and New Guinea, and barely known in Australia. Thirty-two days after leaving Isurava, he arrived at an American camp on the far side of the ranges, having traversed several rivers and recrossed the mountains. As soon as he was back in Port Moresby, Buckler organised a plane to drop supplies and medicines at Sangai, but the plane could see no signs of life there.

In fact, the men he left behind had been found. Someone killed them all, including young Reg Hunter. We don't know who, when or how. If the villagers witnessed the killing, their accounts have not been preserved, but they would certainly have seen who was responsible.

It's possible that someone from the village betrayed the wounded to the Japanese. Alliances were liquid in the area: the villagers did not like the Japanese but they feared them, and no-one knew if they were there to stay. It's also possible that Japanese scavenger patrols, out looking for food, found them.

The murders would not have been unusual for Japanese units in the area: they had already killed another group of captured civilians, including two female missionaries, near Buna. But were the Japanese really responsible?

In 1946, Australian war crimes investigators in Rabaul interviewed a number of mixed-race Rabaul men who had been forced to work for the Japanese in 1942. They told a different story.

One of the men, Joseph Kramer, said he had heard from native carriers on the Kokoda track in 1942 that a mixed-race Rabaul Chinese man – whom I shall call X – had killed the men at Sangai. Kramer said he had encountered X on the track, and that he was working for the Japanese.

'He had two revolvers, one Australian and one Japanese, and I heard from the natives who had been brought from Rabaul to carry for the Japs that there were about six or seven Australian soldiers ill with dysentery in this village and that X had shot them all.'

John Stehr, of Malay mixed race, was also interviewed in Rabaul in 1946. He said that X had been a petty criminal before the war, often in trouble with the colonial police, whom he hated. Stehr and a number of other mixed-race men had been forced to labour in Rabaul from January till August 1942, when they were sent with the Japanese force to Buna. Here they continued to work as labourers during the Kokoda campaign. Stehr eventually escaped and became a radio operator for the Australians. He was interviewed a number of times, and his recollection was that he and his friends had met X one night at a camp near Kokoda, and recognised him from Rabaul.

Stehr said X was wearing a Japanese uniform and carrying a side-arm. He boasted of killing at least seven members of the Papuan Infantry Battalion, the native soldiers fighting with Australia. He also claimed to have killed a number of white soldiers (although Stehr did not

say where). Stehr also said he knew Joe Kramer but did not trust him.

The investigating officer, Lieutenant Richard Tuck, wrote in his summary in late 1946 that efforts to get a third witness, Jerome Madero, to return to Rabaul had failed. Madero, who was working at Finschhafen on the New Guinea mainland, supplied a written statement, taken by his employer, Mr Pentland. He agreed that he had met X between Buna and Kokoda in 1942, that X was wearing a Japanese uniform and carrying a pistol and rifle. Madero said he had heard that X had killed some Australians but he did not remember who told him, or the name of the village.

Lieutenant Tuck concluded that Stehr's evidence alone would not be enough to bring a case against X, who was now living in Chinatown in Rabaul. Since the war, X had repeatedly denied to New Guinea Police Force investigators that he had collaborated with the Japanese. It's clear from Tuck's report that he distrusted Kramer's account, even though it was the most damning of X. Tuck believed that X had joined the *Kempeitai*, the hated Japanese secret police, on his return to Rabaul in November 1942. The investigation appears to have stopped there, stymied by lack of witnesses, or the quality of their recollections. X prospered in Rabaul after the war, his family running a successful business.

'Ben' Buckler retired from the army in the 1970s as a brigadier. He had never forgotten the men who died at Sangai. He kept asking questions, especially after two researchers found the Kramer interview in a file at the Australian War Memorial. Buckler submitted a Freedom of Information request in 1992. He and some senior veterans of the 2/14th Battalion wrote to the Keating government in March 1992, asking for the Sangai case to be reopened. They were angry that the government had earmarked $30 million for war crimes investigations in Europe, but the Sangai murders remained unsolved. They wanted to know if X was still alive, and if so, whether he could be extradited to Australia.

After five months, Buckler received a letter from a senior adviser to the Minister for Defence, Robert Ray, who said that it would be difficult to obtain permission from the Papua New Guinean government to interview witnesses. The adviser considered 'it would not be desirable to pursue the matter any further'. Ben Buckler died in February 1995. Further attempts to lobby successive Liberal ministers went nowhere.

The eight men who died at Sangai were eventually reburied at Bomana War Cemetery near Port Moresby. Reg Hunter lies there under his brother's name, Stanley Robert Hunter.

The real Stanley Robert Hunter survived the war and had two children – one of whom, Rhonda, has tried to have the gravestone error corrected by the Office of Australian War Graves, without success. Stanley, aka Maurie, never knew the details of his brother's death, which was perhaps a small mercy. He died in 1980, before the story of the massacre was told in newspaper reports in the mid-1990s. Rhonda was grateful when the 2/14th Battalion Association placed a plaque dedicated to Reg Hunter near the regimental monument at Heidelberg Repatriation Hospital in Melbourne. He is also mentioned on the Kokoda memorial at One Tree Hill near Tremont, Victoria.

The Japanese were eventually defeated on the Kokoda track and again at the beaches of Buna and Gona, where they had landed six months earlier. The concurrent American campaign at Guadalcanal in the Solomons further stretched Japan's resources, so that resupplying her troops became increasingly difficult. The defeats continued in a series of battles around Lae and the Ramu Valley in 1943. The tide had turned against the once invincible Japanese forces, but it would take another two years to complete the task.

After his court martial, Jack Blackman, the son of the police sergeant at Cootamundra, got his wish to return to the fighting. He reached Port Moresby in December 1942, only to go down with illness, which took him back to Brisbane. He was back in his old unit, the 2/13th, by June 1943, until he got scabies. He landed at Milne Bay at the end of July and fought with his old mates for the next seven weeks. He was killed in action on 22 September at Finschhafen, on the New Guinea coast north of Lae. He is buried in the Lae War Cemetery.

The *Tumut and Adelong Times* of 19 October 1943 reported his death.

'With all that the Cootamundra boy went through, he certainly proved himself to be a soldier and a man.'

That sentence brings us back to the question: was he boy or man? By the time of his death, having been once court-martialled, twice wounded and thrice enlisted, he was still only twenty years of age.

CHAPTER FIFTEEN

SHAPING THE TRUTH

BILLY DAVIS

DOUGLAS TAYLOR

Billy Davis is probably the youngest boy to enlist in the Australian army in the Second World War. He was thirteen years and two months when he signed on in Sydney, early in November 1941. His first enlistment was also one of the shortest, lasting about ten minutes.

'I got as far as the car that was to take me from Martin Place, when a recruiting officer came up and felt my chin,' Bill told a newspaper reporter. 'He caught me off guard. He asked me whether I had shaved and I told him I didn't have to – and that was the end of it.'

Soon after, he tried again for the militia, claiming he was eighteen. The recruiting office told him he should have sent in his registration papers when he turned eighteen, under the new limited-conscription scheme set up by Robert Menzies.

He went away and did that, but routed all correspondence to his local post office, rather than his home. That way, when he was automatically called up, his mother Laura wouldn't know.

William George Davis Junior had a special bond with his mother. She called him Billy. His letters during the war are very affectionate, signed with rows of kisses and little drawings, as he trailed around the Pacific on various ships. It's not clear whether he was as keen on his father.

William George Davis Sr (WG, for clarity) was a less than law-abiding citizen. He was born in 1909, 1910 or 1911 – he gave all three years at different times in different courts. In the Children's Court in 1927, aged somewhere less than eighteen, he was declared uncontrollable and remanded to

> 'I got as far as the car that was to take me from Martin Place, when a recruiting officer came up and felt my chin ... He asked me whether I had shaved and I told him I didn't have to – and that was the end of it.'

the custody of his mother, on probation. In May 1928, charged with receiving stolen goods, he was bound over on a five-year bond. In July 1929, charged with break and enter, he was given twenty-three months with hard labour.

On this occasion, he attracted press attention by representing himself in court, 'aged eighteen'. He had been charged with breaking into the home of one Michael Guerin of Bellevue Hill. The *Daily Telegraph* noted that he 'addressed the jury with the sangfroid of a KC [King's Counsel], and chatted to Judge Curlewis as though he were a bosom friend …'

The judge sentenced him to two years. The defendant responded like a shot: 'Make it a year and eleven months. You know what that means to me. And will you send me to Emu Plains? I can arrange for the wife to shift up there, and I'll be able to see the kid at weekends.'

The judge apparently agreed to the reduced sentence and the choice of Emu Plains gaol. Clearly, WG was a born negotiator, brimming with confidence and guile.

The kid he wanted to see at weekends was William Jr Billy. His parents had married on 31 March 1928, at St Michael's Church of England in Flinders Street, Surry Hills. WG was from Moore Park. Laura was from nearby Paddington, where her father William Stanley Green was a carter. WG and Laura were both seventeen. Their son arrived inconveniently early on 13 September 1928 – six months after the wedding.

Marriage did not reform WG. In December, he was convicted for selling 'sly grog' in Kendall Street, where he lived. Sly grog was slang for illegal after-hours liquor, in the days when pubs closed at 6pm. This was the first of three sly grog charges he received from 1930 to 1933. An undercover constable asked for six bottles of beer, then nabbed him when he produced them. For many working-class men, selling sly grog was a public service rather than a crime.

WG seems to have been only a part-time petty criminal. He was a bus conductor in 1928. There is no violence in his record and the convictions seem to end around 1934. They correspond largely with the worst years of the Depression.

As **WILLIAM DAVIS SENIOR** went off to war in 1940, **BILL DAVIS,** aged eleven, and mother, **LAURA,** posed for a family photo. William returned in February 1942 after serving in Malaya. Billy, by that time thirteen and a half, enlisted soon after.

The family home was not always a happy one. One family member remembers hearing that WG drank too much and could be abusive; she believes that Laura may have let Billy join the army in part to get him away from an unhappy home. The couple eventually separated, either during or sometime after the war.

WG joined the army in June 1940. He sailed with the 8th Division for Singapore in February 1941, as part of the 2/20th Battalion. He was a rowdy sort of soldier: he was fined and confined to barracks for seven days in April for breaking out of the barracks and being found in town in Seremban, Malaya. Having written on his forms that he was a baker, he was sent to work as one, but he acted up again. On 14 August, he was found 'interfering with civilians' and interfering 'with goods in a civilian shop' in Pudu Road, Kuala Lumpur. He copped hefty fines and seven days for both offences. He relinquished the baking and rejoined his unit in September, but by now, the army considered him medically unfit, because of recurring bronchitis. They sent him back to Australia in January 1942 and discharged him in February. He was lucky: many of the 2/20th would soon become prisoners of the Japanese.

The *Sydney Sun* of 10 May 1942 carried a story that made Billy Davis famous for a time. It was reprinted by many other papers. Most of them appeared under the headline: 'Boy of 13½ must leave army'.

The *Sun* told of his two previous attempts to enlist, how he succeeded a month earlier in his third attempt, and was then sent to the same country camp his father had passed through.

'My mother thought I was in the country picking peas, but when I wrote and mentioned that, like Dad, I had found the weather cold, I gave the show away,' he told the *Sun*. 'Mother realised that I was in camp, and now I am on my way out.'

Other newspapers shortened the report and claimed a different ending: WG had returned from Malaya, found his son enlisted and promptly got him out. The problem with that story is that Billy did not enlist until 13 March, and his father had been discharged from the army on 20 February. Unless WG did not go home for three weeks, they would have been under the same roof for some time before Billy enlisted.

The return of a stormy father may have caused Billy's departure. If his mother did let him go, why did he enlist under her surname, as William George Green? And why did he put her address as 92 Gibbs Street, Newtown? When WG went to war in 1940, he listed Laura at his home address, 80 Arthur Street, Moore Park.

Those addresses suggest that Laura had left her husband by March 1942, perhaps temporarily. Billy might have used her surname to stop his father finding him. He listed Laura, rather than his returned father, as next of kin. If that was his aim, it didn't work: he lasted twenty-three days, before someone tipped off the army and had him sent home. That would most likely have been his father. Despite his two setbacks, Billy wasn't done yet.

Who told the newspapers about Billy Davis in May 1942? There are many possibilities, including the army, which was always happy to encourage recruiting by promoting stories that were meant to shame the older men, but the most likely source was his father or mother. Parents were often exceptionally proud of their under-age sons going to fight – especially when they came home safe.

A number of the stories in this book came from newspapers. The trouble is that many of the reports are inaccurate, partly because the reporters were sloppy, or they were fed deliberate falsehoods. Some soldiers felt a strong need to exaggerate their war experiences, and that tendency may have been worse among the under-aged, who craved equal status with the older men. It was difficult for a country newspaper, or even a city one, to check what a soldier said he had done. His records were not public so the only danger was that another soldier might come forward to call out an exaggerator. That was rare, at least until after the war. Consequently, many of the news reports tell a different story to the records. Sometimes the records are wrong, and sometimes it's the soldier, either through faulty memory or a desire

to self-aggrandise. One of the effects of post-traumatic stress disorder, less understood at the time, is that it can be profoundly harmful to memory.

Douglas Alexander Taylor grew up in a family of tough guys. Around Leeton, in the Murrumbidgee Irrigation Area, the Taylors were known as a wild bunch, according to Doug's sister Maxine, who was the last of eight children. Their father, Alexander James Taylor, had been a bare-knuckle boxer and Aussie Rules footballer before the war. His father, William, had once been wealthy, owning a large tract of the land between Leeton and Yanco, but most of that wealth was gone by the Depression.

'My father (AJ) went off to war because they were very poor and he thought that five bob a day was better than starvation,' says Maxine.

AJ had been a fireman at the Yanco power station. He spent his days stoking a large wolf-furnace, hence his nickname, 'Woofie'. He married Elma Mary Farrell on 8 May 1926, when she was seventeen. She grew up near Wangaratta. AJ was almost twenty.

Douglas, their first child, arrived 28 January 1927. Another son, John Victor, arrived in December 1928, so the boys were thirteen and eleven when their father went to war in May 1940. AJ joined the 2/4th Battalion and was listed as 'missing' in the battle for Greece the following April. The family had an agonising wait of almost six months before the news came that he was alive, in a German prisoner of war camp.

'Douglas always wanted to go to war once his father did,' says Maxine. 'Mum always said he was a wild child, a very independent-minded boy. Dad used to let him run, but Mum was always worrying where he was.'

DOUGLAS TAYLOR'S enlistment papers were largely a work of fiction. He did not give his parents' real address, so they could not receive official mail. He had burned his bridges.

When his father left for war, Douglas, now thirteen and a half, declared that, as eldest boy, he was now head of the family. He looked older than he was, Maxine says. He tended to dominate his siblings, of whom there were now four, which caused tension. When the news came that their father was a prisoner, Douglas determined to go to war himself.

'Mum said he just took off, having said he was going to join the army. She took no notice. She thought if she let him go, the authorities would just say no. I think he wanted to join Dad.'

> 'Mum said he just took off, having said he was going to join the army. She took no notice. She thought if she let him go, the authorities would just say no. I think he wanted to join Dad.'

The authorities just said yes when he presented himself at Martin Place on his birthday, 28 January 1942. He was now fifteen, not thirteen and a half, as he would later tell the newspapers. His attestation papers were largely a work of fiction.

He gave himself a new surname – Thompson – but kept his Christian names, Douglas Alexander. He claimed to be an eighteen-year-old labourer from South Australia. For some reason, he said he was married, his wife residing at the Salvation Army Women's Hostel in the city. He listed his next of kin as Elma Mary Thompson. They were his mother's real given names but Maxine does not know why he picked Thompson as a surname.

The army mistook this as meaning that Elma was his wife instead of his mother, but the absence of a real address made it impossible for her to receive any official communications anyway. He had burned his bridges. Two days later he was in a training camp at Dubbo.

After five days, he reported the first of many illnesses. He went to hospital with influenza on 3 February, but when discharged eight days later, the diagnosis was measles. Two days later, he collapsed and was readmitted. After a fortnight, he was on a charge for using obscene language, for which he was given fourteen days' detention – a relatively severe punishment – and sent back to Sydney to convalesce.

On 25 March, he gave himself a day off and was charged with being absent without leave. He was fined a pound on that charge, and another four pounds for having a false leave pass. He now stepped up his absences – AWL for seven days in April, then five days in May. His sentences got longer: for the last he was given twenty-one days' detention.

In July, he transferred to a Brigade Ordnance Workshop in Bathurst – basically a heavy machinery outfit for maintaining all the army's guns and gadgets. In September, they sent him to another workshop in Queensland. Finally, he stepped off the boat in Port Moresby on 10 November 1942, and three days later he was hospitalised with a fever. He worked in an ordnance workshop on and off for the next few months,

between more bouts of sickness. In May 1943, he returned to Cairns.

In June he transferred to the 2/6th Australian Field Company of the Royal Australian Engineers. Again, he found trouble. He was fined five shillings for an undisclosed lapse in conduct on 7 July. On 22 July they shipped him back to New Guinea, where he got sick again, with appendicitis in October and cystitis in December.

By October the Australians had taken Lae and Nadzab on the New Guinea coast and were advancing inland up the Ramu Valley in pursuit of the Japanese. The aim was to force the enemy back over the Finisterre Range and link up with an American force pushing towards Madang. The fiercest fighting for the Finisterre Range would be on Shaggy Ridge, an impossibly steep feature on which the Japanese were well dug in.

Douglas spent Christmas with his unit before transferring in January 1944 to the 53rd Field Park Company, a mobile technical outfit engaged with demolition, explosives, road- and bridge-building,

Australians patrol forward in the Finisterre Ranges near Shaggy Ridge in New Guinea, in March 1944. Illness took a huge toll on the men in this campaign, including **DOUGLAS TAYLOR**.

sawmilling and blacksmithing. They were at Dumpu supplying much-needed supplies, like rope for the assault on Shaggy Ridge. They were near enough to be strafed by enemy planes.

The fight for Shaggy Ridge was another test of endurance. More than 200 Australian soldiers were killed and 464 wounded during the four-month campaign, but 13,000 men of the 7th Division were also evacuated sick. Nearly every man who fought there was succumbing to, or recovering from, illness.

In February, Douglas was evacuated again to the 2/5th Australian General Hospital, diagnosed with 'P.U.O.' or 'pyrexia (fever) of unknown origin'. In the First World War, where it was first recognised, this was called trench fever and was found to be transmitted by lice. It's hard to distinguish from malaria. In Douglas's case, his

diagnosis was later changed to 'enteritis' but he had another problem: the army had found out his real age. In mid-March he was shipped back to Australia for discharge, which eventually took effect on 5 April 1944. He was two months past his seventeenth birthday. He had served for twenty-seven months, and the most obvious result for him was a series of debilitating illnesses.

On 9 May 1943, the *Daily Advertiser* in Wagga – about an hour's drive from Leeton – carried a full report on his remarkable army career. The newspaper said he had enlisted at fourteen (wrong), three weeks after his mother heard about his father being a POW (probably wrong) and he had spent three years in the army (wrong) and saw eighteen months active service in New Guinea (wrong, it was fourteen months).

The report said he had served on the

> He was two months past his seventeenth birthday. He had served for twenty-seven months, and the most obvious result for him was a series of debilitating illnesses.

Kokoda track and at Buna and Gona (possible), and went on to detail what he had seen in the Ramu Valley campaign. 'He was in the thick of the fighting on Shaggy Ridge,' said the report, noting that his weight had dropped from 11 stone 5 pounds (72 kilograms) to 9 stone 2 pounds (58 kilograms), and that he had malaria eight times. 'On the morning that he was leaving Dumpu for Australia, Japanese bombers swooped down in a raid and scattered their bombs, but fortunately he was not wounded.' It's clear that Douglas was the source for the story, although it contains no direct quotes. It may have come from a stringer (freelancer) for the paper, from Leeton. The source of all the errors is difficult to determine. Taylor would have known his own record, but every under-age soldier knew how to shape the truth. They had to tell lies to get in, and keep telling them to stay in.

Billy Davis reappeared in the newspapers in November 1943, eighteen months after he had been sent home from his 23-day enlistment. The story in the *Sydney Sun* of 19 November told of how he faced a court martial the previous day, after making another attempt to get into uniform. This was literal: he borrowed the uniform of another soldier named Blake. He left his parents a note, saying, 'Dear Mum and Dad, don't go pulling me out again … You will think I am young and silly, Dad, but all the same I can't help this feeling inside me. Every time I hear you talk of Malaya, I want to be there … I know this will be hard on Mum but please don't pull me out.'

That note suggests that his parents were together again by late 1943.

Billy's plan this time was ingenious: he knew that John Leslie Blake, whose uniform he stole, was AWL. With his previous experience, Billy thought the punishment would be light, so he gave himself up to the authorities under this man's name. He did not know that Blake had been missing for six weeks and three days. When 'caught', they sent him for court martial.

The *Sydney Morning Herald* quoted the defending officer, who asked the court to consider whether it had any jurisdiction over this boy of fifteen, who was not the real John Blake. 'He had run away from his family to join the army, and had been attested at the age of thirteen years and some months. In April 1942 he had been discharged as Private William George Green as being under age.

'The lad, I am instructed, has not since been attested,' said his lawyer.

The president of the court adjourned proceedings to consider the matter. 'It appears that the accused is not subject to military discipline and that the court has no jurisdiction,' the president added.

This was apparently so, as there is no further reporting of the case. The reporter from the *Sun* quoted Billy's parents. 'His heart is so set on getting into the army, I would let him go if he were allowed,' said his mother.

His father said he had lined up a job for him with a greengrocer in Cronulla, a southern suburb of Sydney, but selling greens was never going to satisfy young William. In February 1944, he joined the US Army Small Ships, signing on until 29 August.

Initially, this makeshift little navy was composed of hundreds of small craft, requisitioned in Australia and New Zealand to support the American war effort in New Guinea and the islands. There were fishing trawlers, pearling luggers, Sydney ferries, tugboats, ketches and schooners, a banana boat that had once been a destroyer and a Tasmanian timber trader, the *Lorrina*, skippered by an Austro-Hungarian who had once commanded a German U-boat. They carried everything and anything north to support the Allied forces, and sometimes brought back the wounded and the dead. In a few places, they landed soldiers on coasts that the bigger American ships could not get into, because of uncharted reefs.

The Small Ships section was initially administered by the US Army Services of

BILLY DAVIS in the uniform of the AIF. He was court-martialled in late 1943 for wearing another soldier's uniform. The court agreed it had no jurisdiction, since he was not actually enlisted.

Supply, and it would take nearly anybody with a desire to serve and sail, including boys as young as fifteen. During 1942 and '43, this became another back door to the war for both the under- and over-aged. The oldest crew member was seventy years old. Some had been gassed in the First World War; at least two had served in the Boer War.

Billy Davis spent most of the next four years on the salty sea. His first ship was the SS *Noora*, a British coastal steamer from 1924, taken over in November 1942 from the Adelaide Steamship Company. *Noora* took him to Milne Bay on the Papuan coast; Buna, Saidor and Finschhafen on the New Guinea coast; and the islands of Manus and Los Negros, north-east of the New Guinea mainland. This was not all plain sailing: at some point in this service, he was wounded and won a citation for bravery under fire. He signed on again in October on the *Beltana*, until August 1945. After the war, he re-enlisted in 1946 in the militia, but continued on their small ships to Bougainville and the Solomons. He made at least seven trips to Japan, in support of the British Commonwealth Occupation Force, through to his discharge in November 1948.

His letters to his mother continued throughout these years, with noticeable American influences that he might not have fully understood: 'Hi there, kid,' he starts, on a note telling her he won't be home for Christmas, because the ship is heading to Wewak. In one of his final letters for 1948, he signs off, 'See you in a week (hubba hubba)'. Photos from the time show him as a trim and well-dressed young man, in a well-tailored American-style uniform. He looks like he is having a ball.

Douglas Taylor rejoined the militia

> Douglas Taylor rejoined the militia in July 1945, giving his correct age for the first time. He was now eighteen, and this time, single.

in July 1945, giving his correct age for the first time. He was now eighteen, and this time, single. He broke his left clavicle soon after, went AWL again for a few hours and contracted scabies. His malaria returned in 1946, along with other ailments and a curious recurring problem with head injuries – concussions, contusions, lacerations. In July, he told the army he had married a woman called Edith, from Singleton. They had a son together. The marriage was not successful.

Doug's young brother John joined the British Commonwealth Occupation Force in Japan in 1947. He was killed there in November 1948, run down at night by an army truck driven by a drunk Australian soldier. Maxine was born five days after he died.

She remembers meeting Douglas once in about 1953, when she was five. He was kind to her and her siblings, buying them toys. Then he disappeared, never to be seen or heard from again. 'His marriage broke up, and he didn't want to pay maintenance for Edith's two earlier kids, so he shot through – possibly to Rum Jungle in the Northern Territory. My mother tried many times to find him.'

After her parents died, Maxine also tried to find him. She believes he ended up in South Australia, living under a different name, possibly Peter Thompson, and that he died there.

Billy Davis got married in late 1949 and had two kids. He worked on the trams in Sydney, then joined the Electricity Commission of New South Wales and remained there until he retired. His daughter Wendy King says he endured a lot of health problems and lived longer than he should have, but he had a strong will. 'He was determined to watch his grandsons grow up.' He died in 2001, aged seventy-two.

CHAPTER SIXTEEN

PARADISE FOUND

FRANK McGREEVY

FRANK McGREEVY enlisted in 1942 because all of his mates in Rockhampton were going. He was not in the least patriotic.

Frank McGreevy didn't like the cold. Most of his war would be in the tropics. Careful what you wish for.

He was born in September 1924 at Toogoolawah, north-west of Brisbane, where the family had a dairy farm. His earliest memory is being sprayed in the face with milk straight from the cow in the milking sheds. He has no memory of his father, who died when he was four.

'He was in the 2nd Light Horse in the First World War and he got some disease over there and never shook it off.'

After Frank's father died, the family moved to Brisbane, where Frank lived long stretches with relatives, partly to take the pressure off his mother, Catherine. It was the Depression. 'If I got a ha'penny, I was excited,' he remembers.

Frank left school in 1939, aged fifteen. He had no plan, and little understanding that there was a war on. His first job, in a factory, was so filthy, he lasted a month. Percy Bremner, a friend of his mother's, gave him a lead to a job at Sidney Williams Ltd in Rockhampton, where Bremner was employed. Their prefab huts, shearing sheds and Comet windmills were famous across the outback, as far as the Northern Territory.

Frank's wage of thirteen shillings a week did not even pay for his bed and board at the Great Western Hotel. He did jobs around the hotel and his mother sent extra money. One of his jobs was to sit outside the pub on a Sunday, when the hotel was not allowed to serve alcohol, acting as the 'cockatoo' who warned the Sunday sippers that 'Waxy' the policeman was coming down the road on his bicycle.

'We all used to go to church first,' Frank remembers. They were all Brisbane men working on construction, most of them Catholic like Frank. Someone gave him a bicycle, so he could keep up with his friends, who were a few years older.

> 'We never talked about the war. The war meant nothing to me. I had no intention of going ...'

'We never talked about the war. The war meant nothing to me. I had no intention of going ...'

By 1942, Frank had been in Rockhampton for nearly three years. All of his friends were enlisting. He was not in the least driven by patriotism – 'not one bit'. He just didn't want to be left behind. He went to the drill hall to register, saying he was born in 1923, not 1924. He was still only seventeen. In due course, a notice arrived, calling him up for compulsory militia service. He was to report in May. He had no idea of what it meant to be a soldier; he had never met one.

The recruiting officer didn't ask for proof of age, but he did have to get his mother's signature. She didn't argue; her boy was almost a man.

The army sent him to Brisbane, then Goondiwindi, one of the coldest places in Queensland. 'It was the start of a camp. All the tents were confiscated from the public because they didn't have any tents ... We had no rifles to train with, we had very little bits of uniform. It was cold and raining and muddy. We were on parade one morning and they called for volunteers, and I said to Dickie Welch, "Come on, we're volunteering for this." Dickie was from Rockhampton, my best mate.

'He said, "Whaddya mean?" I said, "We're outta here, we're not staying here." He said, "What are we volunteering for?" I said, "I don't know, but we're out." So we stepped forward. I suppose there were 250 of us. They hit us with needles, vaccinations, and after about a week, we were on the train again.'

They still did not know what they had volunteered for. So far he had no uniform, no gun, and no idea where they were going. The train rattled north for some days till it reached Townsville. He noticed that large numbers of American soldiers were flooding into Queensland.

'The train took us about thirty miles past Townsville to a place called Calcium. There we were issued clothing – the discarded uniforms of the cane-cutters we were replacing. Cane-cutting was a reserved occupation, so these blokes had been sent back to work in the cane fields. We were to replace them in the 19th Field Ambulance. It was part

of the 11th Brigade, which consisted of the 26th, 31st and 51st battalions. It had the 16th Field Engineers, us, and all the auxiliaries.'

The purpose of a field ambulance unit is to bring wounded out from the battlefield: they are usually the first line of medical treatment. Frank had no medical training. This was the army: aptitude had nothing to do with it. He was now a medic, and about as useful to a wounded man as a get-well card. He soon learned the basics: how to staunch bleeding, bandage a wound and splint a broken bone. He had sulfanilamide powder for infections, and the new wonder drug penicillin, developed in 1939, but no painkillers. The Americans had morphine ampoules for their wounded; the Australian soldier just had to put up with pain.

After about eight weeks, he was put on a train with men from the 26th Battalion, heading north. At Chillagoe, someone told him he was the medic for this unit. 'This was the first time I knew what I was doing. I had trouble putting a bandaid on, but here I am, the aid man for about 150 blokes.'

They were sent to guard a new American airbase carved out of the bush at Iron Range, near Portland Road on Cape York. The Americans were flying Liberator bombers and Flying Fortresses against Japanese targets in New Guinea, including Rabaul. Here he saw his first serious casualty – a gunner who lost half his foot to a stray fragment of metal. He cleaned up the

> Frank had no medical training. This was the army: aptitude had nothing to do with it. He was now a medic, and about as useful to a wounded man as a get-well card.

FRANK McGREEVY and comrades from the 2/19th Field Ambulance dig in on Bougainville, probably early 1945.

wound and took the man to the American hospital. The soldier was Australian 'but we had no doctors up there'.

He rejoined his unit at Kuranda, in the Atherton Tableland, where they were training for jungle warfare. Each soldier was issued with a packet of green dye, to change the colour of his uniform from khaki to green, to match the jungle.

Townsville was the nearest town with entertainment but Frank says it was not all beer and skittles. 'You couldn't get much beer in Townsville. In those days XXXX never even went as far as Rockhampton. XXXX used to stop at Raglan, which is forty miles south of Rockhampton, and Rockhampton had its own brewery, McLaughlin's. There were 60,000 Yanks stationed around Rockhampton.'

Frank preferred the small town of Kuranda, where he used to attend dances. This is where he earned his battalion nickname 'Luvver'. The less said the better.

'You could not go into Townsville on your own, because there were too many troops there and most of them were Yanks. They used to fight amongst themselves.'

In April of that year, Frank transferred to the AIF, along with most of his unit. In effect, they became 19th Field Ambulance of the second AIF. That was necessary to send them to Merauke, in Dutch New Guinea.

They sailed at the end of May 1943. Merauke was a swampy, mosquito-infested outpost with an airstrip that made them a frequent target of Japanese air raids.

'I've never seen so many snakes in all my life.'

> Merauke was a swampy, mosquito-infested outpost with an airstrip that made them a frequent target of Japanese air raids … They spent almost a year there, dodging the bombs, the boredom and the blazing sun.

They spent almost a year there, dodging the bombs, the boredom and the blazing sun. Frank had by now shaved his head to avoid the nits, but he suffered badly from the sun. The soldiers didn't know about the dangers of skin cancer.

His unit returned to Australia in August 1944, for rest and recuperation. Many of them were sick. At Merauke, the daily issue included an Atebrin tablet for malaria, a large salt tablet, ascorbic acid (vitamin C) and various ointments for dermatitis and tinea. Frank had problems with his ears, eyes and skin (from the green dye), as well as dysentery.

By late 1944, General Douglas MacArthur's US forces had landed on the Marshall Islands and Guam and were heavily engaged in the battle for the Philippines. MacArthur's plan was to push the Japanese back across the Pacific, island by island, bypassing and isolating them to cut off their supply routes. He had wanted to take the stronghold of Rabaul, but the Joint Chiefs of Staff in Washington would not authorise enough troops.

In late 1943, US Marines made an amphibious landing at Cape Torokina,

on the west coast of Bougainville in the North Solomon Islands. Here they established a perimeter along 25 kilometres of coastline, with airstrips and naval facilities. These were used to cripple Japanese operations further north around New Britain and New Ireland. By the end of 1944, the Japanese troops on Bougainville were effectively cut off from resupply, but no-one knew how many were hiding in the mountains that ran the length of the island.

Bougainville is 120 kilometres long and 65 to 95 kilometres wide, a Pacific paradise of coconut palms, volcanoes, white sand beaches and crystal-clear water, with a central range rising to 8500 feet (2600 metres). On the western side, the rivers are fed by 2.5 metres of annual rainfall, which made them difficult to ford. By the time the Australians took over at Torokina in December 1944, the war there had reached a kind of stasis. Without resupply, the Japanese would eventually surrender or starve. The Australian historian Gavin Long estimated that as many as 16,000 Japanese died during the period the Americans were at Torokina, and another 8000 in battle.

Torokina was like a small American town, with both static and mobile cinemas, various messes for officers and other ranks, a radio station, printing works and a functioning library. There was also a brief but flourishing black market, between the Yanks, who were better paid and supplied, and the Aussies, who were skilled at deal-making, not to mention theft. American officers had access to whisky (ten pounds), rum and gin (seven pounds), and were happy to trade, despite regulations. Beer was ten shillings. Cigarettes and lighters were popular items of barter. As usual, the Australian Comforts Fund, the Salvation Army and the YMCA were not far behind the Australian troops. All that was lacking was someone to shoot at.

The Australian II Corps, under Lieutenant-General Stanley Savige, consisted of twelve battalions, eight of them from Queensland. The Americans had ceased gathering intelligence on Japanese activities outside their perimeter after a major Japanese assault on Torokina failed in March 1944. They even recalled the coastwatchers who had been hiding in various parts of the island, reporting enemy strengths and movements, with the help of local villagers. The Australians sent new coastwatching units out, to restart the reconnaissance.

At the handover, there were conflicting analyses of how many Japanese were on the island. The Americans estimated 12,000; Australian intelligence said more like 25,000. They were pooh-poohed by the Americans for saying so. After the war, it became clear there were more than 40,000 Japanese on Bougainville at the time.

One question less often asked is why the Australians were there at all. The Australian Commander-in-Chief Thomas Blamey had been sidelined by Douglas MacArthur, whose headquarters were now at Leyte in the Philippines. MacArthur consistently omitted the role of the Australian forces in his communiques about the war, to suit his own purposes and those of an American public eager to hear that their troops were winning the war single-handed.

The Australians took over the American base at Torokina on the west coast of Bougainville in late 1944. It was like a small US town, with a library, two cinemas, a radio station and printing works.

Under an agreement between the Australian government and his headquarters, the Australian press was prohibited from writing about any location of war that had not been first outlined by those communiques. Thus, from late 1944 until March 1945, the Australian public heard almost nothing about what their troops were doing in New Guinea, or the war in the Pacific in general. The American public heard even less. This led to speculation in the Australian press that our men were not being used to fight, so what were they doing up there?

The campaign on Bougainville consequently took on a political imperative, especially for Blamey, who needed to prove

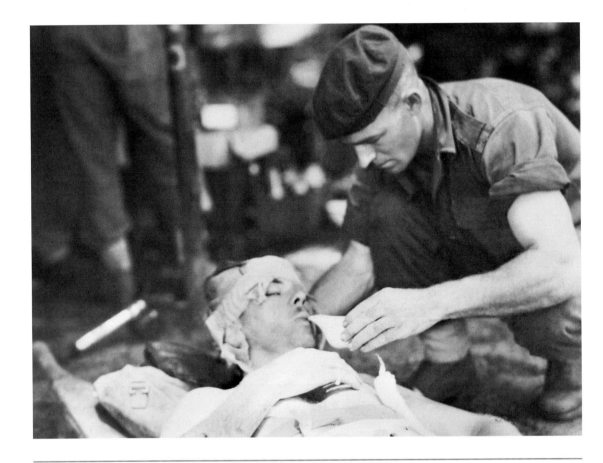

FRANK McGREEVY remembers the photographer taking pictures on this day, 6 February 1945, at Tsimba Ridge on Bougainville. Here, **PADRE CHARLES** of the Salvation Army assists **PRIVATE AC SMITH**. The wounded McGreevy was patched up at the same regimental aid post.

that his troops were doing their job, killing Japanese. The Australians were to take an active role, mopping up the enemy, rather than waiting for them to starve.

Offensive patrolling began, both north and south along the coast, and into the mountains. In truth, that probably suited a lot of Blamey's men. They preferred action to boredom, if they had to be in uniform. But, as in Crete, Ambon and Timor, hundreds were to die to prove his point: 516 men, to be specific.

A number of them were Frank Mc-Greevy's friends. He arrived there as part of the 11th Brigade on 12 December 1944. They were in action soon after.

The battalions had been amalgamated after previous losses in the Middle East, so Frank was now serving beside men of the 31/51st Battalion, and the 55/53rd Battalion. He remembers that the strategy was to leapfrog patrols along the coast: some men would walk the coast for a certain distance, perhaps 10 kilometres, while their relief came up by barge. The relief would then take over and walk the next ten.

'It was a disgraceful operation ... I don't think anyone knows why we were there ... The Japs couldn't hurt us, or do a thing. The Yanks wanted to let 'em starve to death.'

In January 1945, he took part in the attack on Tsimba Ridge, an outcrop

about 120 metres long on the north-west coast of the island, near the Soraken peninsula. The Japanese had trenches and pillboxes along the top of the ridge, and were determined to make a stand. They resisted for two weeks, from 21 January to 9 February.

'At Tsimba Ridge, I got hit on the 6th of February. I was patrolling with the 31/51st, about a platoon worth. A mortar landed amongst us. Bailey, about that far away from me [2 metres], he was laying down, I thought what's wrong with him? One chap said, "Where's all the blood coming from?" I said, "I've got no idea." Next thing I see my wrist pouring blood, so we wrapped it up as best we could, turned Bailey over and his throat was gone. There was shooting and grenades going off and people yelling, "Keep down, keep down". It was my left hand

> 'It was a disgraceful operation ... I don't think anyone knows why we were there ... The Japs couldn't hurt us, or do a thing. The Yanks wanted to let 'em starve to death.'

Tsimba Ridge was the first time Frank had come under direct fire, and his unit's first casualties. He remembers his reaction. 'I was very scared at first, but then you just settle down.'

so I joined in and threw a few grenades with my right.'

At some point, Frank lost consciousness and woke surrounded by Australians in clean, new uniforms. 'I still don't know where they come from … Their uniforms had me tricked because they were all new … I must have been unconscious for a few minutes.'

The dead man was Dave Bailey, from western New South Wales, a member of the ambulance unit. 'I knew him well. We had two Baileys and both of them got killed. The other one was "Sucker" Bailey and he was a good mate of mine.'

Tsimba Ridge was the first time Frank had come under direct fire, and his unit's first casualties. He remembers his reaction. 'I was very scared at first, but then you just settle down.'

Frank helped another wounded man walk down the hill, and back to the regimental aid post. They sent Frank back to Torokina. The *Official History of Australia in the War of 1939–45* says nine Australians were killed on Tsimba Ridge and twenty wounded. The Japanese lost sixty-six men.

Frank spent three weeks at an army hospital at Torokina. He returned to his unit on 3 March.

'They issued me a new uniform so I was the cleanest bloke in our unit. They give me the discharge papers from hospital and when I get back to camp, there's a truck with about a dozen men in the back … they're all givin' me the "coo-ee" for my smart uniform, all my own unit. This medical captain walked round and said, "Get on that truck." I said, "After I go to the Orderly Room and give them my discharge papers, I'm on light duties." He said, "Get on that truck." So I got on the truck and away we went. We pulled up not far along and there was a couple of ambulances and the trail was roped off. What's going on? A bloke says, well that is a minefield. We didn't know anything about this minefield. He said, "We've got two sections in there … and we've gotta go in and bring 'em out."

'So the captain says, away you go. I said to this captain, "Well they will want a doctor in there." And he said, "You bring 'em out here and I'll patch 'em up." So we went in, following the left side of

FRANK McGREEVY believes he is one of the stretcher cases (at left) in this picture of wounded being evacuated from Tsimba Ridge, Bougainville, 6 February 1945.

a ribbon. There was about four or five dead, I don't know how many wounded … oh shit, there were some badly wounded. I said, "We'll patch these ones up but those ones, who are not badly wounded, take them out to that prick." So they took 'em out. I said, "When you get there, roll 'em off the stretchers and come back here and we'll have these boys all bandaged up and ready for you." So back they came and they took them out and this captain said, "Why didn't you bring these out first?"

'So I said, "No, you were safer out here, and they were too badly hurt to be done twice." I said it was "straight to the ambulance" for them. I had hold of a stretcher and one bloke said, "Hey,

you got out of hospital this morning."
He took the stretcher and the captain
said, "Oh, you're bludging again." I just
looked at him like … then someone told
him to shut up. And he swung round,
"Who said that, who said that?" So I
said, "It coulda been me but it wasn't."

'Next morning he come looking for me
and said I've got light duties for you. This
went on for three days, working every
day. So I got a rifle and Bill Cowan, the
sergeant major, said, "What are you doing
with that?" I said, "I'm gonna shoot that
bastard. I'm gonna shoot that bastard
now." He grabbed the rifle and took it off
me and said you can't do that. "Well,"
I said, "you better get me out of here."
There was a truck going up to the front.
Righto, I'm going with them. I was that
upset, I would have shot him, without a …
oh yeah, I was gonna shoot the bastard …
We come back from the front about two
weeks before the war was finished.'

Frank's unit then moved to Rabaul,
where about 60,000 Japanese men were
now prisoners. Frank had his twenty-first
birthday there. His new duties appalled
him: he was sent to a native hospital
where Australian doctors hardly bothered
with wards full of indigenous patients.

'The doctors weren't looking after
them at all … First thing I had to do was
clear about ten dead patients out of their
beds in the wards. I told them where
they could stick their job.'

Frank was discharged from the army in
Brisbane, at the end of January 1946. He
had served for 1348 days.

I asked him what he did after the war.

'I drank beer for about two years. I
couldn't settle down. I went back to
Rockhampton for a while, and walking
down the main street, a chap said, "Do
you want a job?" I said, "We just got
out of the army, don't be silly." He said,
"Ten shillings an hour, today is Saturday,
it will be a pound an hour, loading boats
down at Port Alma." Wharf labourer.'
He had three or four months' casual
labour on the Fitzroy River.

In down times, he drank. 'We used to
just drink, and drink, and drink. I used
to scoot down three or four pots, and
I would go for a piss and it would just
come out like a gusher, and then I could
sit down and drink all day.'

The drinking started in the army, when they could get it. It took off after Bougainville, where he had his worst moments of the war.

'When we did the aptitude test for careers, I put in to be a carpenter. They give us this test and I am just sitting there looking at it, thinking, good god, this must be to fill in time. The sergeant came over to ask, "Are you stuck?" It was to see if you were capable of handling a tradesman's course. He took my papers away and everyone else is still doing the papers, and he says, "The major wants to see you." The major said, "You applied to be a carpenter, what about being an engineer?" I said, "Oh, I don't think so. I'd have to sit there studying and be told … that'll take two or three years. For the last four years I've been told what to do every day, I don't think I could put up with it …" I just wanted to get back on the booze. I would wake up of a night-time shaking and fighting the bed.'

I ask if he had nightmares.

'Oh, I had heaps. My wife Hazel passed away about six years ago and a couple of times, her skin was very delicate and I was kicking, and I put her in hospital twice with my nightmares, just flailing around. About three years before she passed away, I had my last one.'

Our conversation took place at Frank's home in Coolum, more than seventy-five years after the war ended. The symptoms had been with him since the 1940s, and had not lessened with time. 'I don't think it got worse or better. It just keeps bubbling along.'

Even so, he has no regrets about going to war, even under-age.

'No-one forced me to go, and I was quite happy in the army. I had plenty of freedom. Matter of fact, I think my army days were my best days.' ✿

FRANK McGREEVY, photographed at home on the Sunshine Coast in late 2021.

CHAPTER SEVENTEEN

BREAD AND BUTTER AND JAM

DAVID CURRY
ROY CROSSLEY

By late 1943, the signs were clear that Germany and Japan were losing the war in their respective hemispheres. The Allies then began to plot against each other about who would win the peace.

There were many areas of contention, played out across the continents in diplomatic cables. Aviation was a central issue, as it was to the war itself.

Australia wanted to establish an aviation industry capable of building large planes, so the Australian prime minister John Curtin agreed with Britain to build Lancaster bombers in Australia. General Douglas MacArthur, heading the Allied forces in the Pacific, opposed the plan. American aviation companies wanted that market for themselves. The Americans had built airfields all over the Pacific, but Britain informed them that those on Commonwealth territory – in places like Malaya and Fiji – would be owned by Britain. The Americans were appalled: their men were dying to build these airstrips, and they would have to hand them over to the old colonial power once they defeated Japan? It wasn't right.

Having spearheaded the fight against the Japanese in 1942, before the Americans arrived, Australia was now sidelined by MacArthur in his push to retake the Philippines and defeat Japan. The victory should be America's alone; so too the spoils of victory, in terms of influence and territory in Asia and the Pacific. But the Americans could not fight a Pacific war without the food and support provided by Australia. By 1944, Australia was chronically short of manpower for food production. Curtin and treasurer Ben Chifley ordered the slimming down of the armed forces, so that men could return to farm work. In David Day's memorable phrase, 'it was time to start putting butter before guns'.

Curtin could see that the major powers would not easily offer Australia a chair at the peace talks. Australia had to be in a position to demand one, on the basis of what it had contributed to the war. If that meant keeping three divisions in the field, fighting and dying in tropical backwaters far from the tip of the American spear, that was a cost that had to be borne. Not by Curtin or General

Thomas Blamey, who argued strongly for staying in the field, but by men like David Curry and Roy Crossley, who were not yet men at all.

The final year of the war for Australia was about influence, not territory, which is why many veterans were bitter about fighting battles 'that did not need to be fought', in places like Bougainville and Borneo. The words 'mopping up' became bitter in their mouths.

Curry and Crossley were born weeks apart in 1926, at opposite ends of the country – Crossley in Perth in September, Curry in Sydney in December. Both grew up in the school of hard knocks. For them, butter was scarce well before the war.

I met both men in 2020 in New South Wales. David Curry was living quietly in Port Macquarie, crediting golf for his obvious fitness. Roy was less mobile in Pottsville, but full of humour, even after a stroke. Both still had remarkable recall of their war years, and no regrets about going as under-age boys.

It says a lot about the lives they had led before the war that both Curry and Crossley thought army food was terrific.

David Curry remembers that he was hungry through much of his childhood during the Depression. He and his four siblings – three brothers and a sister – lived in North Annandale in a house that was never peaceful. His parents were

> The final year of the war for Australia was about influence, not territory, which is why many veterans were bitter about fighting battles 'that did not need to be fought', in places like Bougainville and Borneo.

DAVID CURRY remembers being hungry through most of his childhood during the Depression. He thought the food in the army was terrific.

from Belfast, in Northern Ireland. His father had fought in the Irish Fusiliers and the Royal Flying Corps during the First World War. His mother had worked in a munitions factory in London, and was an accomplished coloratura soprano. By 1930, they had fallen on hard times.

'Every day was fight day, mainly because my mother never stopped nagging, nagging, nagging. She never stopped talking, you know. I can understand my father getting frustrated … She had a violent temper,' he says.

David remembers her swinging his sister June by the hair.

'Last time she took the whip to us, both my brother Cyril and myself, we were stripped naked … I think that sort of turned me. I just could not understand a mother doing that, and conniving to get us undressed …'

Their crime was stealing peaches from a neighbour's orchard. They had been warned, but David could see fruit rotting on the ground, and food was scarce. He grew up under-sized. Their mother waited until bedtime, till they took off their clothes, then took to them in a locked bedroom with a horse whip. After the ordeal, the boys agreed they would get away from home at the first chance. It took David four years, so he must have been about eleven when this beating occurred.

The family had moved to Bass Hill on the very outskirts of Sydney in 1935, to a new housing commission home. David loved school and reading, but the only books in the house were a Bible and a dictionary. He was the only one of his siblings to qualify for high school but it didn't last. He left school at fourteen and found a job in a tool-making company.

By 1942, he was thinking about joining the war. He was now fifteen. His father had joined the RAAF and been sent to Perth to build airstrips. His elder brother Harry had enlisted. That left David as the eldest at home, the target of his mother's temper.

ROY CROSSLEY went to work on a sheep station near Lithgow at the age of twelve, when his mother could not afford to keep him. He enlisted at fourteen and eight months, still too young to shave.

His first attempt to enlist failed: the recruiting officer said, 'Go home, sonny'. He became more wily. All boys of eighteen had to register for conscription: he went to the recruiting office in Bankstown with a story about having just arrived back from a farm near Lismore. He said he had been born in Belfast and had lost his passport. They told him to return in two days for a medical. A week later he was in the militia. It was November 1942.

He told his mother he was joining the Civil Construction Corps to help build the new road from Alice Springs to Darwin. She soon realised that he was lying and contacted the army, but he had anticipated that. On his forms, he had changed the spelling of his surname and reversed his given names, to become Edward David Currie, so that she would never find him.

Roy Crossley had experienced a similarly tough childhood. His parents had come east from Perth, his fa-ther looking for work as the Depression hit. Jean, his mother, had seven children from a previous marriage. She and Sam Crossley had twins – Roy and Allan.

Sam got a job building Bunnerong Power Station in Sydney but he was laid off. He could not afford the rent on their flat in Kensington, and was about to move the family to La Perouse, to a camp of makeshift shelters known as Happy Valley. A man offered him a shack at a disused quarry in Maroubra: he could be the caretaker, and live rent free.

'The place was full of fleas,' Roy remembered. 'Took 'em three weeks to get all the fleas out. I went there when I was six, and stayed there till I was ten. I went to Maroubra Junction school and got called before the headmaster. He said, "Crossley if you come to school again without your shoes on, I will send you straight back home." I said, "Sorry, sir, I haven't got any shoes." He was dumbfounded, never asked me again. I got winter sores on my feet. Didn't have a great time.'

There was just enough food to go round. 'One day a cat brought in a big rabbit, to show off what she caught, and my mother grabbed it. We had it for stew that night.'

Roy didn't like school, so he stopped going. 'My father hated authority. This truant officer came and said, "Your son Roy hasn't been going to school, we will send him to Mittagong Boys' Home." My dad said, "How can I stop that? If I give him a good hiding, will that do?" The inspector said, "Yeah, that'll do," so Dad belted the shit outta me. ' Roy laughed. 'My mother tried to stop him and he pushed her over and she said, "I'm not staying, that's it." She packed up the two of us and took us to live in Darlinghurst, in one of them places below the footpath …'

Jean told Roy she could not keep both boys. As the stronger one, he would have to go and work. The Lindsays, family friends, owned a sheep station between Bathurst and Hill End. Roy went to work there. He got no wages for the first three months.

'The Lindsays could not believe my father had belted me, but they could see the bruises. He had a piece of timber about that wide and belted hell out of me. He woulda been jailed these days.'

Roy understood why his father had belted him, just not the severity. He had stopped going to school because he got caned all the time. He was not good at English and spelling, always in trouble, although he excelled in mathematics. He thinks he was probably dyslexic.

He was now a twelve-year-old farm worker. There were no luxuries and no women – just the two Lindsay brothers and 2500 sheep. Roy worked hard, getting up at 4.30am. When not working, he trapped rabbits for food. He sold the pelts in Bathurst. He had to buy and cook his own food.

'They had a big old original farmhouse. They used to do the washing up every three months. They would pile up all the plates on the sink. You turned your plate over when you were finished so the rats wouldn't run over it.'

He lasted two years, then returned to Sydney, finding a job in a factory making shells for 25-pounder guns. He gave his mother two thirds of what he earned.

He was now fourteen. 'Yeah, I was a man,' said Roy. 'I was a pretty solid lad because of the work I did on the sheep station.'

He started thinking about the army. He went to the recruiting office at Moore Park in Sydney, early in 1941.

'Every time I went down there the bloke would come along, he had lost one arm in the First World War, and he had a clipboard under his arm, what was left of it, and he would come along and say, "You, you and you, piss off home to your mother. You're under-age." He could pick it straight away. Twice I done that. Third time he come along and he said, "You, you and you, I know youse are only eighteen, you can join the Coastal Defences." They needed men for searchlights and anti-aircraft guns. I said, "That's better than nothing." At least, I was in uniform.'

Roy believes the army always knew he was under-age.

'Course they did. I was only in the army two days, an officer come along at morning parade and asked me if I shaved. I said, "No, sir, I don't shave." He said, "You better start now and get that bum fluff off your face."'

This was May 1941. Roy was fourteen years and eight months old, which makes him one of the youngest Australians to enlist in this war. He was posted to Middle Head in Sydney to learn how to fire a 3-inch anti-aircraft gun. Roy believes that about half of the boys in 1 Anti-Aircraft Brigade were under-age. It was a way of training them so that they could be ready, when they turned nineteen, to transfer to the AIF. His unit was about to be shipped

Roy was fourteen years and eight months old, which makes him one of the youngest Australians to enlist in this war.

Members of **ROY CROSSLEY'S** unit, the 2/2 Machine Gun Battalion, on the way to an amphibious landing at Brunei Bay with infantry of the 2/17th Battalion, 10 June 1945.

to Rabaul when he caught the mumps. It probably saved his life.

Of the fifty-five men of 1 Anti-Aircraft Brigade who went to Rabaul, only six came home. Later in the war, he learned what happened to these men. It gave him nightmares for some years.

Japan entered the war while he was at Port Kembla, training on the 3.7-inch anti-aircraft gun. His application to transfer to the AIF was refused, so in January 1942, he went AWL. He dressed in civilian clothes and enlisted at Martin Place, Sydney, as Roy Lindsay, on 13 January 1942. He was sent to Dubbo to the 19th Battalion reinforcements, destined for Malaya. Most of those who went to Malaya ended up dead or prisoners of the Japanese. He was lucky again – the fall of Singapore in February 1942 stopped the plan to send his unit. Reassigned to reinforce the 53rd Battalion, he finally shipped out in March, to New Guinea. He remembered being so seasick on the trip north that he hoped the Japanese would torpedo the boat so he could swim ashore. His first job was to guard the airport at Seven Mile in Port Moresby.

'We manned Lewis guns against the Japanese fighters who were accompanying their bombers. They flew over and dropped their bombs at about 11am every day. This was followed by strafing from the Zeros. Our guns were fairly ineffectual but that was our only defence until the Americans sent in some P-40 fighters.'

After two months, he came down with dysentery and was sent back to Australia. While he was in Concord repatriation hospital in Sydney, his mother told the

> Of the fifty-five men of 1 Anti-Aircraft Brigade who went to Rabaul, only six came home. Later in the war, he learned what happened to these men. It gave him nightmares for some years.

army that he was fifteen. They discharged him on 15 October 1942, just after he turned sixteen.

Both Roy Crossley and David Curry found army life easy, after what they had known as boys. 'The army was a breeze,' said Roy. 'I thought it was great. New warm clothing, they even give us long underwear, and meals … oh beautiful, three meals a day.'

David Curry had grown up in a house where you could have bread and butter, or bread and jam, but never all three. When he got to the army mess, he saw butter, bread and jam on the table. He had to ask a fellow recruit if he was allowed to have all three at once.

The fall of Singapore also affected David's progress towards the war. The number of young soldiers killed or captured there had been controversial: Curtin had a bet each way. The government dropped the legal age of enlistment in the AIF to eighteen in 1943, but no soldier could serve overseas until he was nineteen years old. They also changed the legislation to allow militia conscripts to fight outside Australian territory. The messages were confusing: young men of eighteen had to enlist, but they couldn't go anywhere till they were nineteen.

David had qualified as a 'Don R' – a motorcycle despatch rider – but he was now relegated to the Army Service Corps, delivering rations to units around Sydney. He bounced around training camps in Australia for most of the next year. He went through the gruelling jungle training course at Canungra, where they used live ammunition to teach the men to keep their heads down, and eighteen-hour route marches to harden their feet. He learned to drive a truck and was sent to the 2nd Australian Beach Landing Group, at Trinity Beach north of Cairns, expecting to be a driver. They sent him instead to a BIPOD unit. Officially, it stood for Bulk Issue Petrol and Oil Depot. Unofficially, the men called it 'Bloody Idiots Pushing Oil Drums'.

Curry quickly put on muscle, to match his already solid dislike of bullies. A run-in with a belligerent officer saw him charged with eleven counts of 'prejudice to good order'. The commanding officer heard him out, dismissed all charges and

ROY CROSSLEY took part in the landing at Green Beach, Brunei Bay, north Borneo, 10 June 1945. Their immediate task was to take control of Brunei Town. An official photographer captured the moment of landing at Green Beach.

sent him to join an 'eye' unit. The 'eye' turned out to be 'I' for intelligence. He was a general gofer, a boy runner, but he loved it. He spent the next twenty months, till the end of the war, running messages and learning how to make maps, interpret aerial photographs with a stereoscope, recognise enemy weapons and paraphernalia, and use explosives. He especially liked learning how to blow things up.

He landed at Morotai (in what was then called the Moluccas) in late March 1945, to prepare for the invasion of the island of Tarakan, in northern Borneo. Most of the American troops had moved on, leaving small populations of Japanese soldiers in the mountains of various islands for the Australians to 'mop up'. It was dirty work, against an enemy determined to fight to the death.

The Tarakan invasion was bloody: there were only 2100 Japanese troops but they fought for every hill and rock. The Australian 26th Brigade had been strengthened with extra units until it numbered nearly 12,000 men. They landed progressively from 1 May. They were expected to remove the Japanese quickly so that airfields and naval facilities could be built to support the coming attacks on Borneo. In fact, the clean-out took more than three months, during which the Australians lost 225 men and 669 wounded. The airfields construction bogged down for months; they were not ready when the attacks started on Brunei and Balikpapan. In a frank judgement, the Australian historian Gavin Long wrote that 'the results achieved did not justify the cost of Tarakan'.

David Curry went ashore on the first day. He wrote later, in an account for his family, that he could not remember much of the next few hours 'except that it seemed like organised chaos'. Ordered to dig in, David and his friend Johnny found the ground too hard, so their slit trench was shallow. David fell asleep in the small 'pup' tent they shared. Johnny woke him soon after. The Japanese were shelling. David grabbed his boots and ran for the trench. He fell twice on the way and jumped in on top of his friend.

'I wasn't scared, I was bloody petrified and I regained my religion.'

When the shelling moved on, he discovered he had his boots on the wrong feet. His name in the unit became 'Wrong-foot Eddie'.

The men were jumpy for the next few nights because there were rumours that the Japanese were infiltrating their lines. He did not believe it, until a Japanese sniper opened fire from a tree, hoping to hit some officers. 'All scattered for cover, then everyone started to fire at the sniper. I was more likely to be shot by friendly fire than the sniper. Soon our would-be assassin was dead and the shooting stopped.'

This was the first time Curry had fired his weapon in anger. Talking about this event later, an old soldier told him the only bullet he had to worry about was the one that had his name on it.

'I thought how lucky I was that I had changed my name, and so my bullet would be flat out finding me.'

Both Curry and Crossley took part in the final campaigns on Borneo. Roy had rejoined the AIF in April 1943, six months after he was discharged for being under-age. He told them he was eighteen, and he didn't have a birth certificate because he was born in Perth. He forged a letter from his mother and signed it himself. Even so, he was too young to go overseas so he spent six months learning the Vickers machine gun. A vindictive commanding officer did not like his attitude and kept making him work as a mess orderly. 'I was fed up so I went AWL and as a result I got twenty-eight days' detention in Orange Detention Barracks.'

In mid-1944 he also went through the ordeal of Canungra. He was posted to the 2/2nd Machine Gun Battalion, training on the Atherton Tableland, while Curry was at Mission Beach, hauling oil barrels. Their paths would mirror each other for the rest of the war. Roy spent three weeks at Morotai preparing for the invasion of Borneo. In June 1945, he was part of the landing on Green Beach at Brunei.

'The second night we were shelled by mortar fire in a rubber plantation and we suffered some casualties; four of us then carried the wounded out to jeeps for evacuation. I fell down a gutter with a bloke on my back and hurt my back.'

This was the first time he had seen casualties in his own unit, men he knew. After carrying the wounded out, they had to find their way back in darkness. 'We deemed ourselves lucky not to be shot by our own troops, because usually anything that moved, you shot at it.'

He took part in the advance along Seventy Mile Beach to Seria, where they found twenty-seven burning oilfields. 'Day and night became the same. The skies were lit up for weeks and we moved on before they were extinguished.'

They set up camp at Badas. 'This is where we spent the remainder of the war mopping up. The war ended and I was still only eighteen.'

At Labuan he helped to patch up Allied prisoners of war. He had done an ambulance course in Australia. 'They were in a pitiful condition, suffering from malnutrition, beri-beri, malaria, tropical ulcers, and any other disease known to the tropics.' He arrived back in Australia in January 1946, disappointed to have missed the Victory celebrations. He received his discharge in June.

Roy could not march in Anzac Day parades for the first ten years after the war. 'As soon as I started thinking of those fifty-five guys who went to Rabaul, I used to bloody well crack up ... Terrible. I met two of the survivors in Concord when I came back from New Guinea and they told me about walking through the jungle for three months and getting picked up by a PT-boat.'

Roy had no regrets about going to war, but it took its toll on his health, mental and physical. 'I'm all right now but I used to lose my block real easy, especially in

> Roy could not march in Anzac Day parades for the first ten years after the war. 'As soon as I started thinking of those fifty-five guys who went to Rabaul, I used to bloody well crack up ...'

Brunei, north Borneo. After taking the town, **CROSSLEY** and his comrades camped at an abandoned Chinese joss house on June 14, 1945. They were able to wash and enjoy a billy of tea.

traffic. Somebody would blow his horn behind you … some idiot, you know, and I'd get outta my ute. I'd go back and really lose it and call them everything and ten minutes later, I would think, why did I do that?'

He became a plumber, working with his father. He married in 1946, aged nine-teen, but it was short-lived. He moved to Western Australia and worked for the housing commission. He moved back to Sydney in the early 1950s and he and his second wife had four children. Roy worked as a plumber on the northern beaches, living at Manly, where he be-came an enthusiastic surfer and diver. He and his third wife Liz moved to Pottsville in 1996, on his retirement.

Roy Crossley died in June 2021, three months short of his ninety-fourth birthday. His ashes were spread at sea off Currumbin on Anzac Day 2022, from a Currumbin surf boat. His last journey was at sea, despite his propensity for seasickness.

David Curry took part in the landing at Balikpapan on 1 July 1945. The Japanese opposition was strong, but the battle was won in three weeks. He was at Banjarmasin, on the southern tip of Borneo, after another landing, when the Americans dropped the atomic bombs and the war ended. Discharge from the army was worked out on a points-for-priority system, and he had few points, so he was still on Borneo at Christmas. He was dreading going home, to a house of arguments. He became very ill, lying in a coma for three weeks, during which he developed double pneumonia. The war had not put a scratch on him, but the peace nearly killed him. He was flown home in an air ambulance. He spent three months in Concord hospital in 1946, and another period in a convalescent home.

David and his first wife Joyce married in June 1947, and had two children. David worked for the post office for several years, then bought a bread run. He spent most of his career as a manager in various bread companies in Sydney, before his marriage broke down. He moved to Queensland with his new wife Nance, and eventually to the Mid North Coast, where he retired. Golf became a consuming passion. He got a hole-in-one eleven days after his ninetieth birthday.

He and Roy Crossley eventually met at an Anzac Day march in Sydney. Both had been invited to become members of the Under 16s Association, a group of veterans who had all enlisted before they were sixteen.

Left: **ROY CROSSLEY** and David Curry eventually met through the Under-16s Association. Here, Roy attends a reception in Sydney on Anzac Day 2012.
Right: **DAVID CURRY**, at home on the Mid North Coast of New South Wales in 2021.

CHAPTER EIGHTEEN

THE MURDER OF INNOCENCE

LEN McLEOD

HERB GARDNER

The artful dodger: **LEN McLEOD** at 15. He enlisted more times than even he can remember. Each time his mother would get him out for being under-age.

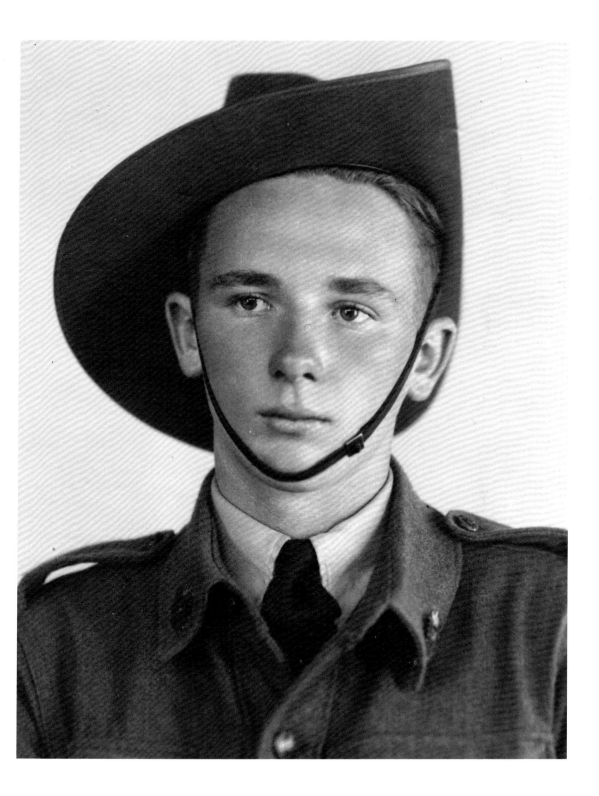

Len McLeod has an unusual military distinction, although it's completely unofficial. He joined the second AIF four times. His mother kept getting him out and he kept going back. He would wait a while and then join up again, using a different name. That is how he was able to join an army he was already in – not once, but twice.

His record is a masterpiece of persistence, and a low point in army record-keeping. It's also an epic tussle with his mother Ruby: a wilful fifteen-year-old determined to do his bit, and a loving mother determined to keep him safe.

On two occasions Len was enlisted under different names at the same time. How did he manage to be in two places at once? The answer is that he didn't. He absconded on more than one occasion, whenever his mother was getting close. His available records are incomplete: they show he went AWL two days after his first enlistment on 7 July 1941, and stayed away for more than four months, at least from his first unit. He doesn't quite remember how he did this, but it required some ingenuity.

Len lives in a small town near Kingaroy, north-west of Brisbane, with his daughter Denise and her husband Barry. In early 2022, Len was a fit 95-year-old, a keen tender of backyard vegetables and a seasoned teller of stories. Those he remembers are well remembered, but there are gaps. Those he would like to forget, he cannot. Parts of his war still trouble him deeply, robbing him of peace.

He ended up in the US Army Small Ships, along with 3000 other Australians, but he gave the army a good shake before that.

One of the powerful forces in this drama was a missing father, whose legend left a profound impression on young Len. John Leopold McLeod served in the 5th Battalion in the First World War, at Gallipoli and in France. He returned with damaged lungs that left him weak and short of breath. In the late 1920s, he was diagnosed with pulmonary tuberculosis.

Len has few memories of him. 'I remember sitting around with him – he could just get from chair to chair. And then, I heard them say they were going to pick him up in the ambulance, and they're going to take him to Caulfield Repat, and he didn't come out.'

Len was five when his father died, in January 1932. He grew up hearing stories of his father's war: how he enlisted so quickly that his army number was 35, how he had fought at Gallipoli and in the mud of France, how he was gassed. When the time came, Len told himself, 'If he could do it, so can I.'

John Leopold died at the height of the Depression. The family sought refuge for a year with the Barlows, Ruby's family at Yarram, then returned to North Footscray, where they had a soldier settlement home. This was a new suburb, a hub for broken men and their families. The McLeods lived on Mitchell Street; over the back fence were Monash and Birdwood Streets. Len grew up surrounded by generals, in name at least.

Len ran free here with a group of older boys, friends of his older brother Don. They would hang out in the early evening on a street corner. For sport, one of them would call the police to complain about 'hooligans' making a nuisance – just to goad the coppers into chasing them around the neighbourhood. They didn't laugh so much when a tough Irish cop lined them all up for a belting with his cosh. Len remembers all the names – Charlie and Laurie Newsom, Billy Bird, the two Hoolaghans, Jimmy and Kevvy, Bill Curran and his brother Tony – the Mitchell Street boys. They always laughed when Billy Bird had to divulge his address on Emu Street. Len was a handy footballer and an enthusiastic supporter of the Footscray Football Club. Then came the

> Len was five when his father died, in January 1932. He grew up hearing stories of his father's war: how he enlisted so quickly that his army number was 35, how he had fought at Gallipoli and in the mud of France, how he was gassed.

war and all of his mates were called up to the militia.

'They didn't call me up … Some of them would come back and say I joined the army today or I'm goin' in tomorrow. Gradually they all ended up in the air force, the navy or whatever. So when the last ones were going too, I went along. That was my first trip down to the drill hall in Footscray.

'I'm not telling you a lie, there was a great long line-up, all young fellas. So I get in the line and get up to the recruiting officer and he said, "How old are you?" And I said twenty-one. And he looked me up and down and said, "I think you better piss off home and come back with your birth certificate." He threw me out.

'So I left it for a fortnight or so, and then I go back again, and again there was a great line-up. The drill hall was in Barkly Street, Footscray. It's still there. Part of the Footscray football ground.'

This time he got in. His mother did not object if he served in Australia, but she would never allow him to join the AIF, to serve overseas. Having lost her husband to war, Ruby was not about to lose her son as well.

'So what I used to do when I'd go home with a uniform, I would take the "Australia" badges off my collar. That was the only difference between the uniforms.'

Ruby wasn't fooled. He wasn't hard to find, given that he used his correct name. When he heard she was coming, Len

> His mother did not object if he served in Australia, but she would never allow him to join the AIF, to serve overseas. Having lost her husband to war, Ruby was not about to lose her son as well.

LEN McLEOD (middle) with two friends from the US Army Small Ships, on leave in Rizal Avenue, Manila, in 1945.

took off and stayed away from home and the army. The army classed him as AWL. When he eventually reported back as Len McLeod, they discharged him (in November 1941). Before that, he had enlisted again, on 25 August 1941, this time as Roy Loft. The Lofts were a neighbouring family in North Footscray. Roy was his middle name.

During his 'Roy Loft' enlistment, a cousin recognised him in camp and yelled, 'What the bloody hell are you doing here, Lenny?'

Len told him to shut up. 'I'm not here and you haven't seen me.'

Somehow, 'Roy' stayed in the army until 5 January 1945, according to one of his four army certificates. Except that he didn't. His mother got him out again sometime early in 1942. His enlistment was not cancelled for another three years, which is a mystery. Until his complete records become available, we don't know where the army thought he was. In body, he was at home in North Footscray, but he soon became restless. On 12 December 1941, five days after Pearl Harbor, he rejoined the AIF as Len

Barlow, his third enlistment. Once again, he was doubling up – enlisted twice at the same time. And once again Ruby found him and brought him home, in late January. This time Len Barlow was properly discharged. His fourth enlistment, his most substantial, began on 24 September 1942. He went in under his real name. He told his mother he had joined the militia. He was sixteen and almost four months old.

'The last time I went home I told her lies, blatant bloody lies. I took my badges out and told her I was in the Home Guard. She had got me out three times and she must have thought, I'll leave him in, it might straighten him up a bit.'

Within thirty-six hours he was on a train to Canungra in Queensland for jungle training. The army would not take his older brother Don. He was a metal-moulder, a 'reserved occupation'. Both Don and Len's sister Jean worked in munitions during the war.

By the middle of 1942, the Japanese were pressing hard in New Guinea: Len believes the army would have taken anyone. Training consisted of about twelve days at Canungra. He could already handle a rifle, from hunting rabbits as a kid. The rest was marching, running, jumping, crawling till you dropped with exhaustion.

'We get to Townsville and they packed us on a bloody old cargo ship. We slept anywhere. Straight up to Port Moresby. They took us to Murray Barracks. We were all under canvas. And that afternoon, everyone is saying, "It'll be on tonight." I said, "What do you mean?" I didn't know. Heard that half-a-dozen times … "Oh it's a nice clear night, no rain, no clouds, they'll be over tonight." And sure as shit, the Japanese came over and blew shit out of the airport and we were a mile from there. We could see the planes coming over and fighter planes going up and into them, searchlights and Christ knows what, everything was going on. There were slit trenches everywhere, so they said, "When you see them coming, make sure you know where to jump into the trench" – but nearly always they were bloody waterlogged and wet.'

Len was finally where he wanted to be, with his mother none the wiser. It would have broken her heart.

Herb Gardner was working on a farm near Townsville when Len McLeod passed through on his way to Moresby. Herb remembers looking up at the troop trains passing the farm, seeing black American soldiers for the first time. The Yanks had arrived.

Had they known each other, Herb and Len would have discovered much in common. Herb was born twenty-eight days before Len, on 5 May 1926. Herb also lost his father just before he was five, from a heart attack.

'I have no memory of my father at all,' said Herb, when I met him at his home near Hervey Bay in Queensland, in 2020. He lives in a house by the sea, with tame butcher birds coming in for a chat on his balcony. His recall of events is tack sharp.

The death of his father impoverished an already poor family. They had worked an orchard and a cane farm at Home Hill, 100 kilometres south of Townsville. They were now reduced

L E N had this portrait taken in Manila, probably just after the war, wearing his US Army Small Ships uniform.

to living in a tin humpy on land they had once owned. Herb remembers they had three cows. The four children (two sisters and an older brother) would milk the cows before school and fill three pint bottles, which they would sell to neighbours on the way to school. Each pint sold for threepence. As far as he knows, that was the only money coming in to the family. Their mother, Beatrice, grew vegetables, churned but-

ter, baked bread. Meat was rare. 'It was tough for everyone.'

The children attended the nearby school at Inkerman, with fourteen other kids.

'We were all poor and we knew it, because this one family had a bicycle. The Smiths. Our sandwiches were homemade plum jam. We never had tomato sauce as kids, but Johnny Smith had tomato sauce sandwiches, and I would always ask him to swap. He didn't mind about mine, because he was always well fed. We were hungry.'

Beatrice's sister ran a hotel at Innot Hot Springs, a small mining village between Mount Garnet and Ravenshoe, inland from Cairns. Arthur, the elder brother, went to work there around 1936. By now, Beatrice had been able to sell the land at Home Hill. Herb became a boarder at Abergowrie Agricultural School at Ingham. He was one of a handful of non-Catholic pupils, so he did not have to attend religious instruction but he picked up all ten commandments anyway.

Herb didn't like school. In late 1939, aged thirteen, he wrote to Jack Munro, who had bought the family farm at

Home Hill. He and Munro got on well. Herb started work at ten shillings a week with bed and board. Beatrice was now working at Hot Springs, so there was no family home to return to.

Herb had no desire to go to war, no understanding of world events. 'We were just kids. In those days, kids were kids.'

Even Jack Munro, who supported the Communist Party of Australia, could not awaken Herb's political sensibility. Herb had not yet owned a pair of long pants. 'I was just a happy country kid, a real bumpkin.'

In the next two years, he moved from farm to farm – dairying at Millaa Millaa, cattle at Bowen, poultry at Townsville. He and a friend, Billy Searle, bought a motorbike together. They would ride into Home Hill to the pictures on a Saturday night. Billy told Herb about the 'US Army Remounts'. All they knew was there was an American unit in Townsville that worked with horses. They rode there on the bike and asked about jobs.

The Remounts was full of under-age boys, working with Americans to break horses for the US forces. The job only lasted until the end of 1943 but it led to him joining the US Army Small Ships.

'I had never been on a boat in my life,' says Herb.

He had picked up some basic skills at cookery while working on the farms. He volunteered for a post on the WT-1 *Kupe*, a 45-foot tugboat that had just arrived from Sydney. He was now a cook and deckhand, one of three men chugging across the Torres Strait towards Port Moresby. It was April 1944, and Herb was now seventeen.

> Herb had no desire to go to war, no understanding of world events. 'We were just kids. In those days, kids were kids.'

The morning after his first air raid in Port Moresby, Len McLeod was on

Out she goes … Three men from 2/160 Supply Depot Platoon heaving cargo from a RAAF Douglas C-47 Dakota supply plane, a 'biscuit bomber', in New Guinea, 1945.

parade when officers called for volunteers to work as spotters: they would be given six weeks' radio training and dropped into remote locations to report on enemy movements.

Len had become friendly with an older soldier on the boat, 'a real good fella'.

'He was standing behind me in the pa-rade. So they called for volunteers for the spotters – you would get an immediate promotion to corporal, which meant an extra two shillings a day, so I stepped forward. He grabbed me by the back of the neck and pulled me back. "Come back 'ere, you young bastard," he said. Pulls me back into the line. He said to me, he said, "You're in the army now, you don't volunteer for anything! If they're calling for volunteers, stand clear."'

When they called for men to work as 'droppers' on the supply planes, Len could not resist. He joined the 'biscuit bombers', flying out each morning at dawn to drop food and ammunition to men fighting on the Kokoda track. They flew in DC-3s, with the doors removed. They were always piloted by one Australian and one American, with a radio operator who could be either nationality. Everything to be dropped was in boxes that were sewn into heavy-duty canvas bags, without padding or parachutes. There were two droppers per plane, supervised by the radio man. Nine planes went up together, climbing to 4000 feet, then flying in rows of three.

'We always had an escort of five or six fighter planes. We never knew where we were going.'

The droppers had no safety harness. Len's job was to lie on his back, feet up against the load, holding onto hand rails above his head, waiting for the signal. The troops below would have prepared a drop zone by cutting down trees. The pilots would come in low, barely above the trees. When he saw the green light come on in the cabin, Len's job was to kick the load out the door in the shortest possible time. He never saw where the bags landed, although many were known to miss their target, or explode on impact. The work was vitally important, but dangerous. During the ten weeks he worked on the supply planes, he lost two friends when one of the planes crashed.

After two months, Len requested a transfer to the infantry. He arrived on the other side of the mountains, just after the 2/7th Battalion had taken Wau – a former gold-mining frontier town – from the Japanese.

'When I arrived, I was disappointed to a certain extent, because I heard a lot of them say, "Jesus Christ, what is Australia doing to us, sending school kids up." Looking at me. See I was snow white, and they were burnt brown, coming from the Middle East, and they were still in their khaki.'

Len lasted seven weeks before illness took its toll. His platoon was on patrol in the mountains, a couple of days walk out from Wau. The medical officer checked his temperature and ordered him back to Wau. The problem was there was no-one to escort him.

'He said, "I can't afford to send anyone with you." He said, "Do you think you can possibly walk back to Wau?" It was a bloody long way but I said, "Yes, I'll make it."

'So he gave me a lecture: it was just a native track, and it rained a couple of times a day so it was always damp. He said, "Don't get off the track, stay on the track, unless you see something you are not sure of, then get off it and wait. Have a look at the track and if you see the shape of the split-toed shoes, you know they are ahead of you or nearby."' Japanese boots fitted around the big toe, separating it from the other toes, so they left a distinctive shape in the mud.

'Then they found out I was under-age. I don't know if it was my mother, I didn't argue. I was out. I went home but there was no-one there. Everyone was in something to do with the war.'

Len walked back down the mountain for a day and a half, his temperature raging, expecting to run into the enemy at every turn. At Wau, they put him on the first plane back to Port Moresby. He remembers joining a flood of casualties from the battles at Buna and Gona. Four days later they flew him back to Cairns, then Melbourne. He had dengue fever and dysentery and had lost a lot of weight.

'Then they found out I was under-age. I don't know if it was my mother, I didn't argue. I was out. I went home but there was no-one there. Everyone was in something to do with the war.'

Billy Bird from Emu Street was still around so they went out shooting together. That is how Len ended up with a leg full of buckshot, when Billy discharged a shotgun by accident. Most of the pellets are still there now, giving rise to ongoing problems.

'I knew I could not get back into the army, but I could still get around a bit. This young fella told me I could have his job on a Yugoslavian ship that was tied up at North Melbourne, the *Olga Topic*. He was a trimmer. All you had to do was shovel coal down to the firemen in the engine room.'

He made four trips back and forward carrying coal from Newcastle to Melbourne. His mother was happy with this job, as it seemed a lot safer than the army. Waiting in Newcastle for the ship to be loaded, another merchant seaman told him about the US Army Small Ships. Len took a train to Sydney, found the American headquarters at the Grace Hotel, and signed on. He never went back to the *Olga Topic*.

Life on the US Army Small Ships was a major step-up after a filthy coal ship. The pay was double, the living conditions and food much better. They had uniforms that fitted.

'They put me on a ship called the *Bopple*. Back in New Guinea, they flew me down to Milne Bay, as a fireman. It only had about three little fires and carried a hundred ton. One of the slowest ships of the lot.'

The S-147 *Bopple*'s small size meant it could get in and out of the shallow waters around Oro Bay and Lae. Enemy planes would often strafe her, if they could be bothered with such small fry. Much of their transport work was done at night.

'Whatever they wanted ashore, we would take it ashore. We spent a lot of time in Finschhafen till it was consolidated, then we moved along the coast to Dutch New Guinea to Hollandia [now known as Jayapura]. I didn't know what was going on. In the bay when we got there, there were very few merchant ships but after several weeks there was over a hundred ships, nine and ten thousand tonners. Quite a few ships from the American and Australian navy too, destroyers, and escorts and cruisers. I thought, Christ, what's going on here. I got talking to the American captain and he said, "We're going north shortly." Eventually we formed up into a convoy of 104 ships.'

At Hollandia, Len was transferred onto the USAT *Armand Considere*, one of twenty-six cement ships built in Tampa, Florida. They were 7500-tons, about 300 feet long (92 metres). This one was launched in May 1944, as a floating stores ship. Len describes it as like Bunnings on the water. He was delighted to be on a big new ship, but daunted when he saw the engine room.

'To me it looked like a bloody hospital. Everything was new and polished, valves here and valves there. I told the young fellow I was supposed to replace, "You've got problems." I said, "I can't take this job, I don't know a thing about it." All I'd ever done was bloody old coal burners. He said, "Don't worry, Len, I'll teach you." It was a lesson to me: if you want to learn and you are dead-keen to learn, you will bloody learn. After two or three shifts, I could do it with my eyes closed.'

At Port Moresby, Herb Gardner's tugboat had picked up a barge and towed it round the coast to Finschhafen.

'We did not know anything about the war, or where the Japanese were, there was no radio or communication to listen to. We didn't know nothing.'

The crew consisted of an American captain and engineer, an Australian deckhand and Herb, as deckhand and cook.

'The hold was full of tinned food, and there was a cookbook and a kerosene-operated stove. I musta managed. Each tin had the Army symbol on it and instructions: Put in hot water for twenty minutes.'

Herb improvised, making stews and pies. The tugs congregated at Finschhafen. Eventually about forty tugs set off together to run up the coast to Hollandia, with empty barges in tow.

'It took us seven or eight days to get there. Our engine must have been already cracking up because in the night-time and morning the others weren't in sight. We were being circled by seven or eight American destroyers, to protect us from Japanese submarines.'

The barges were used to supply the ships massing at Hollandia. Len McLeod and Herb Gardner were now working on sister ships in the same port at the same time. Their paths had finally converged.

Herb enjoyed working with Americans, especially the African-American soldiers who drove much of the transport. 'They knew so much. We had never done anything. They used to bullshit to us kids, I suppose. I learned all about American motor cars, as they came around, like what the symbols were. A Plymouth had a sailing ship on it. I knew all the models …

'So our engine cracked up. One of the other skippers was a negro and our boat had an oven and this man had been a baker in the States, so he would come across to our boat to bake bread. He recommended me to this other ship, to cook for thirteen men, but I couldn't handle it. This ship had come from America and it had a freezer in it, with half carcasses of animals. I didn't know how to cut it up.'

Herb's new boat was a one-hold cargo ship. He discovered that an able seaman on board had been trained as a chef. They swapped jobs. That saw out his six-month contract.

He re-signed and was sent back up to Hollandia on a new 80-foot fast rescue vessel called a QS boat, designed to pick up wounded during battle. It had beds below for casualties, but it was never used for this purpose: the war had moved on up into the islands. Still, Herb saw some of its effects.

'When we were coming back from Biak one time we picked up a lot of Japanese. Prisoners of war. We weren't allowed to go near them, but there were about twenty of them and they were starving. We took them to Hollandia. One poor bloke died on the way. Our captain told us later that they had thought they were fighting in America.'

One of his last boats was the 5000-ton *City of Fort Worth*, a 'lake' boat, commandeered from the Great Lakes in Canada. It had forty-five crew, most of them Australian. It was sent to Mel-

> Herb's war was his education in the ways of the world.

bourne for overhaul. This was Herb's first time in a big city. His first night off was an 'eye-opener'. He had never drunk alcohol or smoked. He ended up at a sly grog party in a bawdy house where someone punched him in the eye. 'I woke up the next morning with an awful headache and a black eye. I was still a bushie, a hick.

'The last trip we did, we loaded up with Red Cross stuff to go to Shanghai. We were handing all these ships to the Chinese, woulda been early '46. While we went ashore they put us up where the racecourse was in Shanghai, and then they put us on a ship that was going to Manila. I had no home to go to, so I got onto the *Octorara*, an American passenger ship taking troops back to America. We ended up in San Francisco, as "distressed British seamen", waiting to get back to Australia.'

Herb's war was his education in the ways of the world. He took on many jobs after the war – from 'roo shooting to installing clotheslines to running a caravan park. He married in 1951 and had two children. He has no regrets about his days in the US Army Small Ships.

The 3000 Australian men and boys (and one woman) who served in the US Army Small Ships received no recognition, by way of medals or privileges, after the war. Herb could not visit an RSL club as a returned serviceman, because the RSL did not recognise the US Army Small Ships as a military operation – even though thirty-six Australians were killed in its employ. After much lobbying, that recognition has now been granted.

The recognition didn't chase away the demons for Len McLeod, whose life was profoundly affected by what he saw

> 'I had a hell of a time in Shanghai. That was the worst I've seen. I had seen the aftermath of battle, the slaughter, but nothing affected me like China.'

while in Shanghai. He arrived during a famine at the end of the war.

'I had a hell of a time in Shanghai. That was the worst I've seen. I had seen the aftermath of battle, the slaughter, but nothing affected me like China. When we got there I went ashore for a walk, and if I think about it now, it will make me cry now. I walked down the main street there, and I seen a lorry, like a farm truck. Up there they had six men in the front pulling it and a couple down the back pushing it – and first thing in the morning, I seen this bloody thing, and they were going into the doorways, all smashed and destroyed, picking up the bodies. Little kids, little babies, women, beautiful looking girls, and they would put the bodies across each other ... men, women and kids. In between that you've got the mothers coming up to you, and little kids, saying some-thing like *che che che* ... wanting food and water. Water, water ... those dirty rotten bastards, the Japs, they just left, evacuated, took the food and destroyed everything. The poor bastards. We were the first ship in there. And I would say

to the captain, "Jesus Christ, we've gotta get some ships in, some wheat and oats, and get anything from Australia." He said it's all under way, they'll be here in a few days.'

Len has been haunted by what he saw in Shanghai. It changed the direction of his life, turning him into a peace activist and committed unionist. He has never been able to rid himself of the memories: the nightmares affect him every month.

Hoping to change that, his daughters Denise West and Suzanne McLean took him back to Shanghai four years ago, to see the new prosperity of the city. They thought it might put his mind at rest. It didn't, but it was a beautiful gesture of love for their father, who has never been able to forget what he saw.

Len McLeod is in some ways the quintessential under-age boy soldier. He was unstoppable in his determination to serve; he found a way after four blocked attempts. It could easily have killed him, but he survived. Just don't say he was unscathed. Every boy in this book came home with scars of one sort or another. Some of the wounds are still raw.

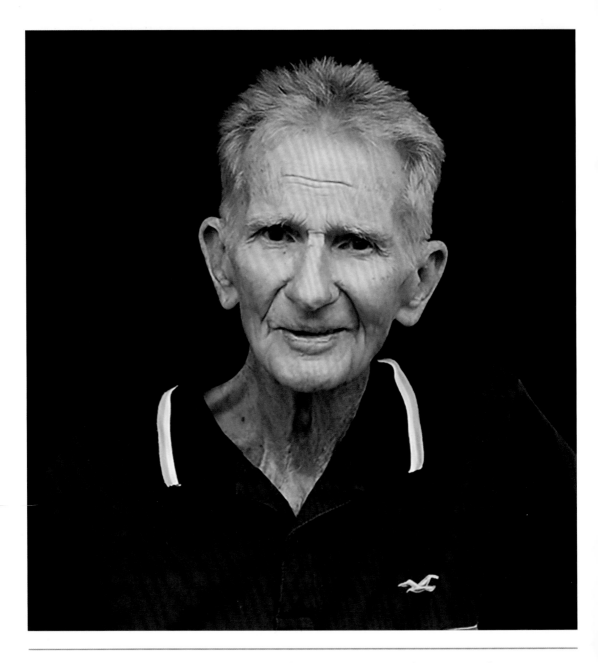

LEN McLEOD became a committed unionist, a lifelong peace activist and a campaigner for many causes. The photo was taken at his home outside Brisbane in late 2021.

HERB GARDNER at his home near Hervey Bay, Queensland, in late 2021.

CODA

There is a pattern to the way young soldiers were used in the Australian forces in the two world wars. In both conflicts, the governments dropped the age at which men could enlist once higher casualties demanded reinforcements. In essence, halfway through, it became acceptable to recruit eighteen-year-olds, when at the start of the war it was not. Morality conformed itself to need.

It's possible that the number of under-age recruits also increased in lock step. We don't know, because no-one knows how many under-aged recruits there were. Each false declaration would have to be tested. Nor do we know how many died. It could be more than in the First World War, simply because there were twice as many soldiers in uniform.

What we do know is that eighteen-year-olds were the majority of *conscripts* in the last eighteen months of the Second World War: 85 to 90 per cent, in fact. The rule changes of 1942 and '43 meant these eighteen-year-olds had to spend at least six months training in Australia, and they weren't supposed to be sent overseas until they were nineteen, but those rules were often flouted. Historian Mark Johnston has pointed out that many of the AIF recruits at Kokoda, Bougainville and Borneo were eighteen and nineteen, which means that many were also below those ages. Some of the boys in this book were in those places.

Another pattern is that the scars of the First World War continued into the Second and beyond. So many of the boys here had fathers who fought in 1914–1918 and came back damaged. The sons of war, in their turn, came back damaged, if they made it back. It would be hard to exaggerate the social and domestic toll that both wars took on those who fought, and their families. The misery, tragedy and conflict are there in almost every chapter.

Some of those who were very young men are now prepared to talk about it. That was the greatest shock for me in writing this book: the hurt has not healed, the damage has not been undone. As I finished writing, on Anzac Day 2022, some of them marched, or appeared at dawn services, to remember their friends who did not make it back. Some of them chose never to march and never would. The memories remain too painful.

ACKNOWLEDGEMENTS AND THANKS

My partner, Mary Dickie, has shared the highs and lows of two books in four years, during which I have been both absent, for research, and absent-minded, when diving down rabbit holes in search of stories. Her forbearance, advice and encouragement were always there when I needed them.

My main interest had always been in the Great War. The two years I have spent submerged in 1939–1945 have been an education, thanks to Martin Hughes at Affirm Press. This was the war in which my father fought. I had walked a bit of the Kokoda Track in 1980, when I was a correspondent in Papua New Guinea, and the whole thing in 2006, but I knew very little about the campaigns in the Middle East, Greece and Malaya. It was a steep learning curve. It has helped me to better understand my country.

The staff at the Australian War Memorial Research Centre were patient and resourceful, as ever. Jennifer Milward, after shepherding my first book, offered valuable assistance

again. Paul Croke and colleagues at the National Archives of Australia provided much help with soldier records. The staff at the State Library in Sydney were diligent, as always. Lane Cove Library became a secret resource: one of the best military history sections in the country. Covid made everything harder, but well-funded libraries are a gift to us all.

Special thanks to those who gave me hospitality in Canberra and Sydney during the research: Peter and Nerida Clarke, John and Ros Rogers, Graham and Stephanie Reilly, Kathy and Ian Pickles, Katy Pickles and Jon Happold, Michael and Kate Grealy, Gary and Colleen Langtry and my sisters, Helen Renshaw and Melanie Robb, and their husbands Pat Renshaw and Paul Robb. Tim Bowden gave generous access to his raw tapes made for the ABC radio documentary series, Australians Under Nippon, during the 1980's.

I offer a special thanks to the old men who welcomed me into their homes to record interviews. Jennifer Ballard, patron of the

Under Sixteens Association, put me in touch with some of them. I was not able to use all of their stories, but nearly all were generous with time and recall. Most were prepared to revisit memories that were still painful. I thank them all: Les Cook, Roy Crossley, David Curry, Herb Gardner, Len Leggett, Frank McGreevy, Len McLeod, Dennis Moule, Jack Tarlington and Keith Williams. The children of other men long gone opened their family records to me. As ever, Trove, the National Library's magnificent searchable database of newspapers, magazines and much more, was an invaluable source.

Many others helped along the way. Their names are acknowledged here in alphabetical order: Michael Adams, Norm Aisbett, Michael Ball, Jill Bear, Joan Beaumont, Michael Bendon, Col Benson, Malcolm Botfield, Sam Byrnes, Nicole Chambers, Brad Cone, Pamela Cox, Norman Cramp, Elizabeth Crossley, Peter Curtis, Anne Davis, Alastair Davison, Helen Dell, Audrey Dodson, Matilda Dray, Barbara Dubois, Peter Edwards, Cathy Every, David Ferry, Tenille Hands, Keith Harrison, Luke Hickey, Rhonda Hunter, Steven James, Penny Harris Jennings, Peter Ford, Anne Forrest, Sean Gallagher, Glenda Garde, Lorraine Graham, Bob Holt, Anita Jaensch, Martin James, Judy Jenkins, Arthur Jiggins, PIE Jones, Sherold Kelleher, Wendy King, Katrina Kittel, Ray Kohn, Peter Lacey, Gail Langham, Greg Larchin, Lynne Leggett, Tom Lewis, Noeleen Lincoln, Luke Litchfield, Guy Lucas, Jeanette Lynch, Paul McAlonan, Stephen McGreevy, Anne MacKean, Heather McMillan, Karen McMahon, Darren Mallett, Ella Middleton, Rod Miller, Vincent Molony, Michael Moule, Annie Mugridge, Leigh Mulgrave, Robert Muscat, John Naismith, Lisa Norris, Dan O'Brien, Anne O'Halloran, Lorane Oldfield, Wes Olsen, John Perryman, Bruce Pollock, Wendy Porter, Ron Pritchard, Helen Priest, Sharyn Roberts, Josephine Rowe, Donald Roy, Caroline Sabin, Mark St Leon, Roxane Scott, Phil Shehan, Lynne Ramsay Silver, Ian Smith, Christina Stubbs, Maxine Taylor, Gary Waddell, Denise West, Chris Whan, Paul White, Ross Wilkinson, Susan Wilson.

Inevitably, there will be mistakes in what I have written. Please write to me via the publisher and I will try to correct them in later editions. ❦

PHOTO CREDITS

Many of the photographs are from the Australian War Memorial collection and appear with permission. They are indicated below by 'AWM', followed by the identifying number used by the memorial. The rest of the photos come from families and private collections, and all are subject to copyright restrictions. None may be used or reproduced without the permission of the owners. I wish to thank all those who gave me access to these images, many of which appear here for the first time. 'Family collection' applies to images belonging to a soldier who has died. 'Personal collection' refers to a soldier who was living at the time he gave permission.

Abbreviations:

AWM: Australian War Memorial
FC: family collection
NAA: National Archives of Australia
PC: personal collection

Foreword: Elson Evered Bell AWM 024225; New recruits AWM 000184/03; School boys AWM 138716; Recruits photographed AWM 058845
Introduction: Bill Davis AWM 009134; First men to enlist AWM 000172
Chapter 1: Boat trip AWM 007445; Elsie Richards AWM 013178; Len Barnes NAA; Boy at parade AWM 139267
Chapter 2: Bob Holt at 15 FC Robert Holt; Battle for Tobruk, AWM 005403; Bob Holt as boxer FC R Holt; Bob Holt as adult in uniform FC R Holt
Chapter 3: Douglas Foster on march FC Douglas

Foster; Teddy Days NAA; Douglas Foster army portrait FC D Foster; Jack Jenkins army portrait FC Jack Jenkins; Jack Jenkins on leave FC J Jenkins; Fall of Tobruk AWM 006642
Chapter 4: Troops at the Acropolis AWM 006797; Diggers on donkeys AWM 006714; Menzies AWM 005732
Chapter 5: Andy Mulgrave FC Andrew Mulgrave; Des Beard, Jim Seiver, Andy Mulgrave and Colin Price FC A Mulgrave; Andy Mulgrave with gun FC A Mulgrave; John Robert Fraser AWM P02466.225
Chapter 6: Andy Mulgrave in the desert FC A Mulgrave; Andy Mulgrave at POW camp FC A Mulgrave
Chapter 7: 'Allan Stuart' army portrait FC Glen Scott; Glen Scott with Weipa Mayer FC G Scott; Glen Scott with motorcycle FC G Scott; 2/1st Anti-Tank Regiment FC G Scott; Glen Scott on return FC G Scott

Chapter 8: John Francis Hayes FC Frank Hayes; Hayes brothers and friends on motorcycles FC F Hayes; Norm Molony army portrait FC Norm Molony; Norm Molony and friend with beers FC N Molony; Frank Hayes in Switzerland FC F Hayes; Shoes of POWs FC F Hayes; Soldiers skiing FC F Hayes

Chapter 9: Thomas Jiggins AWM P06105.008; Alice Blatch FC Tom Jiggins; Jiggins Park photographed by the author

Chapter 10: Dennis Moule portrait PC Dennis Moule; Dennis Moule with young woman PC D Moule; Dennis Moule at Winnipeg Air Training School PC D Moule; Dennis Moule at 94 photographed by the author

Chapter 11: Len Leggett portrait PC Len Leggett; Len Leggett and battalion on troopship PC L Leggett (original negative at AWM 076545); Len Leggett at 95 photographed by the author

Chapter 12: Leslie Edwards at 15 FC Leslie Edwards; Ronald Keith Thomas at 15 NAA; Leslie Edwards at POW camp FC L Edwards; HA Purvis AWM 116269; Ambon cemetery AWM 124983

Chapter 13: Ken Hickey FC Ken Hickey; Alan Pollock FC Alan Pollock; Christmas dinner FC A Pollock; Usapa Besar camp AWM P04801.017; Bicycle camp AWM 123668

Chapter 14: John Blackman NAA; Reg Hunter NAA; Reg Hunter in jungle training courtesy of Rhonda Hunter; Soldier on Kokoda Track AWM 026710; Stretcher-bearers crossing river AWM 013641

Chapter 15: Billy Davis with parents FC William Davis; Douglas Taylor NAA; Shaggy Ridge AWM 016722; Billy Davis in AIF uniform FC W Davis

Chapter 16: Frank McGreevy PC Frank McGreevy, copied by Christina Stubbs; Frank McGreevy and comrades PC F McGreevy; Torokina PC F McGreevy; Medic at Tsimba Ridge AWM 079033; Evacuation from Tsimba Ridge PC F McGreevy; Frank McGreevy in 2021 photographed by the author

Chapter 17: David Curry PC David Curry; Roy Crossley, PC Roy Crossley; Soldiers in amphibious ship PC R Crossley (original negative held AWM 108941); Landing at Green Beach PC R Crossley (original negative held AWM 108948); Tea break PC R Crossley (original negative held AWM 110284); Roy Crossley in 2012 PC R Crossley; David Curry in 2021 photographed by the author

Chapter 18: Len McLeod PC Len McLeod; Len McLeod and friends from US Army Small Ships PC L McLeod; Len McLeod portrait in Manila PC L McLeod; Cargo drop AWM 042734; Len McLeod in 2021 photographed by the author; Herb Gardner in 2021 photographed by the author

INDEX

air raids 158, 207, 213, 226,
    245, 263, 320, 342,
    359, 361
Alamein, El 6, 21, 87, 170, 183
Ambon 26, 238–68, 324
Anderson, Charles, VC 193–7
Anzac Day 54, 117, 160, 348,
    350, 351, 373
ANZAC soldiers (WWI) 8, 11
armies
    American 23, 27, 93, 108,
        139, 140, 142, 170, 191,
        223, 227, 242, 245–6,
        252, 257, 263, 274, 305,
        319, 322, 333, 342, 350,
        361, 367
    British 27, 31, 47, 51, 60,
        70, 72, 74–6, 83–5,
        96–101, 109, 114–19,
        125, 132, 150, 152,
        169–71, 188, 190, 193,
        194, 196–201, 222, 246,
        262–3, 269
    French 27, 134, 150, 152,
        284
    German 26, 27, 60, 72, 74,
        76–84, 108, 113–25,
        129, 132, 135, 137,
        139–43, 149, 150, 156,
        171, 173, 176, 180, 207
    Greek 74, 96, 101, 114, 115,
        119, 129, 160
    Indian 51, 60, 96, 189, 190,
        192–8
    Italian 42, 46, 51–3, 70, 72,
        74, 75–7, 108, 175
    Japanese 26, 53, 170, 188,
        190, 196–201, 210–13,
        223, 226–9, 236–52,
        255–75, 281–95, 305,
        309, 320–9, 333, 342,
        346–50, 358–9, 363–4,
        366–7
    see also Imperial
        Guards Division, Japa-
        nese army
    New Zealand see New
        Zealand
    USSR (Russian) 27, 108,
        135
atomic bomb 350
Australia, politics of 8, 15, 17,
    26, 28, 31
    Australian Labor Party 20,

26, 28, 37, 63, 189
Communist Party of
    Australia 28, 361
conscription 21, 26, 250,
    297, 338
Country Party 15, 97
defence spending 26
fear of Japanese military
    action 26, 188, 189, 191,
    236, 237, 241, 242
foreign policy 28, 101, 188,
    191
post-war plotting 245, 333
relations with Britain 15,
    222
relations with USA 222
unemployment 17, 66
Australian Imperial Force
    (AIF), First 20, 43
Australian Imperial Force,
    Second 10, 12, 20, 21,
    31–8, 43, 44, 49, 70, 81,
    152, 173, 223, 260, 261,
    277, 279, 282, 285, 320,
    340, 342–3, 347, 354,
    357, 358, 373
    6th Division 12, 20, 31, 46,
        49, 53, 70, 71, 74, 165
    7th Division 31, 62, 66, 69,
        70, 71, 76, 140, 156, 308
    8th Division 63, 153,
        188–92, 300
    9th Division 63, 71–6,
        169–73
Australian Military Forces
    (AMF) see militia
incompetence of leaders
    96, 243, 257
military police 49, 74, 152,
    201, 280, 284
    see also battalions, regi-
        ments and companies,
        brigades
Australian Women's Army
    Service 38

Balfe, John 84
Bardia 42, 47, 49, 52–3, 72, 80,
    109, 277
Barnes, Leonard M 34–6
battalions, regiments and
    companies
    1 Anti-Aircraft Brigade
        Company 340, 342

2nd Australian Beach
    Landing Group 343
2/1st Battalion 52, 119, 122
2/1st Anti-Tank Regiment
    146
2/1st Engineers 137
2/1st Fortress Engineers
    259, 260, 264, 270
2/1st Heavy Battery 259,
    261, 263, 264, 270
2/2nd Machine Gun
    Battalion 347
2/3rd Battalion 49, 51–3,
    70, 135
2/4th Battalion 303
2/4th Anti-Tank Regiment
    194
2/4th Light Anti-Aircraft
    Regiment 192
2/4th Pioneers 263
2/7th Battalion 140, 165,
    363
2/11th Battalion 104,
    108–9, 111–12, 114,
    116–22, 129, 132, 138
2/13th Battalion 62, 66, 72,
    75–7, 80, 85, 88, 277,
    285, 295
2/14th Battalion 227, 282,
    284–9, 294
2/15th Battalion 75
2/16th Battalion 287
2/17th Battalion 6, 59, 63,
    66, 71, 75–7, 80–4
2/19th Battalion 188,
    192–8, 319
2/20th Battalion 300
2/21st Battalion 238,
    242–3, 248
2/22nd Battalion 243, 271
2/23rd Battalion 169,
    170–4, 237
2/29th Battalion 169,
    193–200
2/30th Battalion 193
2/40th Battalion 243,
    259–67
19th Field Ambulance
    317–20
36th Battalion 218, 221–3
    229–32
39th Battalion 181, 287
53rd Field Park Company
    305

113th Light Anti-Aircraft
    Regiment 159
battles WWII
    Ambon 26, 238–9, 241–7,
        251–9, 263–8, 324
    Bakri 192–6
    Balikpapan 346, 350
    Barce 74–6
    Bougainville 229, 312,
        319–30, 335, 373
    Buna 218, 226–7, 286,
        292–5, 309, 312, 364
    Gona 226–7, 295, 309, 364
    Guadalcanal 227, 295
    Milne Bay 88, 227, 295,
        312, 365
    Muar 192–5, 202
    Ramu Valley 295, 305, 309
    Sanananda 192, 218, 227–8
    Shaggy Ridge 305–9
    Timor 241–3, 257–63, 268,
        324
Beard, Des 105–8
Bell, Elson E 6
Benghazi 46–7, 72, 74–5,
    92–3, 96, 109, 111–2,
    174–5, 277
Bennett, Gordon 192–4,
    197, 202
Beverley, FG 197
Blackman, Jack 276–95
Blamey, Thomas 70, 74, 87,
    97–100, 116, 222,
    322–3, 335
Borneo 6, 88, 255, 335,
    346–50, 373
Brallos Pass 115–16, 119
brigades
    11th 319, 325
    20th 66, 70–1, 74–7
    22nd 189
    23rd 243, 257, 262
    26th 346
British Empire 15, 27–8, 68,
    92, 96, 101, 189
British government 92–101
brothels 48, 69–71
brothers 10, 36–8, 60, 65–6,
    92, 166, 220, 228, 285,
    335, 339
Brown, Charlie 124
Buckler, Sydney 'Ben' 289–94
Butler, Charles 289

Campbell, Ian 132
Campo 106, Vercelli 176
Campo 57, Grupignano 174–5
Cant, Sydney 138
Canungra Jungle Training Camp 343, 347, 358–9
casualties 53, 84, 118–19, 122, 132, 169, 170, 174, 198, 209, 228, 268, 346
Changi Prison Camp 200–1
Chifley, Ben 333
Churchill, Winston 20, 62, 74, 92–101, 108, 119, 157, 170, 189, 191, 202, 222, 242, 262
Citizen Military Force see militia
Commonwealth War Graves Commission
    Bomana War Cemetery 21, 294
    Lae War Cemetery 295
    Souda Bay War Cemetery 129
Crete 20, 27, 96, 117–9, 121, 125, 128–33, 150, 152, 155
Croft, Ron 200
Crossley, Roy 332–51
Curry, David 332–51
Curtin, John 27–8, 37, 101, 170, 188–90, 222, 236–7, 241–2, 246, 282, 333, 343

Darley Camp 169, 238–9
Darwin 20, 157, 210, 222, 238–44, 259–67, 282, 338
Davis, Billy 296–313
Days, Edwin Raymond 'Teddy' 56–88
Dell, Hazel 38
Depression, the 13, 17, 31, 38, 146, 164, 219, 259–60, 285, 298, 303, 316, 335, 338
disease
    beri-beri 252, 269–70, 348
    blackwater fever 227, 281
    dengue fever 6, 227, 364
    dysentery 13–14, 133–4, 169–70, 174, 218, 262–4, 269–72, 281, 293, 321, 342, 364
    malaria 6, 159, 176–80, 218, 227, 230–1, 262–4, 269–72, 281, 308–9, 313, 321, 348

pyrexia of unknown origin (PUO) 305, 308
    scrub typhus 227, 281
    tropical ulcers 269–70, 281, 348
    venereal disease 48, 70–1, 158, 231
Dowsett, Arthur 124

Edmondson, John (Jack), VC 81–6
Edwards, Leslie 234–55
Elvy, Collin 124
Evans, Bernard 173

Fadden, Arthur 97–8
fathers and sons 6, 10, 11, 17, 20, 43, 54, 146, 160, 303, 339
Finschhafen 293–5, 312, 365–6
First World War 6, 8, 10, 17, 21, 26–7, 32, 37, 60–3, 65, 81, 92, 104, 125, 159, 166, 186, 221, 259, 284, 308, 312, 316, 336, 340, 354, 373
Fish, Charles 135
Fletcher, Tom 290
Foster, Douglas 56–88
Fraser, John Robert 102–29

Gardner, Herbert 352–71
Goorangai, HMAS 33–4
Graham, Calvin 27
Grant, Ron 81
Greece 20, 47, 53, 71, 74, 90–101
Green, Frank 124
Greta Camp 221–2, 226
Grosswenkheim 138–40
Gull Force 243–5, 249, 252

Hack, Frank R 33–4
Hackney, Ben 194, 198–201
Hammelburg 134, 139
Harris, Jack 83
Hasluck, Paul 15
Hayes, John Francis 162–83
Heath, Lewis 195
Hickey, Ken 256–75
Hite, Tasman 32–3
Hitler, Adolf 20, 26, 47, 51, 57, 62–3, 93, 96, 108, 119, 139, 147, 166, 176
Holt, Robert Gordon 'Hooker' 40–55
Honner, Ralph 107, 121–5, 132
hospitals
    army hospitals
        2/2nd Army General

Hospital, Gaza 51
    2/5th AGH, New Guinea 308
    repatriation hospitals 231
    Caulfield (Vic) 355
    Concord (NSW) 87, 295, 342, 350
    Heidelberg (Vic) 182
Hunter, Reginald 276–95
Hunter, Stanley Robert 'Maurie' 285, 294

Imperial Guards Division, Japanese army 192–5, 201
Ingleburn camp 47, 62–3, 66, 146–7
Irish Australians 28, 219, 282, 336, 355

Japan 26, 28, 53, 93, 101, 188–92, 223, 228, 236–7, 241–2, 261, 272, 333, 342
Jenkins, Jack 56–88
Jiggins, Frederick Jr 183, 187
Jiggins, Tom 184–203
Johnston, Charlie 42, 52

Kalabaka 115
Kalamunda 102–5, 143
Kantara, El 70–1, 108, 277
Kempeitai 294
Keogh, Laurence 'Ron' 81
Kilo 89 camp 70, 108, 277
Kingsbury, Bruce, VC 289
Klapalima 261–70
Kleinwenkheim 138–42
Kokoda 182, 218, 226–7, 282–4, 286–8, 290–5, 309, 373
Kramer, Joe 292–4

Laha massacre 241–3, 246, 255
Larissa 115, 277
Lark Force 243, 257, 259, 270–1
Lavarack, John 76
Leggatt, William 262–3, 266–8
Leggett, Arthur 126, 134
Leggett, Len 216–33
Lind, EF 243, 262
Livingstone, Mal 265–6
Louch, Tom 105, 107–8, 112, 116
Luftwaffe 93, 97, 115, 119, 121, 123, 188

MacArthur, Douglas 37, 101, 222, 322, 333

Mackell, Austin 80–4
McDermid, George 124
McGreevy, Frank 314–31
McLeod, Len 352–71
McQuarrie, Alec 137–9
McRobbie, Arthur 116
Maddern, NP 266
Madero, Jerome 293
Maguire, Stanislaus Philip 223, 228
Malaya 153, 188–203, 222, 236, 241, 299–300, 309, 333, 342
Maleme 122, 132
Masakiyo, Ikeuchi 249
Menzies, Robert Gordon 15, 20–1, 27–8, 57, 92–101, 112, 189, 297
Metson, John 290
militia 10, 21, 43, 46
    Australian Military Forces (AMF) 222
    Citizen Military Force 20
Mitchell, Charles 125–6, 132
Molony, Norman Francis 162–83
Morshead, Leslie 71, 74–6, 173
mothers and sons 219, 238, 239, 297, 316, 336, 354–8
Mulgrave, Andy 102–29, 130–43
Mussolini, Benito 46–7, 51, 96, 176–7

Neame, Philip 74–5
Netherlands East Indies, The 210, 222, 239, 241–4
Neuendorf, Keith 171, 173
New Guinea 6, 23, 20–3, 53, 87–8, 159, 182, 213, 218–23, 229, 231, 243, 279, 281, 290, 292–5, 305, 308, 311–12, 319–20, 342, 348, 358, 362, 365
New Zealand 27, 48, 51, 96–100, 114–19, 171, 175, 189, 202, 209, 311
newspapers 36, 38, 57, 88, 236, 301
Nishimura, Takuma 195, 201–2
Noburo, Ando 249
Nooten, John Van 248, 250
Normandie, SS 68
Northam camp 105–7
Norwegian merchant ships 208, 210–12

Oakley, Terry 124
O'Brien, 'Punchy' 49
O'Connor, Richard 74–5, 109
Owen Stanley Ranges 226, 281, 286, 288

Palembang 206, 210–11
Papua 20–1, 37, 223, 226–7, 280–1, 286, 292, 294
Papuan Infantry Battalion 293
paratroopers 27, 119, 121–5, 210, 264, 266, 268
Parit Sulong 192, 195–202
Parkinson, Snowy 49
patriotism 10, 47, 54, 317
Pearl Harbor 27, 170, 190–1, 210, 236–8, 242, 257, 261, 282, 358
Penfui airstrip 262
Percival, Arthur 194, 202
Perivolia 121–32
Philippines, The 23, 190, 222, 236, 271, 321–2, 333
Pineios River 115
Pollock, Alan Sinclair 256–75
Port Moresby 213, 223, 226–7, 286, 292, 294–5, 305, 342, 359, 361, 364, 366
Potts, Arnold 289
poverty 164, 303, 336, 338, 359
Price, Colin 105
prisoners of war 52, 72, 119, 132, 174, 198, 269
Proud, Billy 124

Queen Mary, RMS 68–9, 169, 191, 279

Rabaul 153, 222, 229, 243, 257, 259, 270, 281, 292–4, 319, 321, 329, 342, 348
racism 28, 31, 152, 191
Ramu Valley 295, 305, 309
recruitment 10, 15, 21, 23, 27, 31, 36, 63, 65, 220
  age of enlistment 32, 37–8, 343
  back doors into military 10, 21
  changes to rules 27, 32, 343
  numbers 31, 32, 63
  proof of age 10, 21, 27
Red Cross 134, 137, 175, 368
religion 232, 346, 360
Rethimno 119, 121–3, 132
Returned and Services League (RSL) 183, 230–1, 368
Roach, Len 243
Robertson, John C 194

Rommel, Erwin 72–5, 80, 84–5, 119, 169–70
Roosevelt, Franklin D 93, 96, 222, 241–2
Rowell, Sidney 244–5
Royal Air Force (RAF) 96, 109, 117–18, 132, 212–13
Royal Australian Air Force (RAAF) 15, 32, 86, 188, 206, 211–14, 262–3, 267, 279, 336, 362
Royal Australian Artillery (RAA) 146
Royal Australian Engineers 52, 69, 137, 269, 305
Royal Australian Navy (RAN) 32, 34
Royal Navy 28, 74, 114, 117, 132, 169

Salonika 98, 133, 169
Sandover, Ray 116, 119, 122, 126, 129, 132
Sangai massacre 290–4
Savige, Stanley 322
Scott, Glen Derek 144–61
Scott, William 243–6, 249, 252
Seiver, Jim 105
Shanghai 368
Singapore 28, 157, 188–94, 200–2, 210, 222, 241, 263, 267, 271–2, 282, 300, 342–3
Smith, AC 324
Smith, Edgar 'Ted' 81, 83
Smythe, Edward 60
Snelling, Rewi 198–9
snipers 6, 80, 124–5, 128–9, 143, 194, 289, 347
soldier's lives
  black marketing 322
  desire to travel 28
  discipline 43, 49, 192, 226, 300
  discontent 226, 242, 347
  drunkenness 17, 48, 51–3, 70–1, 75, 153, 158, 192, 229, 313, 329, 368
  going absent without leave (AWL) 66, 159, 169, 192, 226, 279, 280, 305, 309, 313, 342, 347, 354, 358
  in trouble 43, 229, 293, 300, 339
  mutiny 173
  on leave 38, 72, 216, 229, 357
  pay 31, 37, 43, 220, 322, 365

photographs 12, 62, 105, 187, 228, 268
post-war difficulties 54, 87, 255
punishment 49, 88, 135, 251, 272, 305, 309
stress on return (PTSD) 87, 160, 229, 230, 255, 330, 348, 369
under-equipped 113, 243
Souda Bay 117, 129, 132
Sparrow Force 243, 257, 259–63, 266–8, 275
Stalag camp XIII-C 134
Stalin, Joseph 93
Stapf, Therese and Hildrud 138
Stehr, John 293
Stockhein 134–5, 137
Stoneham, Arthur 124
Street, Geoffrey 57
Strickland, John 264
Sturdee, Vernon 243
Suez Canal 47, 69, 70–4, 96, 108–9, 147, 157, 170
Sullivan, Thomas A 36

Tan Tui camp 244, 247, 255
Tandjong Priok camp 271
Tarakan 346
Taylor, Douglas 296–313
Tel el Eisa 171, 174
Thermopylae line 115
Thomas, Ronald 'Baden' 234–55
Thurland Castle, SS 117
Tobruk 6, 42, 46–7, 53, 59–89, 237, 277
Tocra 112
Tol plantation massacre 259
'Tommies' (English soldiers) 149, 152–3
Torokina 321–3, 327
Treacy, Maurice 289
Tripoli, Libya 72, 74, 84
Tsimba Ridge 324–8
Tuck, Richard 293

under-age soldiers
  back doors into military 21, 312
  discharged as under-age 21, 36, 86, 343
  effects of battle 85, 157, 228
  first to die 33
  numbers of 10, 373
  in other countries 26, 27, 32
  policies regarding 8, 10, 21, 86, 343, 373

pride of 13, 23
reasons for going 13, 17, 20, 38, 279
records of 10, 231
secrecy 21
sending home of 21, 192, 277, 301, 309, 358
survival of 21
youngest boy 34, 36, 297, 340
youngest to die 202
Uren, Tom 263
Urspringen Camp 137
US Army Small Ships 311, 354, 357, 360–1, 365, 368
Usapa Besar camp 268–70
Usau Ridge 264, 266–7

Vasey, George 116
veterans' rights 231–2
Vevi Pass 149
Vichy French 150, 284
Victoria Cross 84, 193, 286–7, 289
Vincent, George 80
Volk, Wendelin 142

Wallgrove Camp 188
war crimes trials, Australian
  Ambon 247
  Los Negros 201, 312
Warden, Charles 'Chick' 195, 197
Wau 229, 363–4
Wavell, Archibald 76, 96–100, 119, 170, 188, 262
Wharton, Reginald Arthur 200
White, Ron 124
Whittall, Leslie 229
Williams, Ron 'Splinter' 81
Williamson, George 248
Willoughby, Tom 124
Wilmot, Chester 81–5
Wilson, A 263
Women's Air Training Corps 38
Women's Australian Auxiliary Air Force 38
Women's Royal Australian Naval Service 38
Wood, Stan 108

Yamashita, Tomoyuki 195
Youl, JG 262